STUDIES ON THE TESTAMENT OF JOSEPH

SOCIETY OF BIBLICAL LITERATURE

SEPTUAGINT AND COGNATE STUDIES

edited by

Harry M. Orlinsky

Number Five

STUDIES ON THE TESTAMENT OF JOSEPH

edited by

George W.E. Nickelsburg, Jr.

SCHOLARS PRESS
Missoula, Montana

STUDIES ON THE TESTAMENT OF JOSEPH

edited by

George W.E. Nickelsburg, Jr.

Published by

SCHOLARS PRESS

for

The Society of Biblical Literature

Pseudepigrapha Group

Distributed by

SCHOLARS PRESS
University of Montana
Missoula, Montana 59801

STUDIES ON THE TESTAMENT OF JOSEPH

Edited by

George W.E. Nickelsburg, Jr.

Library of Congress Cataloging in Publication Data

Main entry under title:

Studies on the Testament of Joseph.

    (Septuagint and cognate studies ; no. 5)
    "Working papers prepared for the sessions of the
Society of Biblical Literature Pseudepigrapha Group,
to be held October 30-November 2, 1975, at the
Palmer House, Chicago."
    Includes bibliographical references.
    1. Bible. O. T. Apocryphal books. Testaments
of the twelve patriarchs. Joseph--Addresses, essays,
lectures. I. Nickelsburgh, George W. E., 1934-
II. Society of Biblical Literature. Pseudepigrapha
Group. III. Series.
BS1830.T5S78   229'.914   75-26923
ISBN 0-89130-027-9

Printed in the United States of America
1 2 3 4 5 6
Printing Department
University of Montana
Missoula, Montana 59801

TABLE OF CONTENTS

PREFACE

The articles in this volume are *working papers* prepared for the sessions of the Society of Biblical Literature Pseudepigrapha Group, to be held October 30 - November 2, 1975, at the Palmer House, Chicago, Illinois, under the chairmanship of the undersigned.

I would like to thank the several contributors for their willingness to take on the added burden of an assigned paper. Mr. Harm W. Hollander of Leiden was kind enough to share with us a draft of part of his doctoral dissertation. Prof. Michael E. Stone of the Hebrew University in Jerusalem expended much effort under pressure to prepare a critical edition and English translation of the Armenian version of the Testament of Joseph, which will appear under separate cover (see Bibliography, below, p. 12). My special thanks to Prof. M. de Jonge of Leiden for his counsel, cooperation, and encouragement at various stages in the planning of the session and the preparation of this volume.

George W.E. Nickelsburg, Jr.
School of Religion
University of Iowa
Iowa City, Iowa 52242

INTRODUCTION

The symposium for which these papers have been prepared
is the fourth, and presumably the final in a series on testa-
mentary literature. Previously treated were: The Testament of
Abraham,[1] The Testament of Moses,[2] and The Testament of Job.[3]
The Testament of Joseph was chosen as a representative of the
Testaments of the XII Patriarchs (TP) quite simply because it
presented problems that were of interest to the Group. The
papers deal primarily with the narrative and parenetic sections
of the Testament and with their parallels in the other TP and
in other Jewish literature.

The present introduction is a response to the papers. I
have sought to raise questions (sometimes in the form of declar-
ative sentences!) and to relate the papers to one another in
terms of common issues which arise from them. My purpose is to
be suggestive and catalytic of more substantive and broadly
ranging discussions in the sessions. My comments are arranged
topically, according to issues, rather than with reference to
individual papers.

Interpretation of Scripture

The Testament of Joseph is, at the heart of it, an interpretation of a portion of Scripture. We can best understand
the peculiar contours of this interpretation by comparing it
with the text it interprets. How does it build upon, add to,
delete portions of, diverge from, and reshape this text?

The Joseph stories in Genesis are a collection of materials
whose general outline corresponds to a genre which we may call
the "tale of the persecuted and exalted courtier."[4] The protagonist is a wise man, in this case a seer, whose dreams and
interpretations thereof trigger the hatred and envy of his
brothers, who plot his destruction. He escapes death but is

---

[1]Papers appeared in R.E. Kraft, ed., *1972 Proceedings,
Septuagint and Cognate Studies* 2 (1972), pp. 155-245, to be
reissued in expanded form as *Studies on the Testament of
Abraham*, under the editorship of the present writer.

[2]Papers appeared in G.W.E. Nickelsburg, Jr., ed.,
Studies on the Testament of Moses, SCS 4 (1973).

[3]Papers appeared in G. MacRae, ed., *Society of Biblical
Literature 1974 Seminar Papers*, Vol. 1 (1974), pp. 35-76.

[4]For a discussion, see G. Nickelsburg, *Ressurection,
Immortality, and Eternal Life in Intertestamental Judaism,
HTS* 26 (Cambridge, 1972), pp. 48-70, 93-109.

1

sold into slavery. His revelatory gifts bring him to the attention of Pharaoh, and he is exalted as vizier of Egypt. Even-
tually, his brothers are forced to do obeisance to him, thus
fulfilling the very dreams which had led them to plot his death.
The specifically religious overtones of the story are evident
at a number of points. Joseph's interpretive powers are a divine gift (40:8; 41:16,38). His success in Egypt is due to
God's presence and help (39:2,23; 41:51f.; 45:5-9). The episode
with Potiphar's wife adds another dimension: Joseph is a righteous man whose obedience to God (39:9) leads to (a second)
persecution.

In later examples of the genre (Dan. 3,6; Susanna), the
protagonist's status *qua* righteous person is basic and central
to the action of the story.[5] However, this ancillary and secondary feature in the Genesis cycle dominates the characteriza-
tion of Joseph in TJ. His ability to interpret dreams, which
runs like a thread through Genesis 37ff., is of no concern to
the author(s) of TJ and the other TP, and his wisdom, more
broadly construed, is a minor motif, occurring only in TL (see
Hollander, below, pp. 77-79).[6]

The First Joseph Story

In the first paper, Richard Pervo tests Martin Braun's
hypothesis that TJ 3-9 is a close relative of the Greek Romance.
He disagrees with Braun on the question of genre. TJ 3-9 is
not a continuous narrative (poorly put together, according to
Braun), but a cycle of episodes strung together in homiletical
fashion, a series of haggadic illuminations of Gen. 39:10
("...she spoke to Joseph day after day"). Pervo agrees with
Braun that a goodly number of motifs in these chapters do show
the influence of Hellenistic literature and tradition, although
they function differently here (as Braun also admits).

Harm Hollander brings a whole different set of data to bear
on these chapters. The plight and actions of Joseph have been
influenced by the portrait of the distressed righteous man, as
he is portrayed especially, though not exclusively, in the
psalms of individual lament. Joseph prays, fasts, mourns, and
then glorifies God when he is delivered. One may or may not
agree that chs. 3-9 (and other parts of TJ) are as directly dependent on certain passages as Hollander seems to suggest.
Nonetheless, his cumulative evidence is impressive and would
seem to support his contention that our author's portrait of
Joseph does reflect the type of passage under consideration.
Moreover, we can readily understand why the Joseph story might
be read in the light of these psalms. Taken as a whole, the

---

[5] *Ibid.*, pp. 51-54. See also W.L. Humphreys, "A Life-Style
for Diaspora," *JBL* 92 (1973), 217-23; and J.J. Collins, "The
Court Tales in Daniel and the Development of Apocalyptic,"
JBL 94 (1975), 224-27.

[6] This wisdom, moreover, is construed primarily in terms of
Torah.

Joseph cycle carries a theme very similar to that in the psalms: the righteous man, persecuted and beleaguered by his enemies, but finally delivered by God.[7] In the one case, the theme is carried in a strictly narrative genre, in the other, the narrative is recounted in psalmic form.

Our author's purpose and technique become clearer when we combine Hollander's *Motifsgeschichte* with Pervo's literary observations. Our author has chosen that one story in the Genesis cycle which depicts Joseph as a righteous man. He does not repeat the story, but expands it into a series of episodes. In each of these, the dramatis personae are Potiphar's wife and Joseph. In almost all of these episodes, Joseph counters the Egyptian woman's action with a response that Hollander characterizes as the act of a pious man in distress. In capsule form, these episodes are as follows:

3:1ff.:   she threatened, promised / I prayed, fasted

3:6bff.: she embraced / I was sorrowful, lamented

4:1ff.:   she flattered / I put on sackcloth, besought God

4:4ff.:   she sought instruction / I fasted, prayed

5:1ff.:   she promised to kill / I rent my garments

6:1ff.:   she brought gifts, etc. / I wept

7:1ff.:   she threatened suicide / I prayed, knelt, wept

8:2ff.:   she seized my garments / I fled (no time for
                                          prayer)

9:1ff.:   she sent, saying / I did not incline...fasting

9:4ff.:   she bared herself / the Lord guarded me

The pattern is clear: the righteous man's response to the distress that confronts him.

The precise emphasis in these episodes is further clarified when they are compared to the series of episodes presented in capsule form in TJ 1:3-7, where the pattern is: I was in distress / but God delivered me. In the first story, by contrast, the second element is not God's deliverance (except at the very end of the series), but Joseph's response *qua* righteous man. Furthermore, the nature of the distress is different. The list in ch. 1 begins by listing his brothers' actions (they fill the role of the persecutor in the main part of the Genesis story) and the ensuing consequences. Then, as Hollander indicates, some stereotyped troubles are listed, which do not really fit the Genesis story. Only in vv. 6c-7b do we have matters relating to the Egyptian woman, and these are *consequences* of her frustrated attempts at seduction. Chs. 3-9 are totally different. Here distress and response involve ethical opposites: the actions of the Egyptian woman evince ἀκολασία, in which she invites Joseph to participate; his refusal is due to his σωφροσύνη .

---

[7] Hollander cites, e.g., Pss. 22, 34, 69, 118.

Chs. 3-9 are introduced as an account of Joseph's ten temptations, in the face of which he "endured" and hence was approved by God. Thus, at least in their present context, chs. 3-9 are understood as exemplifying Joseph's patience and longsuffering. The parallel in Abraham's ten trials (Jub. 17:15-19:9) has been noted, and there, too, Abraham demonstrates his patience and long-suffering under trial (19:3f.).[8] If TJ is dependent on the Abraham tradition, it is noteworthy that we have a new type of material introduced here. Jubilees does not depict Abraham as a *persecuted* righteous man. Rather, it builds on the common motif of Abraham's faithfulness. TJ is not unique in its combination of "endurance in trial" with the figure of the persecuted righteous one. The Testament of Job, which writes ὑπομονή over Job's experiences (1:3; 4:6), superimposes on the traditional story of Job elements from the description of the persecuted and exalted righteous man in Wisdom of Solomon 2-5.[9] Moreover, the description of Job's destruction of the idol temple (chs. 3ff.) are reminiscent of the parallel story about Abraham in Jub. 12. Conversely, a Joban type heavenly prologue has been superimposed on the story of the Aqedah in Jub. 17. Thus Jubilees' stories about Abraham, TJob, and TJ appear to reflect a traditional conflation of traditions and motifs under the canon of "patience" and "long-suffering." Moreover, ὑπομονή as a characteristic of the persecuted righteous occurs in what Hollander calls the "martyr traditions" (p. 54).

Both Hollander and Pervo have noted the continuous nature of Joseph's trials. It is possible, though perhaps not demonstrable, that Joseph's patient endurance implies his putting up with a constant bombardment of tribulations and trials. If so, the virtue of ὑπομονή may be inherent in the intentionality of the author of chs. 3-9 (and evident in the episodical structure), whether or not he also composed 2:7 and 10:1ff.

In 2:1-3, Hollander sees the influence of martyr traditions. Joseph "struggles" against the woman who seeks to lead him into παρανομία. That is, the story of the persecuted righteous one is superimposed on Joseph's engagement with the woman. The woman assumes the role of the persecutor, and Joseph must suffer for having chosen to obey the law. On Joseph's distress as an ἀγών --in addition to the many parallels cited by Hollander, the same idea (though a different word) occurs in Job 4:8f. in the context of trial-endurance-obedience-reward. Hollander notes that although the idea of struggle is present in martyr literature, it is also found in the context of a struggle for virtue and against the passions, "an idea that originally belonged to Hellenistic moral philosophy." The two contexts, however, are not really antithetical. Fourth Maccabees, which he cites as a prime example of the martyr tradition in this context (n. 61), has in fact, rewritten the stories of 2 Macc. 6-7 in the key of Hellenistic moral philosophy, and the author describes his work as a demonstration of the victory of reason

---

[8]Lat.: *patiens, patientissimus, in longanimitate spiritus;* Eth.: *yet'ĕgaš, 'egusa, bate' egesta manfas*

[9]Cf., e.g., Wisd. 5:4 and TJob 36:2; 49:13; Wisd. 2:17 and TJob 37; Wisd. 5:4 and TJob 30.

(Λογισμός) and certain of the virtues (including σωφροσύνη) over the passions (1:1-6). Similarly, Wisd. 4:1f. (cited by Hollander), and its mention of the struggle in behalf of virtue, stands in the midst of a discussion about the persecuted and exalted righteous man.

The introduction to TJ (1:3ff.) summarizes in repeated parallelism the basic structure of the Genesis story, stressing, however, God's active role in Joseph's deliverance, and (as Hollander has shown), using language from the context of righteous man psalms and allied literature. Hollander is perhaps right in calling this a hymn of thanksgiving, albeit of a late sort that differs considerably from the classical biblical *Gattung*. He notes the lack of a "Toda-Formel," which would make it *explicitly* a psalm of thanksgiving. (p. 56). It should be noted that with one exception (Ps. Sol. 13), all the examples of late psalms which he cites have such a formula (sometimes repeated) or at least mention of the motif of thanks. In any event, Joseph is, in fact, reciting in the midst of his brethren the Lord's deeds of deliverance--something which the psalmist does in his song of thanks.

To recapitulate: in TJ 1-10, emphasis is placed on the one story in the Genesis cycle which stresses Joseph's righteousness. The story itself is expanded into a series of episodes involving the struggle between the righteous and the wicked. To this story there have been accreted numerous motifs and elements from various genres all of which are concerned with the troubles (variously described) of the righteous. The wise courtier has here become the righteous man, persecuted, put to the trial because of his piety, but persistent and victorious in his struggle for virtue, and *therefore* delivered by God.

The Second Story

Here again we have a major expansion on a biblical text. Indeed, different from Gen. 39:6-18, which is a self-contained unit, this text (Gen 39:1) is but one event in the Genesis sequence. As in chs. 3-9, the biblical text is expanded into a whole series of episodes, but here, they are in chronological sequence. Nonetheless, it is not really a story with a plot that resolves itself. The narrator relates a series of events illustrating his point and then drops the thread of his narrative (16:6), though after a bit of parenesis (17:1-3) he wanders on again, making his point (17:4-8). The use of this technique here may corroborate Pervo's suggestion that the first story is employing a rambling sort of sermonic style, the purpose of which is not to tell a self-contained story, but to narrate events which illustrate, by repetition, the moral the author wishes to convey to his audience. The principal difference between chs. 3ff. and chs. 11ff. is that the latter narrates the events in chronological sequence, while in the former they are in haphazard order.

The parenesis attached to this story ascribes to Joseph a deep love for his brothers (so Harrelson and Hollander), evident in the story in his continually keeping his silence (so

especially Hollander). Again the technique of relating repeated
episodes *underscores* the author's point and may be implied in
the ascription once more of patience and endurance to Joseph.
As in the first story, the two main characters are Potiphar's
wife and Joseph. The Memphian women functions as a foil to
underscore that characteristic of Joseph which the author wishes
to demonstrate. She is depicted as manipulating other people
to obtain her ends, this in contrast to Joseph, whose prime concern is how not to put others to shame. Thus, as in the first
story, we see the contrast of vice and virtue.

The thread running through almost every one of the episodes
is: Joseph's silence--lest he put someone to shame. This motif
is all the more surprising in view of Gen. 40:14f.:

> But remember me...for I was indeed stolen out of the
> land of the Hebrews

That is, in the one place in Genesis where Joseph speaks of his
past, he does exactly the opposite of what our story has him do
time and again. Thus our story witnesses to a deliberate manip-
ulation of the biblical text in order to make Joseph into the
kind of person the author wishes to present as an example.

In summary: Joseph is depicted as a righteous man, whose
celebrated virtue here is self-efacing love. To accomplish his
purpose, the author picks up an action of Joseph in Genesis and
has him do just the opposite, and do it numerous times. Whereas in the first story, the portrayal of Joseph *qua* righteous
man is rooted in the biblical story, here the author's purpose
causes him to break totally with the biblical account.

Finally, a note about Joseph's exaltation. In Genesis, it
is implicit in the beginning of the story and forms the climax
around which the last half of the story revolves. In TJ,
Joseph's exaltation is mentioned occasionally (1:7-2:1; 10:3;
18:1).[10] More important, the motif is presented in its opposite
form (I did not exalt myself). What is an integral part of the
action in Genesis is used as a device to emphasize Joseph's
loving character.

*The Composition of the Testament of Joseph
and its Relationship to the Other Testaments XII Patriarchs*

Both Harm Hollander and Anitra Kolenkow support the basic
unity of TJ. Hollander argues for the unity of 1:3-2:6, using
a combination of form criticism and an extended analysis that
demonstrates a unity of content and a common background in certain types of Jewish literature. He then sees this section as
an introduction to the whole of TJ. Common materials and motifs
in the various parts of the Testament support an argument for
unity. He is doing a kind of *Redaktionsgeschichte*. Kolenkow's
argument is different. It is basically structural. How do the
two stories function within the structure of TJ, and how do they

---

[10]See Hollander below, pp. 65-66.

relate to the structure of a wider number of TP? There are analogies of testaments which emphasize two virtues (or vices), and
the same ones found in the two stories in TJ. In the broader
context of TP, TR, and TS form antipodes to the two Joseph stories. Reuben contrasts his fornication with Joseph's avoidance
of that sin. Simeon describes his envy and depicts Joseph as
one who bore no malice, but loved. Moreover, TR and TS are further related to one another in that each brother also warns
against the sin of the other brother. Here is an interesting
methodological difference between Kolenkow and J. Becker. Material in any given testament not related to that patriarch is
excised by Becker as interpolation. Kolenkow takes precisely
the same material as evidence that that testament is inextricably
bound to the other two testaments. She seeks further to support
her analysis by the use outside TP of contrasting pairs as ethical examples to be emulated or avoided. Kolenkow's argument
has the advantage of explaining why the same pairs, or triads,
appear in different testaments. If it is not a compositional
principle, as she suggests, it is certainly a very neat redactional device. One wonders why the effort was expended, it is
an artistic flourish, but adds nothing of *substance* to the respective testaments.

Kolenkow sees this triadic arrangement as evidence that
TR, TS, TJ formed the core of an earlier, smaller collection of
patriarchal testaments, to which she would also assign TL, TZ,
and TB. In all these testaments she finds passages promising
or speaking of a "reward like Joseph." The argument is worth
considering, for it provides an internal connection to TJ, which
is the hub of the three other testaments according to the hypothesis. As further evidence she points to Becker's observation
that certain of these testaments have the same full forms of
preamble. Here the argument is a bit more slippery, for certain
of the testaments which do not belong to Kolenkow's original
group have fuller forms of the preamble than some in her original
group. So, e.g.:

The words	which	x spoke	before death	at age x	Jos's age
R x		x	x	x	x
S x		x	x	x	x
L x		x			
J x		x	x		
I x					
Z x		x		x	x
D x		x	(x)	x	
N x		x	x	x	
G x		x		x	
A x		x	(healthy)	x	
J x			x		
B x		x		x	

Becker's observations may be more of a hindrance than a help to
Kolenkow's hypothesis. There is not room here to pursue the
question at length. We may ask this, however: given the

importance of Joseph to the scheme, could an original collection
have included those testaments in which Joseph appears as an
exemplary figure (TZ, TD, TB--so Hollander)? Or might it have
included testaments that contain fragments of the Joseph story
(TZ, TD, TG, TB)? Do these narratives have anything in common
with the content and technique of the two stories in TJ? Could
a single author have distributed among a number of testaments
portions of a common haggadic tradition? In any event, it is
noteworthy that in certain of TP Joseph does not figure prom-
inently. Finally there is the question of the relationships of
Aramaic TL and the Hebrew TN to a putative earlier collection--
a question the answer to which will be governed somewhat by
one's agreement or disagreement with Martin's proposal of a
Semitic *Vorlage* for the whole of TJ.

The Original Language

The application of Martin's approach to TJ raises some
methodological questions. It is surely a valid statistical
principle that the larger the sample, the more accurate one's
findings are likely to be--if the sample is being interpreted
as a part of a larger whole. A proper sampling of 25% of the
population will better reflect the whole of public opinion than
a sampling of 10%. In the case of TJ, however, we are dealing
with a different question. We have the statistics on 100%.
But if one entertains the possibility that the whole is made up
of heterogeneous parts, then the statistics regarding the whole
are, in fact, an average, whereas the statistics on the parts
reflect more accurately the situation in the given section.
Thus a poll of a whole city reflects a complete tally of opinion
pro and con a given issue, but a breakdown according to dis-
tricts or groups will reveal the specific contours of that opinion. Now, the built-in difficulty with Martin's method is that
the smaller the section or subject, the more ambiguous the
interpretation of the data. But if one grants the possibility
of heterogeneous origins for various pericopae, one is simply
"stuck" with that ambiguity, and the larger sample, being an
average, is a less than valid criterion.

An obvious question is raised by the difference in the
statistics in the first story and various other parts in TJ.
Martin may rightly point to certain translation Greek with
counts very close to those in the first story, or to certain
translation Greek in which sections vary between very wooden
and very free and idiomatic translation. As long as we have
the Semitic *Vorlage*, the issue is settled. But the problem
here is precisely that we do not have the *Vorlage*, and hence
the fluctuation can be interpreted in different ways. Hellenistic influences can be, and are found in Semitic writings,
but one ought not *ignore* the fact, when discussing the language
question, that it is precisely the section in TJ with the least
Semitic Greek which shows clear influences from the Hellenistic
world--including the repeated use of σωφροσύνη , for which one
must find a reasonable Semitic counterpart.[11]

---

[11]U. Luck suggests מִּזְמָר , TDNT 7, 1100, but σωφροσύνη
never occurs in the LXX in translation Greek.

Evidence of the Use of Traditions

Even if one grants the compositional unity of TJ, it is
questionable to what extent the author has composed his materials
de novo, and to what extent he has used traditions and in what
form they existed?
A. *Internal Evidence.* Hollander suggests, e.g., that the open-
ing psalm is an introduction to both of the stories. Moreover,
its very contents requires something like a testament of Joseph
for an initial literary *Sitz*. With regard to the stories, themselves, do they not presume or require the following parenesis,
or something very similar to it. Pervo, while granting the
possibility that the first story could reflect an older, more
ordered story, argues that the present order (introduction,
narrative section, parenetic conclusion) makes a nice homiletical
structure, although he cites no analogies for the structure.
The homiletical *Sitz* is a (reasonable) extrapolation. But that
would be record brevity for a sermon! Perhaps the material is
a compression of longer homiletical material of the same theme
and outline. The analogy of the "sermons" in Acts suggests itself. Would the device of narration in the first person have
been used, or is that a device of the testamental form? Alter-
natively, might the whole of TJ be one single homiletical piece?
A difficulty here is the introduction of the Memphian woman,
the wife of Pentephri (12:1), as if she hadn't been heard of
before in the present context (i.e., in TJ). This suggests we
are near the beginning of a block of tradition.
B. *External Evidence.* The rabbinic and Samaritan materials
offer little concrete help for the present question. The case
is different with the other three, Philo, Josephus, and Joseph
and Asenath (see Hollander, Harrington, Smith).

	TJ	Philo	Josephus	JA 7:2-6
σωφροσύνη	4:1f.; 6:7; 9:2f.	40, 57, 87	II.48,(50), 69	(4:9)
contrast: ἀκολασία	7:1; 9:2	40		
threats	3:1		49-50	(J's)
benefits	3:2		48	
remembers father	3:3			x
exhorts her	4:6f. 5:2; 7:5ff.		51-52	
gifts	5:4			x
illness	7:1-2		45-47	x
ὑπομονή	passim		43	
J's silence	10:6-16:6	237, 247-50	60	

Josephus knows the first story in some form. All the more
significant, therefore, is his use of the silence motif, although he applies it to Joseph's silence about the woman's
actions. Philo knows both of Joseph's σωφροσύνη and the
woman's lewdness, and of Joseph's silence regarding his

brothers. This combination of motifs from the two stories make it tempting to posit a knowledge of TJ, and the possibility cannot be certainly disproven. Nonetheless, Joseph's σωφροσύνη is an all too obvious Hellenistic interpretation of the story, and the contrast of the woman as ἀκόλαστος is not unnatural. Particularly striking is 247f., according to which Joseph held his silence regarding his brothers during his imprisonment. This is a direct contradiction of Gen. 40:14f. Can we explain the appearance of this motif in the Joseph tradition as such an intentional contradiction? In such a case, Philo has the more primitive form, and TJ, a secondary expansion of the tradition. Or should we understand the motif as rising in loose relationship to the Genesis passage (so TJ) and then being brought into direct contradiction with Genesis (so Philo)? The former may be the more probable. Joseph and Asenath shows some knowledge of a form of the first story. Reference to his recollection of Jacob's words is especially noteworthy. We cannot ascertain whether JA knows TJ. Reference to Joseph's chastity fits well with the theme of the writing. Lack of reference to his silence proves nothing, since there is no special reason to develop that theme in the book. Our conclusions as to dependence on TJ or its traditions remain uncertain, but closer scrutiny may bear more positive results.

Provenance

The evidence from Philo and Josephus indicates that at least the traditions in TJ were known in first century Palestine and Egypt. (In view of Josephus, the silence of Ps. Philo and the rabbis is no argument against a Palestinian origin). Joseph and Asenath does not help us, since its place of origin is uncertain. The language question enters in, but is not decisive. A Semitic origin could indicate Palestine, Syria, or the Eastern diaspora. A Greek origin might favor Alexandria, but surely does not exclude Palestine and Syria. A more certain determination of the relationship of TJ to other of the Testaments would provide a broader base of evidence. The anti-Samaritan polemics in certain of these (cf. Purvis' paper) are most easily understood in a Palestinian setting. The Semitic testaments of Levi and Naphtali have been found in Qumran.

An origin in the diaspora is supported by Harrelson. He, along with J. Thomas and K.H. Rengstorf, sees Joseph as a symbol for the diaspora Jew.[12] The constant identification of Potiphar's wife as "the Egyptian woman" and "the Memphian woman"--almost an archetypal "foreign woman"--may support the hypothesis of non-Palestinian origin.

---

[12]J. Thomas, "Aktuelles im Zeugnis der zwölf Väter," in *Studien zu den Testamenten der Zwölf Patriarchen, BZNW* 36 (1969), pp. 106-14; K.H. Rengstorf, "Herkunft und Sinn der Patriarchen-Reden in den Testamenten der zwölf Patriarchen," in *La Littérature juive entre Tenach et Mischna,* ed. W.C. Van Unnik (Leiden, 1974), pp. 140.

One final matter. The lack of rabbinic parallels has led Barbara Geller to write the following throw-away sentence:

> The absence of greater similarity between the portrayals of Joseph in the tannaitic Midrashim and TJ is not surprising, given the very different spheres of Judaism from which they emerged, and the different literary vehicles the author selected.

On the difference in genre, there is no debate, although elements of the tradition could have been included at appropriate points, were they known, and had the compilers wished to include them. More interesting--and worthy of discussion--is the question of "the very different spheres." What is the sphere of TJ or its traditions? Josephus attests knowledge in first century Palestine of at least the tradition. Pervo argues convincingly for a homiletical format or *Sitz*. Who is doing the preaching and/or teaching, and where? And how do such persons relate to the rabbis?

The Question of Hellenization

It is commonplace and fashionable to speak of the wholesale Hellenization of Judaism. In the present case, Braun has shown --and Pervo agrees with him--considerable influence from Greek romantic literature. But borrowings from Hellenistic sources do not a work Hellenistic make, and both Braun and Pervo indicate that some of the Hellenistic motifs have been transformed, taken on different functions, or exist as mere vestigial remains, clever window dressing. Should we define Hellenization as the substantial transformation of the Jewish tradition? How and where has this happened in TJ? Is it to be seen in the rewriting of stories to exemplify abstract virtues and vices, to depict a virtuous hero who engages in a "struggle" against an opponent who is the personfication of the vice to be avoided? Hollander (following Becker) suggests the origin of such ideas in Hellenistic moral philosophy. In any event, given the voluminous parallels to both native Jewish psalmic and wisdom literature and to Hellenistic literature, the question of Hellenistic *essence* can be profitable raised in respect to TJ.

A Parallel in the New Testament

I have suggested that influences from the psalmic literature can be understood as the superimposition upon the story of the persecuted and exalted wise (righteous) man of materials from psalms that carry the same theme. In TJ, the genre in which this combination is effected is neither psalmic (except perhaps ch. 1) nor is it the traditional story of conspiracy, accusation, trial, deliverance to death, rescue, exaltation and vindication. Nonetheless, the process of combining material from thetwo sources is of significance for students of the NT. The shape of the passion narratives is precisely that of the story of conspiracy, persecution, deliverance etc. Yet interspersed in this narrative framework are numerous references, often explicit, to the righteous man psalms. For this conflation we have an analogue in TJ--albeit in a different genre.

A Bibliographical Footnote

No complete bibliography, even of recent works, can be attempted here. For a good starting point, see:

M. de Jonge, "Recent Studies on the Testaments of the Twelve Patriarchs," *SEA* 36 (1971), 77-96.

On the Armenian version, see now:

Michael E. Stone, *The Armenian Version of The Testament of Joseph: Introduction, Critical Edition, and Translation. Texts and Translations, Pseudepigrapha Series* 5 (Missoula, 1975).

Forthcoming very soon is:

M. de Jonge, ed., *Studies on the Testaments of the Twelve Patriarchs* (Leiden, 1975).

In addition to numerous articles on the text of TP, are:

M. de Jonge, "The Interpretation of the Testaments of the Twelve Patriarchs in Recent Years"

-----,"Christian Influence in the Testaments of the Twelve Patriarchs" (reprint)

-----,"Notes on Testament of Levi II-VII" (reprint)

Th. Korteweg, "The Meaning of Naptali's Visions"

George W.E. Nickelsburg, Jr.

SEMINAR PAPERS

THE TESTAMENT OF JOSEPH AND GREEK ROMANCE[1]

Richard I. Pervo

I. Summary and Introduction

Martin Braun discovered in T Jos 3-9 an important example of what might be described as a "missing link" in his theory on the origin and development of Greek narrative fiction. Braun attempted to demonstrate that the "First Joseph Story" in the Testament betrays clear influence from the Phaedra legend "or one of its variants."[2] Whereas the account in Genesis 39 is a "novella," T Jos represents a transformation of literary genre, to a "longer narrative with much in common with what we call Romance," the source of which might be novels or novelle or cycles of novelle.[3] Braun's findings, especially his detection of ultimately Greek influence, have received general critical approval.[4]

Against Braun I argue that T Jos 3-9 is not a "story," a cycle of connected episodes. These chapters do not present a continuous narrative. The passage rather appears to be, in large part, an illumination of Gen. 39,10, a sermon-like presentation of "The Ten Temptations of Joseph by Potiphar's Wife." The entire pericope, which probably extends from 2,1 to 10,4, may exemplify a type of synagogue preaching that utilizes elements from popular entertainment and ethical exhortation.

II. T Jos and Ancient Fiction: Martin Braun

M. Braun published two monographs during the 1930's dealing with widely divergent aspects of narrative fiction in the Greco-Roman world. His dissertation, Griechischer Roman und Hellenistische Geschichtschreibung (Fors. z. Rel. & Kul. d. Ant. 6), 1934, attempted to delineate the influence of erotic fiction upon "rhetorical" historiography. Josephus' Antiquities were his principal subject. Braun's second, and better-known, work, History and Romance in Greco-Oriental Literature, 1938, was a critical response to the classic hypothesis of Erwin Rohde regarding the origin and background of the Greek Romance.[5] Rohde, who found little of value in ancient novels, argued that they were a product of the Second Sophistic, i.e., rhetorical display, and that the genre came into being through the deliberate fusion of two motifs popular from the Hellenistic era onward: romantic love and fictional travel literature. Papyrological recoveries soon destroyed both the absolute and relative chronological underpinnings of Rohde's thesis. Romantic novels were, in fact, written during the Hellenistic and early Roman periods, and Sophistic influence upon their style was secondary. In seeking to outline a new genesis for this literature, Braun pointed to the traces of nationalistic hero-romances, developed from Oriental legendary tradition and issued in Greek to present the claims of proud old peoples in response to the Hellenistic domination.[6] Competition among various national groups encouraged an eventual uniformity in the content of these novels and stimulated a process of literary and cultural assimilation and evolution which resulted in the dissipation of their national character. The eventual outcome was, as the surviving fragments of the Ninus-Romance suggest,[7] the depiction of the quondam Oriental hero as a conventional bourgeois lover. Similar transformations of local legends and stories may lie behind other novels, including the

15

<u>corpus</u> <u>classicum</u> of Greek Romance.[8]

The second chapter of <u>History</u> <u>and</u> <u>Romance</u>, which is largely a study of T Jos 3-9, pursued the line of development proposed above in a critical engagement with another of Rohde's influential theories: that novels cannot be developed from a novella.[9] The T Jos pericope assisted Braun in his refutation of Rohde by testifying to a middle stage in one process through which he thought that Greco-Roman novels had developed. A rather bald schematization of his theory might look like the following:

1. Local or National Legend or novella (e.g., Gen. 39,6b-20)
2. "Popular" Romance   (e.g., T Jos 3-9)
3. "Literary" Romance   (e.g., Jos. Ant. 2:39-59)

It would not be fair to suggest that Braun calls T Jos 3-9 a "romance," <u>tout court</u>. He rather saw this pericope as an example of a process of literary development. The ultimate source of T Jos could have been one or more of several literary types, including a novel or a novella or a collection of stories.[10]

Historians of religion have been primarily interested in Braun's postulation of motifs ultimately derived from Greek sources. The putative value of these findings would seem to relate to the important questions of date, provenance and original language. Braun's personal opinions in these matters did not differ from the views offered by Charles. Braun operated with the hypothesis that T Jos was a Jewish work, written in Hebrew (or Aramaic) during the Second Century BCE.[11] As the title of his work suggests, Braun worked with the category of "Graeco-Oriental" literature. He did not regard "Greek" or "Hellenistic" or "Jewish" as impermeable oppositions. The basis of Braun's research was that the Oriental contribution to the development of ancient romances had been underevaluated by previous investigators. Here, too, he was opposed to the prevailing judgment of Rohde.[12]

Within this context Braun advanced his detailed and rather persuasive hypothesis that T Jos 3-9 betrays influence from the extremely popular Phaedra legend. The shape of the legend attested in the <u>Hippolytus</u> of Euripides was widely employed in later times.[13] Braun recognized that, because of the continual re-use of the Phaedra story and its associated cluster(s) of motifs in New Comedy, Mime, Romance, Apocryphal Acts and Hagiography, there was no need to claim that either the writer of T Jos or even its source were directly dependent upon Euripides. The intermediate medium have included story-telling, i.e., popular oral tradition.[14]

The character of the Joseph story in the <u>Testament</u> is well-suited for the type of Phaedra story current during the Hellenistic and Roman periods. In place of the original problem of servile loyalty, which is the key issue in Gen. 39, adultery has become the major temptation faced by Joseph.[15] This is certainly no surprise, but it does conform to the general focus upon illicit sex in the Greco-Roman parallels. Secondly, the religious motivation for steadfastly rejecting the woman's proposal does not distinguish T Jos and the other Jewish accounts from their pagan counterparts. This is already a factor in Euripides' drama, where Hippolytus' refusal is based upon his cultic chastity in honor of Artemis. Sophrosyne is mentioned in the novel of Xenophon of Ephesus 3,12,4, and in Apollonius of Tyana, 6,3, for example. The novella contained in Apuleius' Met. 10,2-5 (one of the best parallels in content to T Jos), takes note of the lad's pietas and modestia, (10,2). Fidelity to one's spouse or fiancée and the general incest taboo are other common reasons for declining the proposed relationship.

The real power of Braun's claim that elements of this popular story-type have been assimilated into T Jos 3-9 does not lie in his lists of parallels, impressive as these may be, but in his demonstration that inappropriate motifs have been adapted, apparently for their own sake, into an alien context. The implication of his findings is that these alien motifs have been absorbed to make the story "competitive" with its pagan rivals, that we have an instance of syncretism in the sphere of edification and entertainment rather than religion.

The inappropriate motifs identified by Braun are frequently unmotivated or even illogical situations in the "story." The woman promises to make Joseph 'Lord of the manor.' (3,2). Her offer would fit logically at the conclusion of ch. 5, since it depends upon her husband's demise. Seduction under the guise of parental affection, which is suggested in 3,6b ff., is a perennially popular approach. In the current setting, however, the probability of its success has been greatly diminished because she first tries the "step-son" subterfuge after her lascivious and dastardly intentions had been fully revealed. This device could be a logical "Step I" in the plans of a capably evil Phaedra. The phenomenon of love-sickness occurs ad nauseam in popular literature, but its role in 7,1ff. is rather obscure. If feigned, it does not really provide a necessary occasion for an intimate meeting. The suicide threat in ch. 7, with its sentimental and psychological coloration, is almost indisputably derived from the popular culture of Hellenism.[16] The poison/aphrodisiac incident related in ch. 6 also fails to play the decisive role for which it is suited. (See the discussion of "Episode VI," below.) Braun points to the incongruity of these motifs in their immediate context and suggests that they were introduced because they were popular. The lack of integration was assigned to a poor narrator. The problems identified by Braun in his analysis of the use of these "alien" motifs constitute one point of departure for my critical discussion of his conclusions.

Despite occasional temptations to see parts of the story as "derived from the literary tradition founded by Euripides,"[17] Braun rejected the notion of a purely Greco-Roman basis for the "new information" in T Jos 3-9. Identifying the "conversion" passage, the miraculous deliverance from poison and the erotic display of skin as "Jewish" or "Oriental," he judged the use of Greco-Roman motifs as quite external, not affecting the character or message of the document.[18]

III. The First Section of T Jos is more like a "Sermon" than a "Story": A Critique of Braun.

With regard to the question of so-called "Hellenistic influence" Braun's judgment, with all its qualifications, appears sound. One can, to be sure, invoke the universality of

the story, point out that the oldest preserved account is the
Egyptian "Tale of Two Brothers"[19] or note the existence of the
Hellenistic-Syrian story of Stratonice and Combabus in the _Dea
Syria_ ascribed to Lucian.[20] The decisive factor, however, is
not the mythical or legendary background (Gen. 39 is certainly
"Oriental"!), but the cultural situation observed by Braun. In
particular, the motif of threatened suicide, amoris causa, for
sentimental and romantic reasons, is characteristic of popular
literature after Alexander, and represents a cultural setting
in which individual feeling and happiness become prevalent
values.[21] Joseph's psychological insight in 7,8 "For if a man
hath fallen before the passion of a wicked desire and become
enslaved by it, even as she, whatever good thing he may hear
with regard to that passion, he receiveth it with a view to his
wicked desire" (tr. Charles), is also, as Braun observes, typical of romantic fiction.[22] The older Oriental stories offer
only general stuctural and material similarities.[23]

My most significant quarrel with Braun is of a form-
critical nature. He described T Jos 3-9 as a "longer narrative
which has much in common with what we call a romance." This
pericope, which is in fact merely four pages in length, is not
a continuous narrative, a story. One cannot treat this passage
as an expanded edition of Gen. 39,6b-20. The reader is probably
expected to know the Genesis account, the details of which are
summarized rather than elaborated. The section from 2,1 to
10,4 is a general treatment of the Genesis story with especial
attention to illustrations of Gen. 39,10. ויהי כדברה אל יוסף
יום יום... ἡνίκα δὲ ἐλάλει τῷ Ιωσηφ ἡμέραν ἐξ ἡμέρας...
Joseph, an extraordinary model of obedience to the Sixth Commandment, survived no less than ten temptations at the hands et
al. of Potiphar's wife.[24] The actual form of the passage in
question is made obscure by Braun's attempted resolution of
chs. 3-9 into discreet episodes. I will attempt to refute his
analysis in some detail. My principal objections are that a
number of the alleged "episodes" relate to typical or habitual
behavior rather than specific, sequential incidents, and,
furthermore, that the logical incoherence of the material cannot be attributed to a lack of narrative skill.

Episode I 3,1-5[25] (Braun, pp. 48-50)

Two rhetorical exclamations are supposed to introduce
this "episode," as well as the entire "story." No setting or
narrative introduction is provided. One is expected to be
familiar with "the Egyptian woman." In addition to these
structural problems, the repeated ποσάκις and the impf. ἔλεγε
contradict the notion of "episode." The threats and punishments, which are not described, and the concomitant enticement
are not to be seen as an isolated event within a narrative sequence, but as samples of what poor Joseph had normally to
endure on a daily basis. There is no interaction between the
two "characters," and no dialogue is recorded. The data given
in this section set the pattern of her wonted wantoness and his
pious perseverance. (Note the series of impfs. and related
ptcpls., etc. 3,1 ἔλεγε... 3.ἐμνησκόμην ...προσηυχόμην...
...4. ἐνήστευον ... ἐφαινόμην ...5...ἔπινον... ἐλάμβανον
... ἐδίδουν .) Because this section is not an episode,
the logical sequence is unimportant, and Braun is incorrect in
chastising the stupid narrator for not realizing that the
woman ought to have suggested killing her husband before offer-
ing to transfer his property and her obedience.

Episode II 3,6b-10 (Braun, p. 50f.)

There is no narrative transition at this point. At 3,6b, following more impfs., we learn of her nocturnal visitations, conducted initially under the guise of pseudo-maternal concern. The great difficulty in reading this section as continuous narrative is confirmed by the textual tradition. Charles prints ἠνόχλει μοι· καὶ γὰρ ἐν νυκτι Some mss. and Charles omit 7b καὶ ...ἄρρεν as obtrusive.[26] The longer text appears to contain two elements: A.) Joseph as the loyal and obedient servant who aids his owners by prayer, and B.) The ingenuous youth who does not see the actual motivation of his perfidious mistress. The piquant contrast between these two was evidently more significant to the longer text (which includes b here) than any concern for a smooth-flowing story. Without gar and the answered prayer the text is smoother and the possibility of a narrative construction is opened up.

The major problem in this section is, of course, the impossibility of her actual desires eluding Joseph at this juncture, when her true intentions had been fully established. Braun again looks at this problem as an example of poor narrative ability. Chs. 11-17 show, to the contrary, that the editor of T Jos was perfectly capable of telling a coherent story and that he or she understood the requirement of sequential development.

Episode III 4,1-3 (Braun, pp. 51f.)

This segment, like the first "episode," is based upon frequentative impfs. and refers once again to her customary deceit and his chaste endurance.[27] Exemplary piety is the point and repeated stress the leitmotiv of the entire pericope.

Episode IV 4,4-8 (Braun, pp. 52-55)

This incident is also to be seen as repeated. Note once again the use of impfs. Despite the snatch of dialogue, this passage is presented as still another typical situation.

Episode V 5,1-4 (Braun, pp. 55-57)

Chapters 5-8 do contain narrative episodes pertaining to specific incidents. In this section "Joseph stories" or legends have been utilized and strung together. The introduction... ἐν ἑτέρῳ χρόνῳ ... "on another occasion" proves that we are dealing with a string of items and not sequential episodes. The promise made in 3,2 "Thou shalt be lord of me and all that is in my house, if thou wilt give thyself unto me and thou shalt be as our master" (tr. Charles) would have been located at this point if the plan of the work had called for a chronological order.

Episode VI 6,1-8 (Braun, pp. 57-72)

This story seems to possess some logical sequence. 5,4, which mentions her gift-giving, provides a setting for the proffered dish. In terms of plot development Joseph either A.) having rejected her offer to kill Potiphar, has dangerous knowledge and must be liquidated, or B.) is immune to any blandishments and requires chemotherapy.[28] Whichever plan is intended (and the confusion supports my analysis of the peri-

cope as a whole), the action should bring their relationship to
a climax of one sort or another. This is the case in the similar situation of Apuleius Met. 10,4f. Although ch. 6 is the
most detailed and coherent unit within the passage under consideration and clearly is an independent Joseph legend, this
section still presents problems within the broader context.
After her attempt at seduction by magic or at assassination
fails, the woman simply reverts to new variations of her former
tactics. This scene is not part of a narrative plot, but is
rather one of a concatenation of cruel temptations.

Episode VII 7,1- 8 (or 8,1) (Braun, pp. 72-85)

Reverting to her previous style, the woman falls ill with
love and threatens suicide. Misinterpreting Joseph's sage
advice, she decides he really does love her, after all, and
provokes a psychological reflection.

As Braun correctly notes, the love-sickness plays no real
role in the "plot." In similar stories the illness might be
feigned to provide a basis for assignation, or it could be mis-
taken for physical sickness. Unfortunately, while 7,2 "And
when her husband saw her, he said unto her: Why is thy counte-
nance fallen? And she said unto him: I have a pain at my
heart, and the groanings of my spirit oppress me;" (tr. Charles)
is an explicit avowal of emotional illness, the final μη
ἀσθενοῦσαν   suggests a sham. The illness appears to be a
case of employing a popular motif for its own sake, without
clear relevance to or significance for the story.

7,3 complicates the issue to a further degree. τότε εἰσεπήδησε πρός με, ἔτι ὄντος ἔξω τοῦ ἀνδρὸς αὐτῆς.
Is τότε supposed to mean "after the (assumed) illness had been
treated"? How does ἔτι ἔξω   ...fit? One could reconstruct
a hypothetical source that has been quarried in chapter 7. The
presumption--which does not apply elsewhere in the pericope--is
that contact between the two is not easy to effect. In that
case the sham illness could become a pretext for sending her
husband off to find a doctor, or the like (however inappropriate such conduct would be for a ranking bureaucrat), thereby
providing an opportunity for liason.

Whatever the motives of an underlying source, the editor
of the passage used in T Jos is only interested in retailing
the motifs as peirasmoi of Joseph. Ch. 7 takes up the topic of
emotional pressure. Any problems thereby created for the "plot"
of the pericope as a whole are insignificant. The longer text
appears to have attempted to introduce clarity and consistency
into this chapter and to integrate it with a "plot." At 7,1ff.
Charles prints ἔτι δὲ ἡ καρδία αὐτῆς ἔκειτο εἰς τὸ κακὸν καὶ
περιεβλέπετο ποίῳ τρόπῳ με παγιδεῦσαι· στενάζουσα δὲ συντόμως
συνέπιπτε μὴ ἀσθενοῦσα...   3. τότε οὖν εὐκαιρίαν
λαβοῦσα, εἰσεπήδησε...29   The underscored words,
none of which appear in the shorter recension(s), rationalize
the events into sequence and relate them to the previous sections. The illness is definitely feigned and represents another
one of the many wiles she will use to achieve her objective.
The sickness is also depicted, however unclearly, as the cause
of an opportunity for a meeting. The longer recension appears
to try to homogenize the woman's character, to make her con-
sistently conspiratorial.

The greatest inconsistency in ch. 7 is indeed in the character of Mme. Potiphar. Her previous and subsequent self was aptly described by Braun as the 'type' of an "Oriental slave-keeper whose brutality in the enforcement of erotic desires knows no bounds."[30] In 7,3-6, however, she suddenly appears as a sentimental lover grasping desperately at straws of affection. The tension thus generated has affected the incident about her love-sickness. We cannot discern whether it is supposed to be sentimental and consonant with vv. 3-6 or feigned and in harmony with her character elsewhere (i.e., the longer text is only a partial harmonization of her character). T Jos probably draws from different sources which utilized either a 'tragic' or a 'romantic' adaptation of the Phaedra legend.[31]

Episode VIII 9,5 (Braun, pp. 85-87)

In order to achieve a narrative composed of separate and sequential episodes, Braun has to relocate this passage. His rearrangement is based upon his conclusions regarding the author's incompetence rather than proposed textual corruption.

I disagree. The placement of this verse clearly indicates that T Jos 3-9 does not present a series of episodes so much as a chain of temptations. The location may suggest that provocative nudity was the most potent weapon in Mme. P's arsenal.[32] This "episode" also portrays typical behavior rather than a specific incident (Note the frequentative impfs.). As Braun observed, her tempting beauty would be mentioned at the onset of a plot as a means of heightening tension.[33]

This was the final episode discussed by Braun. He quietly dropped his detailed study and analysis and suggested a few more parallels to other verses.[34] There is, of course, no structural or formal basis for omitting ch. 8 and the balance of ch. 9 from consideration. They are neither more nor less "episodic" than the preceding seven chapters.

Chapter 8

New material probably begins at 8,2. The major difficulty is the lack of logical transition. Joseph's antagonist is once again the brutal mistress who will stop at nothing. Her ἄρκει μοι μονον (7,6) has been forgotten. In 8,2, without preparation or transition, there is a brief allusion to her ultimate wickedness, attempted rape. Braun was surprised at the brevity of this "scene" and trots out, as usual, the hapless narrator.[35] If T Jos 3-9 were a "story," the rape scene would have received the detailed treatment appropriate to its climactic significance, as is the case, for instance, in the accounts of Philo and Josephus. The correct explanation must be that the audience is presumed to be familiar with the details of the Genesis story. The failure to capitalize upon this scene, which amounts to "throwing away" the climax of the whole tale, is destructive of Braun's thesis that T Jos is something like a romance. In place of the most important scene we have in 8,2-4 a rapid resumé of Gen. 39,11-20. T Jos supplies details where Genesis summarizes and summarizes where Genesis gives detailed information.

Chapter 9

This section continues the series of Joseph's temptations and deliverances. The frequentative πολλάκις and ποσάκις

are used in 9,1 and 9,4. Vv. 4 and 5 are not connected to one
another or to vv. 1-3. There is no narrative sequence. Ch. 9
is another string of typical _peirasmoi_. (On 9,5 see "Episode
VIII," above.)

T Jos 3-9, then, is not a continuous narrative. Although
it contains stories, it is not itself a "story." Logical sequence is absent, consistency of character is lacking, typical
scenes are preferred to specific incidents and the climax is
ignored. These "flaws" do not stem from what would have to be
the most woeful absence of narrative or editorial acumen; they
do point to a different form. The most likely candidate
appears to be the sermon or, more properly, a homiletic style.[36]

I propose that T Jos 2,1 to 10,4 is a homiletic passage
rather than a narrative, containing haggadic illuminations of
Gen. 39,10 and dealing with the topic of resisting the temptation to adultery. If these structural limits are accepted,
then chs. 1 and 10,5f. would be the linkage between 2-9 and
11-17 from the viewpoint of the composition of the _Testament_.
A tentative outline of the sermonic passage would be:

2,1-7. Introduction. Joseph as a type of the Virtue of
Chastity in conflict with wantoness and violence.

3,1-9,5. The Conflict. Ten Temptations (or "heats") and
Ten Triumphs through _Hypomone_.

10,1-4. Conclusion.

They hypothesis of a homiletic structure would seem to
give a very probable explanation for the formal and material
disparity of the content. Although the sources of T Jos 2-10
were evidently quite varied in form, meaning and cultural context, the passage was probably oriented toward an audience
accustomed to the attractions and temptations of life in the
Hellenized East.

Braun's concern with his own interesting theory about the
origin and historical development of Greek Romances led him, I
believe, to misdirect the significance of the literary parallels
he found. T Jos is not a romance, but it shares in common with
Romances, New Comedy, Mime, Acts and Hagiography the literary
interests of what we would call the "lower-middle class" population of the Hellenistic and Roman East. Sex, miracles,
sadism, superhuman virtue, tyrannical slaveowners, sentimental
lovers and last-minute escapes are stock items in the repertory
of ancient popular entertainment. The use of these motifs in
this sermonic pericope seems to provide a possible example of
how synagogue preaching could be made attractive, competitive
with the surrounding environment and appealing to both Jews and
any interested Gentiles.[37] The appeal to a population influenced by Hellenization extends beyond the plundering of popular
motifs, since T Jos 2,1-10,4 also appears to evoke the concept
of an _agon_ and to make use of traditional Greek popular ethical
ideas.

The metaphorical use of _agon_ for moral struggles was a
normal feature of the popular philosophical diatribe.[38]
Stauffer speaks of "many examples from Hellenistic Judaism" of
heroic struggles which the pious must endure.[39] Martyrological
and thus eschatological applications follow as a matter of

course. The use of the agon-concept in T Jos 2,7 is the same as that found in Philo and the popular philosophers: A moral struggle.

The virtue inculcated is Sophrosyne, in its popular sense of "chastity."[40] As antagonistai we meet akolasia (7,1 9,2) and bia (8,3). These contrasts are ethical commonplaces in the Hellenic world and ultimately derive from Greco-Roman cultural influence.[41]

According to my hypothesis the literary genre underlying T Jos 2,1-10,4 represents an interesting sample of one type of Jewish preaching in the Hellenistic or Roman period. Joseph's encounter with Potiphar's wife has become a triumph of virtue against all odds, a message of edifying content presented in popular philosophical and ethical terms and accompanied by a full range of entertaining diversions. Although one cannot call the passage under discussion "romance" in the sense of genre, it is suggestive of one approach to the difficult task of writing the history of popular forms. The various Gospels and acts indicate that the relationship between the "oral tradition" of preaching and story-telling and popular literary forms like novels is reciprocal. The first part of T Jos is an example of haggadic material which could either be utilized in a Joseph-Romance or be derived in part from such a novel. Whatever its deficiencies, the work of Martin Braun remains an important contribution to our understanding of the affinity between popular stories and literary fiction in the ancient world.

Richard I. Pervo
Seabury-Western Theological Seminary
Evanston, Illinois

NOTES

[1] I am grateful to Prof. John Strugnell, Mr. David Levenson and the Chairman of the Seminar for their critical comments and suggestions.

[2] History and Romance, p. 72.

[3] Ibid., pp. 89f.

[4] Some examples are: W.F. Albright, in his review, AJP 66:100-104, 1945, p. 104: "...his analysis...must be considered in general as eminently successful." Similarly, M. De Jonge, The Testaments, 1953, p. 103f., M. Hadas, Hellenistic Culture, 1959, p. 154, M. Hengel, Judaism and Hellenism, Tr., 1974, 1:111, and J. Becker, Untersuchungen z. Entstehungsgeschichte, 1970, p. 236. For a review from the perspective of Braun's views on the development of the ancient romances, see B. Perry, CJ 37:537-540, 1942.

[5] Rohde's thesis was developed in Der Griechische Roman und seine Vorlaeufer, 1876 (cited by pagination of 3d edition of 1914 and following). Two important early critiques, not based on revised chronology, are R. Heinze, Hermes 34:494-519, 1899 and K. Buerger, Studien z. Gesch. d. griech. rom. zw. Teil, 1903, pp. 4-10. One of Rohde's component elements, the love-elegy, is given primary significance by G. Giangrande, Eranos 60:132-159, 1962. Historiography as the basis of ancient novels was suggested by E. Schwartz, Fuenf Vortraege, 1896, J. Ludvikovsky, Recky Roman Dobrodruzny, 1925 (with Fr. summary) and R.M. Rattenbury in New Chapters, ed. J. Powell, 1933, pp. 211-257. Ludvikovsky emphasized the popular character and social setting of the ancient novels. Rattenbury gave an important survey of the then extant papyrus fragments. B. Lavagnini saw local legends as primary sources, Studi sul romanzo greco, 1921-50. (See also n.8, below). K. Kerenyi related ancient novels to religious literature. According to his theory the primary type was a secularized form of aretalogy; Die Griechische-Orientalische Romanliteratur, 1927. His last work on this subject, Der Antike Roman, 1971, was much more modest in scope and theory. R. Merkelbach, Roman und Mysterium, 1962, argued that the romances were, in fact, aretalogy, covert portrayals of cultic practice and belief. Cultural conditions, rather than formal antecedents, were stressed by F. Altheim, Lit. und Gesellschaft, V.1, 1948, pp. 13-48, and by B. Perry, The Ancient Romances, 1967. An excellent recent discussion of the problem is B. Reardon, Phoenix 23:291-310, 1969. One valuable brief survey is O. Weinreich, Der Griechische Liebesroman, 1962 (from 1932). E. Haight's Essays, 1943 and More Essays, 1945, contain useful summaries of plots and some survey of research.

[6] The fragments of Artapanus are one of Braun's chief examples of this largely hypothetical genre.

[7] For the Ninus fragments see F. Zimmerman, Griech. Roman-Papyri, 1936, and Wiss. Ztschr. d. Univ. Rostock 3:175-181, 1954.

[8] The corpus classicum refers to the novels ascribed to Chariton, Xenophon of Ephesus, Achilles Tatius, Longus and Heliodorus, all in Greek and relatively complete. Braun failed

to give Lavagnini credit for an earlier version of his own
theory (Studi, pp. 177-183). If Rohde's analysis of ancient
romances into the constituent motifs of love and travel were
taken seriously, two of what are usually considered to be the
"best" surviving novels, Apuleius' and Longus' would have to be
"dis-genred"!

[9]Other important attempts at refuting this dogma include
O. Schissel v. Fleschenberg, Entwicklungsgeschichte, 1913, B.
Lavagnini, Studi, S. Trenkner, The Greek Novella, 1958, and F.
Wehrli, Mus. Helv. 22:133-154, 1965. Rohde's views are stated
on pp. 5-8 and 583.

The terms "romance" and "novel" may be used interchangeably
with regard to ancient literature. By "novel" I mean a relatively lengthy work of (essentially) prose fiction. A "novella,"
on the other hand, is a relatively short story, without sub-
plots, possessing substantial unity in conception, time and
space.

[10]See n.3, above. Braun's study of T Jos is on pp. 44-93.
On collections of novelle in antiquity see W. Schmid's appendix
to Rohde in 1914 and later editions. Lucian's Toxaris and
Philopseudes are extant representatives.

[11]Braun, pp. 79f. 90.

[12]Rohde discusses the Oriental influences on pp. 40-59 and
578-601. Braun's own view is in the minority here. Kerenyi
also sees Oriental influence.

[13]For discussion of the Fortleben of the Phaedra story in
its varied settings, see, in addition to Braun, pp. 23f.,
Rohde, pp. 31 n. 4, 34-36, J. Ilberg in Roscher's Lexicon,
3:2223f., P. Wendland, De Fabellis Antiquis, 1913, pp. 11-15,
R. Soeder, Die Apokryphen Apostelgeschichten, 1932, pp. 141f.,
S. Thompson, Motif Index, 1934, K211 (=4:481), S. Trenkner,
Novella, pp. 64-66, M. Hadas, Culture, pp. 151-157, and T.
Gaster, Myth, Legend and Custom, 1969, pp. 217f. Illustrative
texts are Paus. 1,22,1 "...every foreigner, even, who has
learned Greek, is aware of Phaedra's love..." and Seneca,
Controv. 6,7 "Audite rem novam: fratrem crudelem, novercam
misericordem."

[14]On Story-Tellers in Greco-Roman antiquity see especially
Trenkner, Novella, Rohde, pp. 590f., A. Scobie, Aspects of the
Anc. Rom., 1969, pp. 20-29, and J. Thomson, The Art of the
Logos, 1935. Trenkner contends for the influence of popular
novelle even upon Euripides. Her important work sharpens
Braun's observations and cautions against trying to write the
history of genres by identifying the alleged sources of their
motifs.

[15]Adultery is also the problem in Jubilees 39,6, Philo De
Jos. 40-53, Josephus, Ant. 2:39-59 and Bereshit Rabbah 87,3
(in cultic terms).

[16]The suicide threat in Tobit 3,7ff. is not sentimentally
developed. Braun may be correct in suspecting the influence
of Greek literature on Tobit, p. 75.

[17] E.g., p. 56.

[18] Braun, pp. 47. 91f.

[19] Text in The Literature of Ancient Egypt, ed. W. Simpson et al., 2d ed., 1973, pp. 92-107 (New Kingdom Period).

[20] Dea Syria 20-27, on which see W.F. Albright, JBL 37:111-143, 1918. See also n.31, below.

[21] The Phaedra of Euripides' surviving (seond) edition does not threaten suicide because she can't have Hippolytus, but so that she won't. Her actual suicide resulted from the exposure of her desire.

[22] Pp. 76, 85, with references.

[23] This statement must obviously be qualified by the lack of appropriate Oriental sources from the period in question. Ruth has sentimental appeal, however different from Greco-Roman fiction. Esther, Judith and Tobit may be influenced by Greek literature. The Egyptian Petubastis-Romance and related cycles clearly are: A. Volten, Mitth. aus d. Pap'smmlg d. Oest. Natl. 5:147-152, 1956. In any case, the cultural context of T Jos 3-9 is Hellenistic or Roman.

[24] The motif of ten trials of Abraham is presented in Jubilees 17-19, esp. 17,17f. and 19,8. In both T Jos and Jubilees the traditional number is more important than the actual temptations listed, since a division into ten is difficult in each case. In Aboth 5,4 the ten trials, נסיונות, of Abraham are alluded to in a Stichwort series on "ten." Num. 14,22 could be a model for this pattern. Becker, pp. 234f. tries to outline the ten temptations in T Jos.

[25] Braun does not give the limits of his episodic divisions. I have tried to reconstruct chapter and verse divisions from his comments.

[26] R.H. Charles, The Greek Versions, 1908, p. 186. (In fairness to Braun one must note that he basically accepted the text printed by Charles.) My hypothesis does not depend upon a text-critical theory. Acceptance of even the fullest (usually Charles' "Alpha-Recension") text as primary would not invalidate the arguments put forth in this paper. The longer text does incline toward a logical narrative sequence. This is form-critically secondary and could be secondary in the history of the textual tradition. Even if the longer text of 3,7 is an interpolation, it is congenial to the form of the passage.

[27] Hypomone, patient endurance, is a theme which pervades T Jos (E.g., 2,7 10,1 17,1). Endurance is also the key-note in Abraham's victory over ten temptations (Jubilees 17,18, see n.24). The term is also frequent in 4 Macc. and Test. Job and martyrological literature. See F. Hauck, TDNT 4:583-585 and n.39, below. Peirasmos, agon and hypomone appear to be elements of a common pattern.

[28] The goeteia is probably poison, although love-potions

and poisons were confused in antiquity. See Braun, pp. 58f.
T Reub 4,9 and T Jos 6,2 give the impression of an aphrodisiac,
but 6, 5-9 seems to related to a fatal poison and introduces an
irresoluable ambiguity. Two motifs may have converged here.
The meaning of the miracle story, which is of a familiar type,
is that true believers are immune to poison. Cf. Acts 28,6,
Prochorus' edition of the Acts of John 8f., Mk. 16,18, Lk. 10,
19, Braun, pp. 70f. and Hennecke-Schneemelcher 2:206. (Contra
Braun, Propertius 2,1,51f., Seu mihi sunt tangenda novercae
pocula Phaedrae/ Pocula privigno non nocitura suo, does refer
to fatal poison, as the context makes clear.)

[29]Versions, pp. 191f.

[30]P. 50, with references.

[31]Sentimentalized suicide threats are not found in Phaedra-
type episodes in ancient novels. These threats are almost exclusively reserved for the principals and their allies. Braun
overlooks this. Dea Syria 22 is a close parallel to T Jos 7 in
terms of motifs. Both love-sickness and a suicide threat are
present (without sentimental ornamentation) and fit the story
suitably. Some may wish to find a Semitic tradition here. For
feigned illness see also 2 Sam. 13,6.

[32]For the powerful (and morally mitigating) effects of
nudity see T Reub 3,11-15. Braun, pp. 85f., overstates the
case in finding this verse too indelicate for a Greek romance.
The tactics are typically "barbarian." In the superlatively
chaste novel of Heliodorus, the Phaedra-type, who is also the
wife of an Egyptian official, employs the same technique (7,9).
Christian censorship has severely limited the survival of
ancient romances to the more sentimental and delicate type.
Petronius' Satyricon survived, only in fragments, because of
its latinity. For an example of a risqué novel, see the
Lollianos-fragments published by A. Henrichs, 1972. Achilles
Tatius in antiquity, like Fielding in the 19th Century, parodied
the puritan aspect of the sentimental romance.

[33]P. 85,n.1.

[34]P. 87.

[35]P. 74.

[36]Becker, p. 230, also sees the style of a synagogue
sermon.

[37]The possibility of Gentile listeners is left open by the
reliance upon common moral values and metaphors, the absence
of particular Jewish issues and legal formulations, the failure
to stress sexual relations with a "foreign" woman as especially
sinful and the use of hypsistos as a divine title.

[38]So E. Stauffer, TDNT 1:134. See also Becker, p. 233,
and R. Heinze, Philologus 50:458-468, 1891. Dio Chrysostom Or.
8 is a very interesting example of a similar diatribe from the
Greek world. This oration, Peri Aretes, uses the agon motif
illustrated by a sermon on the Ponoi of Heracles. The traditional Cynic criticism of Greek gymnastics could enhance the

appeal of this topos to Jews.

[39]Ibid. Among his examples are Philo, Agric. 119 (Loeb 3:168), Praem. et Poen. 5f. (Loeb 8:314-316), 4 Macc. 12,15 and Wisdom 4,1f. The Testament of Job develops this motif in detail. The Passion of Ss. Perpetua and Felicitas 10 is a noteworthy example from hagiography. Asceticism is prominent in 4 Esdr. 7,125-127.

[40]On "Chastity," see U. Luck, TDNT 7:1097-1104, Tuerk, RE 5:1106, D. Philipson, JE 3:680f., D. Feldman, Enc Jud 5:363f., I. Burns et al. ERE 3:494-499, G. Moore, Judaism, 1930, 2:267-272 and Kerenyi, Romanlit., pp. 224-228. As a virtue of Joseph: Philo, De Jos. 40, Josephus, Ant. 2:48 and Joseph and Asenath 4,9. The evils of illicit sex are stressed in T Reub 3,10-6,4, T Simeon 5,1-4, and T Judah 13,1-17,2. Cf. T. Issachar 4,4 7,2.

[41]See H.W. Hollander, below, pp. 61f. and references in his note 177, and Rohde, p. 343.

PATIENT LOVE IN THE TESTAMENT OF JOSEPH

Walter Harrelson

I. Scope of the paper

This paper offers a brief analysis of the second
narrative in the Testament of Joseph (10:5-20:6).
Other questions, of which there are many, will simply
be given a tentative answer at the start of the paper.
It is not possible in this short study to deal indepen-
dently with them. The analysis of the story will
disclose some items that support the general conclusions about the Testaments of the Twelve Patriarchs with
which the paper opens.

II. Judgments regarding the Testaments of the Twelve
Patriarchs

I am persuaded by those interpreters who, earlier
and more recently, place the Testaments in their
original form in the period prior to the Maccabaean
uprising. The author in all probability wrote in Greek
to Greek-speaking Jews in the diaspora, especially in
Egypt, although it is not at all impossible that his
writing was in Hebrew and was early translated into
Greek. The author comes from the early Hasidic movement in Palestine. His thought has connection with
that of the later Essene and Pharisaic movements and
reflects influence from Hellenistic wisdom as well as
from apocalyptic. But it is a Jewish work addressed
to Jews; its author is significantly influenced by the
division of authority between a priestly and a "secular"
figure as characterized by the prophet Zechariah in
chs. 3-6.[1])

The Testaments consist of three distinguishable
parts: 1) narratives portraying the life of the
respective patriarchs, drawn in part from the Hebrew
Bible and in part from popular haggadic tradition;
2) judgments concerning the future of Israel under the
guidance of descendants of Judah and Levi; and 3)
ethical counsel to the descendants and brothers of the
respective patriarchs. Of these three elements, the
last clearly dominates in the Testaments.

The author is a real author, although he used some
sources primarily as a compiler of tradition. The
conception of the work as a series of "last words" of
the twelve patriarchs is apparently his creation. It
seems highly probable that this conception initiates
the long sequence of testaments of ancient worthies,
since it would appear that the Testaments of the Twelve
Patriarchs is the earliest of the testaments from
Jewish and Christian sources of the period 200 BCE to

CE 200.

The author's work was particularly well suited in form and content to be supplemented in the course of its transmission. Jewish additions to the original Testaments seem clearly to have occurred, probably especially as it circulated in Egypt. Significant and extensive Christian additions were made after its incorporation into Christian literature and for many centuries thereafter. While it may be said that the Testaments, as preserved by the Christian community, represent a Christian document, it is possible to move back from the Christian work to its likely original contents and then forward to trace the Jewish and Christian additions to the work. Such an approach to the study of such Jewish literature with major Christian additions is more workable than the effort to move from the Christian work back, step by step, to the presumed original.

III. The second story in the Testament of Joseph

The second story in the Testament of Joseph (10:5-20:6) in all likelihood is the original testament of Joseph of our early 2nd century BCE author. To him we can assign 1:1-2, the introduction, and all of 10:5-20:6 with the exception of the clearly intrusive section, 19:1-12.[2] That section is certainly not alien in thought to our author, since he unmistakably wishes to underscore the continuing significance of Judah and Levi. It seems highly probable, however, that in a testament of Joseph the author would not wish to underrate the significance of Joseph or in any way to subordinate the words and work of Joseph to those of Judah and Levi. A Jewish addition, probably made in Egypt, accounts for the early form of this addition. A Christian interpolator added the Christian references.

The remainder of this paper is devoted to an analysis of this second story, with references drawn to the first story and to other parts of the Testaments.

1. The theme of the story

We begin by stating the theme of the work. It is unmistakable. Joseph loves his brothers with a kind of love that refuses to press its own claims. Joseph will not save himself or ease his sufferings by relating to his captors that his own brothers sold him into slavery. This misdeed of the brothers whom he loves must not be made public, not by Joseph. Joseph is motivated not just by the desire to preserve the honor of his father and his family, although he has that desire. He is motivated by love of the brothers, by love of those who have wronged him. His understanding of Torah is one that requires him to be faithful to the divine requirements, but chief among those requirements is that of love for the other person. Others must be given preference over oneself. One's own suffering and humiliation cannot be eased by the simple expedient of pressing one's own justice and innocence no matter the consequences upon those one loves. Love must be marked by patience, by endurance in suffering, by refusal to harm others for the sake of one's own wellbeing.

2.   The structure of the story

Formally, the Testament of Joseph in its original shape is quite closely akin to the other testaments. In 1:1-2, the original introduction, we are first told that we have before us a copy of Joseph's testament. The term _diatheke_ clearly means "testament," not "covenant," even though covenant form may have been employed in the testaments, as Baltzer has maintained.[3]

Joseph called his sons and brothers to him at the time of his death and summoned them to hear his last words. These last words in the original testament begin at 10:5. The words open in the familiar way with a brief account of events in the life of the patriarch that illustrate and make graphic the kind and quality of life to which the patriarch is committed. From these events the patriarch draws words of counsel to those gathered around as to how they are to live their lives. This makes up the body of the testament.

Its conclusion appears in ch. 20. A brief word about the future points to the coming oppression of Israel in Egypt and God's deliverance of the people from bondage. Brief instructions to those gathered concerning Joseph's burial and the burial of his wife conclude the testament. Note is taken that Joseph then died at a ripe old age, and a note is given that in fact Joseph's bones were taken up from Egypt and buried in Hebron (this against the clear biblical tradition that Joseph was buried near Shechem, Josh. 24:32).

As noted above, such a structure, with its inter-leaving of historical narrative and words of instruction drawn from the events related, is particularly suited to later expansion. Such expansion clearly occurred in this instance as in those of the other testaments. But the body of the testament is discern-ible and has the familiar structure found in the others.

3.   The figure of Joseph

The clue to an understanding of the entire Testa-ments of the Twelve Patriarchs is the way in which the author treats three of the patriarchs: Levi, Judah, and Joseph. This point has been widely recognized. Our concern is with the figure of Joseph in the present story, although of course Joseph is a prominent person in several of the other testaments as well.

Levi is presented as a visionary and as the custodian of Torah. He is not singled out for blame in the destruction of the Shechemites, nor is Simeon. Levi and Joseph are the particularly exemplary patriarchs in their conduct, although Issachar, Zebulun,

Naphtali, Asher, and Benjamin are portrayed as faithful to God as well. But Levi's special significance lies not in his upright life but in his custodianship of Israel's worship and interpretation of Torah.

Judah is a vivid example of sins to be avoided, but he is at the same time the one on whom is to rest the responsibility for leadership over God's people. The original Testaments of the Twelve Patriarchs may well not have been concerned with the fulfillment of "secular" messianic hopes, but it certainly viewed the promise of a descendant from the tribe of Judah as certain of fulfillment.

Judah and Levi, then, represent the figures upon whom the author places his hope for Israel's political and religious future. But Joseph is the figure around whom clusters the author's most fundamental judgment. God's people Israel will survive and prosper in the world if it is ready to follow the example and the admonitions of Joseph.

It is remarkable how the author is able to make of Joseph an example for the individual Jew to follow as to conduct in an alien culture and at the same time to let Joseph stand as a paradigm for the entire people of God. This extraordinary way of addressing the need of the individual for moral guidance and at the same time holding fast to the Jewish sense of community arises, in part at least, from the form of the Testaments of the Twelve Patriarchs, as I have sought to show elsewhere.[4] The patriarchs on their deathbeds give counsel to their children and other relatives. Each individual has counsel provided for his personal existence, but he has this counsel from the forefather, addressed to the entire assembly of his family and associates. What applies to the individual applies to the whole people. And the inclusion of the author's picture of Israel's future under the leadership of Levi and Judah underscores the communal character of the ethics of the Testaments. Levi, Judah, and Joseph cover respectively the religious, political, and ethical commitments and hopes of God's people.

4.   Patient love in the Testament of Joseph

Let us now examine the teaching of the author with regard to love of others. It is a constant theme in the entire Testaments of the Twelve Patriarchs, of course. In our story, however, it has its most distinctive features. That is so, I believe, because of how the figure of Joseph functions in the Testaments. Joseph represents the Jewish community and the individual Jew in a situation in which the temptations of diaspora Judaism are at their height: to compromise one's allegiance to Yahweh alone; to live by Torah half-heartedly; and above all, to forget one's membership in the community of God's people.

Our story of patient love on Joseph's part underscores this last point. Readers can see that the woman of Memphis is aflame with lust for the young slave, but Joseph is quite unaware of all this. His concern is fixed not upon his own life or upon temptations that may await him in the house of Pentephri; it is on the love of his brothers, on the need to demonstrate love for others even when they do one harm. Such a concern not to expose others to shame and disgrace applies to the eunuch of the woman of Memphis (16:6) just as it applies to one's own brothers. While Joseph may be ignorant of the designs of the Memphian woman, the story may also be implying that Joseph rightly does not suspect her motives; he gives to her conduct the benefit of the doubt.

I consider this picture of love to be the most remarkable teaching in the entire Testament of the Twelve Patriarchs. It goes beyond the love of others that is commended in the other testaments. It is interiorized, made constituent of the very life of Joseph that he prefer others to himself, put himself at the disposal of others, and never forget that the witness of God's people Israel in the world, especially in the world of foreigners, requires patient, long-suffering love.

IV. Implications from the second story

This picture of Joseph in Egypt seems to me extremely well suited to convey the author's message to fellow Jews, individually and collectively, who find themselves among the diaspora, as well as to those who live under the domination of foreigners who rule in the homeland. The author's basic concern is with the health of the people of God. Levi must be given authority in the interpretation of Torah. The hope in God's raising up a righteous king from the line of Judah is not to be abandoned. The conduct of God's people, wherever they are, is to be marked not only by obedience to the letter of Torah. It is to be marked by active love of the brothers, love of one's fellow Jews, of such a sort that it becomes constitutive for the life of each individual.

But this is not to say that the author has handed over Jewish concern for the health of God's people to individuals within the community. Joseph is addressing all of his children and relatives; his words apply to all of the people of God. His concern is not with himself. He is not saying that love of others inevitably brings the favor of God and therefore prosperity. He is not teaching the Stoic view that the self is enhanced through love of others. He insists that such a readiness to suffer harm for the sake of love of others, and especially God's people, is a style of living that "spills over" into one's conduct with all persons, Jew and pagan alike. Thus, love of others characterizes the faithful member of the community of God's people, in whatever circumstances that member may find himself.

The author does not shrink from the statement that in fact God did prosper Joseph in Egypt. He does not fail to stress his special interest in Joseph's love of his own brothers who have sinned. But the author should not be faulted for that special interest in the health of God's people. The faithful Jew, loyal to the covenant and to Torah, lives a life from which non-Jews also draw benefit. The non-Jew will learn something about Yahweh from the faithful witness to Yahweh borne by those Jews who live in his presence and locality. The Testaments of the Twelve Patriarchs is not a missionary document. It does not aim at the bringing in of many proselytes from the non-Jewish world. The author is concerned with the fidelity of God's people to Torah. One of the central ways of fidelity, in his view, is that of active love for the members of the covenant community, an active love that, once constitutive of the life of an individual, cannot be turned off when one deals with non-Jews.

V.   Conclusion

In this story from the Testament of Joseph we confront the special concern of our author regarding the conduct of God's people in the world. The fabric of the Jewish community has been badly rent, by internal dissension, by corrupt priests, by envy of the way of life found in the Hellenistic culture that now pervades the land of the promise. Our author does not call for active political efforts to overthrow the foreign rulers. He does not call for a withdrawal from public life so that God's people may be faithful to Torah and be a true witness to God until the consummation breaks in. He does not counsel compromise and a holding up of the letter of Torah, thus effec- tively separating the religious and the secular dimensions of Jewish life. Rather, he addresses the inner qualities of the life of God's people. They are to avoid fornication, envy, the love of riches, the desire to lord it over others. They are to live by Torah, trust in God's promises, and love one another. They are to be ready to let the other prosper at one's own expense, if necessary, counting upon God's own righteousness and God's own mercy to carry one through times of trial and temptation. Nothing is more central to our author than patient, self-sacrificing love.

It is often thought that such teaching cannot appear in Judaism. Becker goes to great lengths to distinguish the author's teaching on love from Christian love.[5] I see no need or warrant for such efforts. Thomas[6] rightly points out that such under- standings do occur for a first time, and we have no way of insisting when they are permitted to occur. Christian love does of course have a universal setting, connected with the impulse of the Christian movement to share what it has seen and heard with all peoples in all times and places. Our author has, I believe,

stated with extraordinary originality and power some
of the fundamental dimensions of "Christian" love in
his document from a time two centuries earlier than
the establishment of Christian communities in his
locality. He has done so in connection with his pro-
found understanding of what was required to enable the
Jewish witness to the God of the covenant to endure
and to thrive in an environment in which God's people
no longer had political authority at their disposal.[7]

Notes

1. I am combining elements of the views of Juergen Becker,
    Untersuchungen zur Entstehungsgeschichte der Testa-
    mente der Zwoelf Patriarchen (Leiden: Brill, 1970) and
    Johannes Thomas in Christoph Burchard, Jacob Jervell,
    and Johannes Thomas, Studien zu den Testament der Zwoelf
    Patriarchen, ed. Walther Eltester, BZAW 36 (Berlin: A.
    Toepelmann, 1969). I am not persuaded by the inter-
    pretation of Marinus De Jonge, The Testaments of the
    Twelve Patriarchs (Assen: Van Gorcum, 1953), that the
    work is a Christian document making use of Jewish
    traditions or of the interpretation of Marc Philonenko
    (see Cahier de la RHPhR 35, 1960) that the work is in
    essential character Essene.

2. This is the view of Becker and is well argued and
    demonstrated; Untersuchungen, 239-243.

3. Klaus Baltzer, The Covenant Formulary (Philadelphia:
    Fortress Press, 1971), 141-163. Transl. by David E.
    Green from Das Bundesformular, 2nd ed. (Neukirchen-
    Vluyn: Neukirchener Verlag, 1964).

4. See my brief essay in Essays on Old Testament Ethics,
    J. P. Hyatt Festschrift, ed. J. L. Crenshaw and J. T.
    Willis (New York: KTAV, 1974), 205-213.

5. Becker, Untersuchungen, 381-401.

6. Thomas, 94-95.

7. The extensive paper by Harm W. Hollander, "The Ethical
    Character of the Patriarch Joseph: A Study in the
    Ethics of the Testaments of the Twelve Patriarchs,"
    has been highly suggestive for me in the preparation
    of this paper, although I did not have time to examine
    Hollander's findings in detail.

Walter Harrelson
Divinity School
Vanderbilt University
Nashville, Tennessee 37240

THE NARRATIVES OF THE TJ AND THE ORGANIZATION OF THE TESTAMENTS OF THE XII PATRIARCHS (TP)

Anitra Bingham Kolenkow

The stories of TJ 1-10:4 (3-10:4) and 10:5-18:4 are dissimilar and therefore are often considered incompatible. The occurrence of the dissimilar stories together in one work has generally been explained as the product of one or more interpolations into an originally one-motif oriented work. However, this theory does not explain certain charac- teristics of the structure of TP as a whole. One must therefore seek a different answer which explains these characteristics in TP as well as the individual motifs of TJ 1-10:4 and 10:5-18:4.

A. The Argument that One of the Two Stories of TJ Must Be an Interpolation

The TP have many inconsistencies and awkward connections between materials, at least some of which may be the result of interpolations. However, the theory of interpolations has been overstressed in the analysis of TP. The TJ has been a particular victim of such analysis.[1] Critics have used differences in type of story or emphasis to prove that either TJ 1-10:4 or 10:5-18:4 is an interpolation -- without consi- deration of the possible structural use of the story or passage. R. H. Charles noted that the two stories were not presented in proper time sequence and he considered the second story an interpolation.[2] More recently, J. Becker calls the first story an interpolation because it resembles Hellenistic romance and emphasizes σωφροσύνη (unlike the rest of TP).[3]

Studies of apocalyptic structure and literature should, however, have taught critics that there are times when appropriate materials (which use language that is not that of the author) have been used at the appropriate structural point in a text. One criterion for deciding "whether a piece of material is interpolation or part of a coherent structure" should be whether one can find in the work an integral structural purpose for the use of the particular material. If one can find such a structural purpose, then the likelihood is that the material was used in the work by the person who composed the work and its structure. Using such a criterion, is it possible to find a structural purpose for the two stories of the TJ?

37

B.   The Possibility of a "Several Virtues" Emphasis in a
     Testament

     In addition to Becker's postulate that "TJ 1:3-10:4 is
an interpolation because of its similarity to Hellenistic
romance," Becker also uses another tool to strengthen his
argument that TJ 1:3-10:4 is an interpolation. He rightly
stresses that the TP emphasize the virtue of love of the
brethren throughout their combined extent. Therefore, since
TJ 1:3-10:4 (and especially 3-10:4) does not stress brotherly
love, Becker says that TJ 1:3-10:4 must be a secondary interpolation. Becker further argues the probability of his
interpolation thesis by noting that not only his "non-interpo-
lated TJ" but also the testaments of Jub 20 and 36 emphasize
the virtue of brotherly love or love of neighbor. Thus Becker
argues that the single virtue of brotherly love is suitable
as the major subject of a testament. (384)

     However, Becker's examples of "one virtue" testaments
illumine the problem to be attacked in questioning whether
TJ 1:3-10:4 is in fact an interpolation. One example, Jub 20,
not only emphasizes the virtue of love of neighbor (20:2)
but also speaks against fornication (20:3-6). Thus a testament does not have to emphasize one virtue such as love of
brethren. Therefore, part of Becker's argument may be incorrect.

     The possibility of several emphasized virtues (or vices)
in TP's testaments is, of course, evident from numerous passages in TP. The particular possibility of stressing brotherly
love (or opposing jealousy and being angry) together with
"not fornicating" (as does Jub 20) may also be illustrated in
TP. TJud 13:3 speaks about "the spirits of jealousy and
fornication." TB (a somewhat summary work) asks for love of
neighbor (3:3-5:4) and speaks against fornication. (Note
that 8:1-9:1 is a crossover passage moving from discussion of
hatred of brethren to a discussion of fornication.) The first
two testaments also show the possibility of combining an
emphasis on lack of jealousy and fornication. TR emphasizes
fornication, but then (in a crossover passage) says, "In
fornication..... all jealousy dwelleth in the lust thereof."
(6:4) and forecasts jealousy towards the sons of Levi
(6:5). TS emphasizes jealousy and envy of the brethren and
then warns against fornication and says he knows the sons
will be fornicators (5:3-4) and will do harm to the sons of
Levi.[4] TL seems to justify Levi's (with Simeon) Gen 49 sin
of anger by a vision ordering Levi's action against the
circumcised (5:3, 6:6) and also warns of fornication (9:10).[5]
Thus several testaments (besides TJ) show a unifying of
materials about fornication and jealousy (envy, anger).
This occurs in several types of material -- in short phrases,
in crossover presentations and in crossover materials between
emphasis on one sin and emphasis on another. Thus the material of TP suggests the possibility is not to be excluded
(and indeed is quite probable) that TJ would argue against
the vices of fornication and hatred of the brethren (or for
the virtues of chastity and love of the brethren).

C. The Particular Emphases of Certain Individual Testaments
   as Evidences against the Hypothesis of Interpolation

The recognition of the possibility of uniting opposition
to two or more vices (and especially those of jealousy-hatred
and fornication) in TP frees the critic to look at the possibility of a structure for TP which unites criticism of two
vices with affirmation of two virtues. Is there any point,
essential to the structure of TP, which would argue for a
presentation of both pro-chastity and pro-brotherly love
motifs in TJ? As is evident from the above study, the answer
is "Yes." The first two works of TP are concerned with a
person who was a model of fornication and another who was
angry with his brother. In both testaments, Joseph's virtue
is contrasted with the brother's vice. TR, the testament of
the first brother, emphasizes his fornication (1:6, 4:6).
Reuben says that Joseph (in contrast) purged himself from
fornication (4:8). (Thus part of the testament is concerned
with setting up Joseph as a model of one who does not fornicate.) The children are also asked to beware of fornication
and, in order to be pure (a characteristic of Joseph[6]),
to guard their senses (6:1). TS, the testament of the second
brother, emphasizes jealousy of brethren and envy (2:7, 3:1-6)
with wrath (2:11). Simeon also gives a picture of Joseph as
one who bears no malice[7] and loves Simeon (4:4, 6). Simeon
then warns against jealousy and envy so that his children may
have the reward of Joseph (who did not have these sins 4:5).
Thus, both the testaments of Reuben and Simeon use the major
sin of the patriarch to warn against it and they each contrast
the sin with the particular opposite virtue of Joseph (seeking
that their sons follow the virtue of Joseph).
    Becker has declared that such contrasts and "urgings
to follow Joseph" are interpolations because he says
that they are not common in TP (246 on TB 3:1).[8]

These contrasts are important for an understanding of the
structure and origins of TP. The comparison in TR is specifically with the picture of Joseph given in the first story of
TJ (3-10:4); the term "Egyptian woman" is used and magic is
mentioned. The comparison in TS is with the Joseph "love of
brethren" story, the second story in TJ. Thus, one may argue
that the testaments of Reuben, Simeon and Joseph are deliber-
ately set up in contrast to each other, with the two stories
in TJ corresponding and opposed to the characteristic sins of
Reuben and Simeon. In TJ, Joseph's story of chastity and
continence effectively serves as a contrast to Reuben's story
of fornication. Joseph's second story of love of brethren
contrasts with Simeon's story of anger and jealousy. As has
been noted, TR and TS also contain admonition against not only
their own sin but also against the sin of the other brother.
The total effect of these features is that of purposeful
combination of warnings and affirmations. In TR, Reuben warns
against his own sin of fornication, praises Joseph's virtue
of purity and also warns against Simeon's sin of jealousy.
The testament of Simeon warns against his own sins of anger,
envy and jealousy, contrasts this with Joseph's love of
brethren and warns against Reuben's sin of fornication.
Thus, there is a conscious intertwining of these three testaments -- intertwining which involves the two stories of TJ.

This is the structural basis for the use of the two stories in TJ. (As noted above, TB also combines emphasis against the sins of fornication and envy. TL may also be related to this intertwining since TR and TS relate the other brother's sin to action against Levi -- and there seems to be a motion in TL to absolve Levi from the joint sin of Simeon and Levi in Gen 40.)

Recognition of the structural use of such contrasts explains the difficulties noticed by Charles and Becker. Charles noted that the stories of TJ were not in "proper" time sequence -- and that the stories might be reversed in order. However, if the author of TJ wished to present in TJ a parallel but contrasting presentation to the presentation and order of topic of the first two testaments, then the present order would be natural -- an antifornication story (corresponding to TR's emphasis on fornication) followed by an anti-hatred of brother story (corresponding to TS's emphasis on jealousy and hatred toward a brother). The order is required by the order in age of the elder brothers -- cf. Gen 49. Becker raised the problem that TJ 1:3-10:4 is a story with an (unique for TP) emphasis on σωφροσύνη -- an emphasis common in Hellenistic romance. Therefore, Becker argues that the story must be secondary interpolation. However, the above structural suggestions for the composition of TP suggest that TJ 1:3-10:4 may be a primary part of TJ rather than a secondary addition. In view of the common use of Joseph as a model of anti-fornication (cf. Jub 39:6) and σωφροσύνη (Philo De Jos 57, 87), a story about Joseph's σωφροσύνη would be a natural foil to the fornication story about Reuben.

Thus this paper would argue that the two stories of TJ are part of a structural whole in which the sins of Reuben and Simeon are contrasted with the two virtues of Joseph shown in the stories of TJ. This hypothesis explains both the order of the stories in TJ and the reason for use of stories in TJ about σωφροσύνη and love of brethren.

Note: Although this theory would invalidate Becker's solution to the problem of the two stories in TJ, it may strengthen Becker's hypothesis (172) that the original of TP was in Greek. If TJ 3-10:4 was originally a pre-TJ Greek composition, as might be argued likely from the σωφροσύνη emphasis, then the original of TP might spring from a Greek speaker who knew the σωφροσύνη motif (or story) in relation to Joseph. Becker would not seem correct that 1:3-10:4 is a separate piece added later as a whole. TJ 2:7b and 10:1, 2 seem to be crossover materials composed by an author who wishes to combine an emphasis on purity and patience with the emphasis of a story on chastity -- and sees these virtues triumphing over envy and slavery (really the topics of the next section). Such crossover material would be similar to the passages in TR and TS which unite in one sentence emphases on jealousy and fornication (see above) -- and would seem to be typical of the author. Also TJ 1:1 does not have to lead directly into TJ 10:5, but quite as logically leads into 1:4.

D. The Contrast Emphasis as Suggestive of the Original
     Structural Format of TP

Although Becker suggested that the combining and contrasting materials of TP were secondary, the above hypothesis
sees them as primary. The complicated combination of compli-
mentary vices and virtues, however, is indeed limited to certain testaments. If this is not chance, does the argument
suggest that there may have been a smaller group of testaments
(with an emphasis on contrast) prior to the present configura-
tion of twelve testaments? Although the testaments have been
overlaid with interpolated materials, is there any other evidence that TR, TS, TJ and TB (and possibly TL, TJud and TZ
-- since parallels can be or have been made between these
testaments and TJ, TR and TS material) are part of an original
smaller grouping?

As has been often noted, certain of the TP have stricter
testamental structure than do others. TR and TS are particularly noted for such structure -- and these are the only
ones which seem to have the complicated internal parallels
with each other and with the TJ. Certain internal parallels
may also be noted between a limited group of testaments:
     TR and TJ are the only testaments which address brothers
     as well as sons. TR and TS are the only works which
     give a definite period of prayer and fasting after sin
     (seven years TR 1:10; two years, TS 3:4 -- which may
     be compared with a seven year period of fasting before
     endurance in TJ 3:4 and a twelve day fast before con-
     ception in TB 1:4. Only TR, TS, TL, TZ, TJ and TB have
     "reward like Joseph" passages.[10] The significance of the
     above noted similarities in certain of the TP is emphasi-
     zed when compared with Becker's elaboration of "testa-
     mental feature" study. Becker notes that of the works
     which have one set of preamble features, TR and TS have
     all five elements (159). He also notes that TR, TS and
     TL have all three elements of the tale part of the pre-
     amble (160). He then notes that in the "death section"
     TR, TS, TL and one version of TB belong to a particular
     group of "form A" which may be differentiated from a
     "form B" found in TJud, TI, TN, TG, TA and a type of
     TB (164). TJud also has features of form A; TZ is basi-
     cally form A (168) and TJ also uses parts of form A (167);
     TD is mixed (166), but more like "B" (159).[11]
The combination of differentiable structural presentations
with particular sets of contrast and "reward like Joseph"
presentations (where both the contrasts and the testamental
structure are most clearly delineated in the same works, TR
and TS) fosters the argument that there was indeed a smaller
group of testaments in the original form of TP. This group
differs both in form and contrast emphasis from other sections
of the present TP. Thus the contrast phenomena, which seemed
only sporadic and secondary to Becker, may be argued to be
essential to the original construction of the TP. A less
exact use of testamental form and a lack of contrast-reward
usage would seem to be characteristics of the writer who
added to the smaller group of testaments to produce a group
of twelve testaments.[12]

E. The Use of Contrast for Paraenesis

Recognition of the use of contrast between Joseph and certain of his brethren -- especially in regard to fornication and brotherly love -- gives explicit direction to the search for parallels to (and the origin of) TP's structure. What one is looking for is "uses of contrast between biblical figures (and especially Joseph and certain brothers) as a method of paraenesis."

The presentation of lives of contrasting figures to support demands for righteousness would seem not uncommon in Hellenistic Judaism. The testament of Tobit shows one example. Tobit compares the lives and fates of Aman and Manasses (Nedab and Ahikar) to end his testament with a vision of the value of righteousness (Tob 14:10). Both Philo and the Epistle of Aristeas present Moses as one giving accounts of exemplary lives and punishments. Philo (De Prae 2) says that Moses gave accounts of good and evil lives and their punishments and rewards as examples for life. Ep Arist 13 says, "Our lawgiver first of all laid down the principles of piety, not merely by prohibitions but by the use of examples as well, demonstrating the injurious effects (of sin) and the punishments inflicted by God on the guilty." In a later period, 2 Bar 62-66 shows the parallel setting up of the contrasting deeds and rewards of Jeroboam, Hezekiah, Manasseh and Josiah.

The "exemplary" use of Joseph and certain brothers for paraenesis about sexual sins occurs in Jubilees. Joseph and his brothers Reuben and Judah are used as examples of obedience and disobedience to laws of intercourse (33:2-20, 39:6, 41:23-26) -- and Jubilees commands punishment for those who now disobey these laws.[13] (Cf. also Jub 30:1-19 where Simeon and Levi serve as examples of those who rightfully [commanded by heaven, as TL 5] kill those defiling a virgin of Israel.) The rabbis and Samaritans also make use of traditions presenting Joseph with only certain of his brothers (especially Reuben, Simeon, Levi and Judah). The rabbis (following Gen 42:24) emphasize the sin of Simeon (and Levi) against his brother Joseph, while vindicating Reuben and Judah (Gen R 99:7, cf. 84:16). The Samaritan Memar Marqah speaks of the purity of Joseph in contrast to the sexual sins of Reuben (and Judah) and the sins of Simeon (and Levi) who acted as did Cain against his brother.[14] Thus Jewish literature shows paraenetic use of contrasts between Joseph and certain of his brothers on the issues of sexual sins and hatred of brethren. Such occurrence in Jewish literature of the type of literature postulated from the study of the peculiarities of certain of the TP is added evidence for the validity of the above postulated origin and basic form of the TP.

Thus a search to explain the use of the two stories in TJ, one about chastity and the other about brotherly love, has led not only to a rationale for the use of the two stories but also to a new understanding of the original basis and structure of the TP. The two stories in TJ fit tidily into an intricate presentation of contrasts in TR and TS -- providing a foil for the vices of Joseph's two eldest brethren, Reuben and Simeon. The intertwining structural use of contrast occurs in a limited group within the TP which also have a stricter testamental form than other of the TP. The use of both contrast and testamental form in a limited group of works (which emphasize major brothers and their sin, TR and TS) suggests that the original structure of the TP was a presentation in testamental form of a limited set of contrasting portraits used for paraenesis about sins.[15]

These contrast portraits became the basis of a group of six or more testaments in TP which both use a particular testamental structure (similar to Becker's type "A") and emphasize contrast between Joseph and his brethren while further urging the addressees to seek a reward like Joseph (two points that Becker felt were redactional because they did not occur in all testaments) -- TR, TS, TL, TZ, TJ and TB. The later additions to this group (to form a group of 12) are characterized by a less strict testamental style and a short paternal command about burial (as Becker's type "B") -- (TJud), TI, TD, TN, TG and TA.

A study of Jewish paraenetic literature shows that there are Jewish materials which used contrasting pictures of the virtues of Joseph and the sins of certain of his brothers.[16] This literature helps define the background out of which the TP arose. Study of this literature also leads to a further understanding of why TJ emphasizes purity and love of brethren -- these are the virtues which paraenetic Jewish literature used as foils for the sins of Joseph's brothers.

NOTES

[1] Two exceptions to this tendency are M. de Jonge (*The Testaments of the Twelve Patriarchs* [Assen, Van Gorcum: 1953]) who argues for a Christian author bringing together various materials and J. Thomas ("Aktuelles im Zeugnis der zwölf Väter," *Studien zu den Testamenten der zwölf Patriarchen* [Beiheft 36 ZNW; Berlin, Alfred Töpelmann: 1969], 93) who argues that if 3-10 is interpolated it yet fills a lack in the TP.

[2] R. H. Charles, *APOT II*, 290, 346.

[3] J. Becker, *Untersuchungen zur Entstehungsgeschichte der Testamente der zwölf Patriarchen* (Leiden, Brill: 1970). Becker bases his comparison with Hellenistic romances on the work of K. Kerenyi (*Die griechisch-orientalische Romanliteratur in religionsgeschichtlicher Beleuchtung*, 1927) and M. Braun (*History and Romance in Graeco-Oriental Literature*, 1938). However, TJ 3-10:4 does not have the features of length, travel or tension emphasized in Hellenistic romance (cf. recently R. Söder, *Die apokryphen Apostelgeschichten und die romanhafte Literature der Antike* [Darmstadt, WBG: 1969] and T. Hägg, *Narrative Technique In Ancient Greek Romance* [Stockholm, Svenska Inst: 1971]). The story is shorter and more exemplary and should be compared to Philo De Jos 40-58.

[4] These passages also use similar expressions. Both TR 4:6 and TS 5:3 speak of fornication as separating from God. TS 5:4 and TB 9:1 both give Enochian forecasts of fornication.

[5] TL also contains evidence of stories condemning Levi's anger (2:2, 5:1-7, 6:1-7).

[6] Note that the command to stay away from fornication is united with a story of Joseph showing that God protects those who do not fornicate from the wiles of Beliar. On the term "purity" used of Joseph, see particularly Memar Marqah 1:9 and 2:8 which show Joseph's characteristic as purity טהרה when listing characteristics of patriarchs. (Cf. also MM 4:8, 6:4 and footnote #14 below.) Philo *De Jos* speaks of Joseph's purity καθαρεύω (44, cf. TR 6:1) and Moses is said to characterize Joseph as καρτερικός (54). As in TJ and Hellenistic romance, De Jos 40, 57 and 87 use σωφροσύνη as a characterizing virtue and contrast it to ἀκρασία (57). Cf. further discussion of the use of σωφροσύνη in H. Hollander's paper, which also cites Jos Ant 2:48, 50 and 69. Philo, in contrast to both Memar Marqah and the rabbis (cf. #14 below) tends to represent the patriarchs as exemplars of virtues and cites only by number those patriarchs who sold Joseph.

[7] Cf. TZ 8:4. Note discussion below on the relation of TZ to an original limited group of testaments.

[8] Becker does compare TR 6:5-7, TS 5:4-5 and TD 5:4 and says that they might be traditional. However, he says that TR 6:5-7 must be late because of its too early mention of Levi and that TR 6:4 is late crossover material (195-6, cf. 329-30 on TS).

[9] Cf. parallels of thought between TJud 18:2-4 and TS 4:8 where soul and body are said to be destroyed and sleep is driven away -- in TJud by fornication, in TS by envy. Cf. also the above noted combination of jealousy and fornication in TJud 13:3. The major problem, as noted below, in considering TJud as part of a smaller group is its use of short command of the fathers -- as other members of Becker's "B" group -- and its lack of "reward like Joseph" passages.

[10] These occur in TR 4:8-11, TS 4:5-6, TL 13:8-9, TZ 8:4-5, TB 3:3, 5:5, TJ 9:2-3, 10:3, 18:1-4. Becker (as noted above) considered such passages late because of their limited use. However, their limited use corresponds to a limited group of testaments with inner and early coherences.

[11] The growth stages of the early forms of the TP seem markable by the "contrast-reward like Joseph" and testamental usages described above. The original paraenetic contrast would seem to be between Joseph, Reuben and Simeon (and also possibly Levi and Judah). In the "six" version of TP the composer has added "good" patriarchs, Zebulon and Benjamin, stressing rising and judgment (TZ 10:2-3, TB 10:7-11, cf. TJud 25). To this group of 6 or 7 testaments (characterized by "reward like Joseph" passages), are added several more testaments (of Becker's type "B"). These type "B" testaments concern less important brothers and have distinct differences

(both lacks and additions, cf. #12) from the earlier group of testaments.

[12] As Becker remarked of his type "B," this group has the "positive" characteristic of a short command of the father. The secondary compiler (of the 12 group) seems to have added these commands on the model of the command of Joseph to take his bones away from Egypt so that the Lord may avenge Joseph (cf. TJ 20:1-2 and the more complete explanation in TS 8:3-4 -- another parallel between TS and TJ). The short commands of the lesser patriarchs have no such rationale and would seem the work of the secondary compiler. Thus, in addition to the differences in testamental form between groups of testaments, the short command also serves as a criterion for group membership. The later testaments, as noted, also do not use "reward like Joseph" passages. Thus one has a group of "strict form" testaments with "reward like Joseph" motif and a later group of less strict form and short command motif.

[13] Cf. the exemplary use of the punishment of Jacob's sons in CD 3:4, "The sons of Jacob went astray through them (thoughts of an evil imagination and ....fornication, 2:16) and were punished according to their straying."

[14] MM 4:8, cf. #6. In MM 4:9, Judah is said to bring adultery into the world, Simeon to cause distress to Joseph and Reuben to be like them. Memar Marqah generally speaks of Reuben and Simeon, sometimes also of Judah and Levi. On the rabbi's treatment of what brothers opposed Joseph, cf. L. Ginzberg, *The Legends of the Jews* (Philadelphia, JPS: 1925) V, 329. He notes that only TP uses Gad rather than Levi in combination with Simeon (TG 2:3, instead of Judah; TZ 2:1, 3:2 and 4:2). Cf. esp. Gen R 99:7 where Simeon and Levi are associated in the selling of Joseph -- and Reuben and Judah are vindicated.

[15] The use of warning by a father (or exemplary figure) about his deeds and their punishment (and the contrasting picture of the reward of the righteous) is, of course, a feature of Greek nekyia from the time of the Odyssey. Such literature influences Enoch and other Jewish literature. Plutarch (On Divine Vengeance 561d, e, 565 a) gives a useful picture of why the Hellenistic world considered the father particularly suitable as the giver of warning. Plutarch says that the son is predisposed to the sin of the father. Plutarch then shows a son's visit to the other world. The father appears, confesses his wickedness and tells of his punishment. The son is overwhelmed.

[16] Thus, in contrast to those analyses of TP emphasizing a twelve brother structure as the basic form of TP, this study would stress that common Jewish paraenetic contrasts (between Joseph and certain sinning elder brothers) were the bases for TP. The twelve brother structure is only formed by secondary additions.

Anitra Bingham Kolenkow
University of California
Santa Cruz, Calif. 95064

THE ETHICAL CHARACTER OF THE PATRIARCH JOSEPH :

A STUDY IN THE ETHICS OF THE TESTAMENTS OF THE XII PATRIARCHS [1]

Harm W.Hollander

Introduction

In I, I shall analyse the first two chapters of T.Joseph. The next two sections will treat Joseph's attitude as described in T.Joseph 3,1-1o,4(II) and 1o,5-18,4(III).Attention will be given to the mutual relationship of the two sections and especially to their relationship with T.Joseph 1-2. In IV I shall treat those paraenetic passages in the other Testaments where Joseph is held up as an ethical example, and I shall indicate parallels to Joseph's attitude in T.Joseph. In these sections the biographical material about Joseph (and his brothers) will be discussed only when it is useful to our understanding of Joseph as an ethical example.[2] The results of the investigation will be summarized in V.

I.T.Joseph 1-2;T.Joseph 1,3-2,6 : an individual thanksgiving

A.

After the usual introduction(1,1f.),in which ἠγαπημένου ὑπὸ 'Ισραήλ [3] is a striking phrase[4],the patriarch Joseph points to the 'envy' and 'death' that played an important role in his life.In T.Joseph envy is mentioned again in 1,7(ἐν φθόνοις συνδούλων -b is not correct) and 1o,3.Elsewhere,it is particularly Simeon's attitude towards Joseph which is characterized by envy.[5] The thought of imminent death is also frequently found in connection with Joseph.Above all his brothers want to kill him.[6] Others who threaten him with death are the Egyptian woman(T.Joseph 3,1;6,5 [7]) and the leader of the Ishmaelites (T.Joseph 11,3).[8] Despite all these difficulties,the patriarch was not diverted from the truth of the Lord(1,3b).[9]

In his study Die paränetischen Formen der Testamente der Zwölf Patriarchen und ihr Nachwirken in der frühchristlichen Mahnung.Eine formgeschichtliche Untersuchung [10],H.Aschermann distinguishes three parts in T.Joseph 1,3(4)-2,6 : 1) a 'Lobpsalm' in a poetic style(1,3(4)-7);2) a prose section(2,1-3); 3) a final poetic part in the style of a psalm(2,4-6). J. Becker,in his study Untersuchungen zur Entstehungsgeschichte der Testamente der zwölf Patriarchen[11],takes over this conception and draws from it some far-reaching conclusions: a) 1, 3-1o,4 as a whole is secondary with regard to 1,1f.;1o,5ff.[12]; b) the prose part(2,1-3)is prominent,because it is found between two poetic parts;c) not only is 2,1-3 in prose,but also it contains as its central theme the story of Joseph and the Egyptian woman (the 'Tugendkampf Josephs'),a story which has absolutely nothing to do with the original T.Joseph.[13]

I believe that these opinions are for the greater part incorrect and therefore also give a wrong idea of the figure of Joseph in T.Joseph. Surely there are three parts in the passage under discussion(1,3(4)-7;2,1-3;2,4-6),but the second part is closely connected with the first one.Not only do both parts share the same central theme(God's salvation of the pious man from his oppressions),but this second part is related to the whole of T.Joseph,and not just to the story about Joseph and the Egyptian woman.Furthermore,these three parts form a whole,a unity that can be described as an individual thanksgiving,as I shall attempt to demonstrate in the analysis that follows.

B. 1,4-7

The first part(1,4-7) is composed of four subdivisions. Three of these(vs.4,5,7) consists of three small sentences which are built up in parallel,and one(vs.6) consists of four such small sentences.[14] All these small sentences are constructed according to the same two-part pattern.The first part describes (in the first person [15]) the situation in which the patriarch found himself; the second part mentions God's saving activity (in the third person).Thus,e.g.,'I was in trouble,but God saved me.' We find this style in the psalms,specifically in the individual thanksgiving [16]: Ps.118(117),13,'They thrust hard against me so that I nearly fall;but the Lord has helped me' [17];18,18(17,19),'They confronted me in the hour of my peril,but the Lord was my buttress' [18];and 116(114),6,'...I was brought low and he saved me' [19].Although we do not find these sentences typically constructed in series as in T.Joseph 1,4-7,there do occur in the psalms series of small sentences which describe God's saving activity: e.g.,Ps.4o,1f.(39,2f.), '...he bent down to me and heard my cry.He brought me up out of the muddy pit [20], out of the mire and the clay;he set my feet on a rock and gave me a firm footing.'

Another characteristic of individual thanksgivings is the use of the third person to speak about God.[21] So,e.g.,the above quoted Ps.4o,1ff.(39,2ff.);Ps.66(65),16ff.,'Come,listen, all who fear God,and I will tell you all that he has done for me;I lifted up my voice in prayer,his high praise was on my lips.If I had cherished evil thoughts,the Lord would not have heard me;but in truth God has heard and given heed to my prayer.Blessed is God who has not withdrawn his love and care from me.' Joseph also addresses himself to others(namely to his sons) and speaks about God in the third person;thus it may be concluded that T.Joseph 1,4-7 has the style of an individual thanksgiving.[22]

The contents and terminology of 1,4-7 are also typical of an individual thanksgiving.In individual thanksgivings,God's saving activity is often described in terms like φυλάσσειν (cf. T.Joseph 1,4), βοηθεῖν (cf.1,5), ἐπισκέπτεσθαι (cf.1,6) and esp. ῥύεσθαι (cf.1,7). [23] We also find in T.Joseph some other words that are less common in individual thanksgivings.So we read in Ps.4o,2(39,3),'He brought me up (LXX, ἀνήγαγέν με) out of the muddy pit...' [24] The terminology in T.Joseph 1,4(εἰς λάκκον με ἐχάλασαν,καὶ ὁ ὕψιστος ἀνήγαγέ με) may be derived in the first instance from the story about Jeremiah in Jer.38(45),1-13. Jeremiah is thrown into a pit and is pulled up out of it thanks to Ebed-melech [25].The LXX uses not only λάκκος (45(38),

6f.1of.13) and ἀνάγειν (45(38),1o.13),but also χαλᾶν(45(38),6),a
word seldom used in the Old Testament.The motif,however,that
it is God who saves (and therefore is subject of ἀνάγειν),is
not found in Jer.Undoubtedly this motif comes from the psalms;
for this passages as Ps.4o,2(39,3) may have played an important role. [26]

Other terms in T.Joseph 1,4-7 are undoubtedly derived
from the psalms. [27] διατρέφειν(vs.5) occurs several times;e.g.,
Ps.33(32),18f.,'The Lord's eyes are turned towards those who
fear him...to deliver them from death,to keep them alive in
famine (LXX,ῥύσασθαι...καὶ διαθρέψαι αὐτοὺς ἐν λιμῷ)' [28];31,3(3o,4),
'Thou art to me both rock and stronghold;lead me and guide me
(LXX, διαθρέψεις με) ...';55,22(54,23). For παρακαλεῖν see,e.g.,
Ps.71(7o),2of.,'Thou hast made me pass through bitter and deep
distress (LXX, θλῖψεις) ... Restore me to honour,turn and comfort me (LXX, παρεκάλεσάς με) ';86(85),17,'...let those who hate
thee see...that thou,O Lord,hast been my help and comfort
(LXX, ἐβοήθησάς μοι καὶ παρεκάλεσάς με)' [29]. In the same kind of
context we find λύειν several times;so,e.g.,Ps.1o2,19f.(1o1,
2of.),'The Lord...surveys the earth to listen to the groaning
of the prisoners and set free (LXX, τοῦ λῦσαι) men under sentence of death';146(145),7,'...The Lord feeds the hungry,and sets
the prisoner free (LXX,λύει πεπεδημένους)';Job 5,19f. [30]

Thus,in T.Joseph 1,4-7 God's saving activity is described
in terms that are derived,for the greater part,from the psalms,
and in particular from individual thanksgivings. [31] The same
can be said of the terms used in this passage to describe
Joseph's troubles.The psalmist's distress '...besteht in vie-
len Fällen in einer schlimmen Krankheit,durch die er dem Tode
nahe gekommen ist.Andere Fälle werden Ψ 1o7 mitgeteilt : da
sind es Wanderer...Gefangene,im Kerker verschmachtend... An-
fechtung durch Feinde...' [32] In T.Joseph 1,4 the brothers are
as it were the enemies who threaten Joseph(the oppressed man)
with death. [33] This (imminent) death is an important motif in
the psalms (sometimes death is described as an actual fact);
so,e.g.,in Ps.56,13(55,14),'for thou hast rescued me from
death to walk in thy presence...';116(114),8,'He has rescued
me from death...';Dan.3,88 LXX [34].

Whereas especially in the first part of T.Joseph 1,4-7
(vs.4) Joseph's troubles are described in terms that are
partly derived from the Genesis-story [35],this is not the case
in the following verses.Although the contents of vs.5ab may be
connected with the Genesis-story,the terminology is different
[36]. Moreover,from vs.5c onwards both the terminology and the
contents differ from the Gen.-story. [37] Some of the terms used
here are derived without any doubt from the situation of
distress described in the psalms.We have found in Ps.33(32),
19 not only διατρέφειν but also λιμός. [38] The idea of being
lonely (see T.Joseph 1,6, μόνος ἤμην)occurs in the same kind of
context in Esther 4,17(1)LXX, Κύριέ μου...βοήθησόν μοι τῇ μόνῃ καὶ
μὴ ἐχούσῃ βοηθὸν εἰ μὴ σέ.... [39] Illness or weakness (ἀσθένεια -see
T.Joseph 1,6) is a term that often describes the distress of
the oppressed : Ps.6,2(3),'Be merciful to me,O Lord,for I am
weak (LXX, ἀσθενής εἰμι) ...';Lament.1,14,'...my strength failed
beneath its weight (LXX, ἠσθένησεν ἡ ἰσχύς μου)...';cf.Ps.3o,11
LXX;88,9(87,1o);1o7(1o6),12;Judith 9,11;T.Job 25,1o. [40] For
φυλακή and δεσμός see,e.g.,Ps.1o7(1o6),14,'he brought them out

of darkness,dark as death,and broke their chains (LXX, τοὺς
δεσμοὺς) ';142,7(141,8),'Set me free from my prison (LXX,
φυλακῆς),so that I may praise thy name...';116,16(115,7).[41] The
terms in T.Joseph 1,7 which describe the distress of the
oppressed Joseph are probably also traditional,although less
easily traced; for διαβολή see,e.g.,Sir.51,6.[42]

In summary : in T.Joseph 1,4-7 we hear Joseph speaking
about his distress and his salvation by God; this speech has
a form that in both style and terminology belongs to the genre
of an individual thanksgiving.The fact that some terms occur
in individual thanksgivings as well as in other kinds of
psalms,and particularly in individual laments,is,of course,
normal.In an individual thanksgiving the poet thanks God for
salvation from distress,whereas in an individual lament the
poet prays and asks God for salvation from distress.In both
cases the distress is the same.[43]

Before investigating T.Joseph 2,1-3 I want to make two
remarks. First : does T.Joseph 1,3 belong to the individual
thanksgiving ? Although this problem cannot be solved with
any certainty,it is quite possible that even vs.3 belongs to
the individual thanksgiving.[44] Whereas the style of vs.3 does
not directly correspond to the following verses,its terminology and contents are closely connected with them : we find
the φθόνος again in vs.7;the θάνατος is connected not only with
vs.4 (ἀνελεῖν) ,but is also a known motif in the psalms to
describe the lot of the oppressed.Besides this,the typical use
of καὶ οὐκ ἐπλανήθην in this verse belongs to the same kind of
context : see,e.g.,Ps.119(118),110,'Evil men have set traps
for me,but I do not stray from thy precepts (LXX,καὶ ἐκ τῶν
ἐντολῶν σου οὐκ ἐπλανήθην).' Secondly : some terms used in T.
Joseph 1,3-7 recur in the first story (about the Egyptian
woman),and others in the second story (about the selling of
Joseph).So we find λάκκος,φυλακή,δεσμός,ῥύεσθαι,φθόνος only in the
first story [45],whereas οἱ ἀδελφοί,πιπράσκειν,δοῦλος (and αἰχμαλωσία)
only occur in the second story [46]; ὑψοῦν and θάνατος,however,
occur in both stories.[47]

C. 2,1-3

In the second part(T.Joseph 2,1-3),the style differs from
that of 1,4-7.Most strikingly,the sentences are much longer;
we no longer have the nice construction in small sentences.
Nonetheless,as each of the preceding verses (except vs.6)
consists of three sentences each containing two parts,the same
can be said of 2,1-3 as a whole.Leaving vs.1 out of consideration for a moment - vss.2 and 3 consist each of two parts,of
which the second one describes God's saving activity(in the
third person) and the first one describes Joseph's distress,
again -as in 1,4-7- in the first person. Vs.1 does not fit
into this scheme;it consists of only one part,which may be
considered as parallel to vss.2b and 3b.[48] The description of
Joseph's distress,however,is lacking.Why is there such a
lack ? And is there any link with the previous sentence(s) ?
The answer to both these questions may be found in the use
of the introductory words καὶ οὕτως.These words mostly refer
back to the preceding phrase(s) and are frequently used in the
very beginning of sentences or parts of sentences which

mention a conclusion or a final action or describe an action or a situation which must be considered as a more or less logical consequence or illustration of an action or a situation mentioned in the previous sentence(s).See,e.g.,T.Zeb.3,7, '...and so(καὶ οὕτως)they were put to shame before the Egyptians';Acts 7,8,'He then gave him the covenant of circumcision, and so(καὶ οὕτως),after Isaac was born,he circumcised him on the eighth day...';see also T.Jud.4,3;T.Zeb.4,13;T.Gad 2,4;T.Joseph 5,1;T.Benj.2,5;Sir.33,15;I Macc.13,47;IV Macc.12,19 (2o);Acts 28,14.Such a use of καὶ οὕτως is also to be found in T.Joseph 2,1,which describes the fact that Photimar entrusted his house to Joseph : this action is closely linked with the last short sentence in 1,7,'Envied by my fellow-slaves,and He exalted me.' The verb used here(ὑψοῦν) is not only a mere parallel to other verbs which describe the act of salvation, but is also used in connection with the idea of reaching a higher status:exaltation to authority.[49] T.Joseph 2,1 serves as a consequence and an illustration of this 'exaltation' (in the latter sense).Therefore,it is obvious that Joseph's distress could not be mentioned in this verse.

Therefore,I am of the opinion that it is not right to separate 2,1-3 from 1,3(4)-7 in such a strong way,as Aschermann and Becker do.[50] From the following investigation concerning terminology and contents it will be obvious that some of the terms used in this passage also are derived from situations we usually find in the psalms,esp.in individual thanksgivings and individual laments.

It is noteworthy that the expression ἐπίστευσέ μοι τὸν οἶκον αὐτοῦ (vs.1),which is not found in the Genesis-story,recurs word for word in the second story in T.Joseph (11,6),which cannot be accidental.[51]

According to vs.2,Joseph 'struggled' against the shameless woman who urged [52] him to transgress the law with her, but God delivered him from the burning flame. The Egyptian woman is introduced here; she is the subject of the whole first story in T.Joseph. Here,in vs.2, she is called ἀναιδής, a term which the wisdom-literature applies to the 'bad' woman, the πόρνη,who attempts to bring men to πορνεία [53]; so,e.g.,Prov. 7,[54],tries to seduce (young) men.In vs.13 we read,'She caught hold of him (LXX,ἐπιλαβομένη [55]) and kissed him;brazenly she accosted him and said (LXX,ἀναιδεῖ δὲ προσώπῳ προσεῖπεν αὐτῷ)...'[56] Therefore,it is very likely that the Egyptian woman in T.Joseph is to be seen as a πόρνη.

This woman wants to bring Joseph to παρανομία.[57] This idea comes from a combination of two closely related motifs.On the one hand παρανομία is connected with fornication and women;thus, e.g.,Philo,Vita Mosis I 3ol,where in connection with the fornication committed by many Israelites,it is said,'...And this continued until Phinehas,the son of the high priest,greatly angered at what he saw,and horrified at the thought that his people had at the same moment surrendered their bodies to pleasure and their souls to lawlessness(τῷ παρανομεῖν) and unholiness...'(see further I 3o8;Decal.129).[58] More important, Philo connects this motif with Joseph.The patriarch says to the Egyptian woman,'To this day I have remained pure,and I will not take the first step in transgression (παρανομεῖν) by committing adultery...'(De Jos.44). In De Jos.52,Philo remarks that,after the woman's false accusations,Joseph's master gave Joseph no opportunity to defend himself,and '...convicted unheard this entirely innocent person as guilty of the greatest misconduct (ὡς τὰ μέγιστα παρανομήσαντος)...'

On the other hand,we find the motif of a challenge to παρανομία in the martyr-traditions. The tyrant tries to bring the martyr to transgress the law,e.g.,by charging him to eat forbidden food.In IV Macc.5,13 Antiochus says to Eleazar,'For consider this,too,that even if there be some Power whose eye is upon this religion of yours,he will always pardon you for a transgression done under compulsion (ἐπὶ πάσῃ δι'ἀνάγκην παρανομίᾳ γινομένῃ)',to which Eleazar replies,'Therefore we do surely deem it right not in any way whatsoever to transgress the Law(παρανομεῖν) ' (5,17;see further 5,2o.27;8,14;9,3f.).[59]

In T.Joseph 2,2 both motifs are combined.On the one hand there is the traditional relationship between fornication and παρανομία.On the other hand the special setting comes from the martyr-traditions;like the tyrant,the woman wants to bring the pious man to transgress the law. Moreover,the motif of a mortal threat (T.Joseph 3,1) can also be found in the martyr-traditions.When the pious man does not want to transgress the law,the tyrant threatens him with death.In IV Macc.9,5 it is expressed in terms very similar to those in T.Joseph 3,1 : ἐκφοβεῖς δὲ ἡμᾶς τὸν διὰ τῶν βασάνων θάνατον ἡμῖν ἀπειλῶν...[60]

In T.Joseph 2,2,Joseph's attitude towards the Egyptian woman is described by the term ἠγωνισάμην. The idea of the pious man's struggle (ἀγών)is wide-spread in the martyr-traditions.[61] On the other hand,however,this idea is very often [62] found in the context of a struggle for the sake of virtue and against the passions(e.g.,ἡδονή and ἐπιθυμία),an idea that originally belonged to hellenistic moral philosophy[63] and which in Judaism can be found especially in Philo. [64] It is, however,very important to note that Philo also uses it in connection with Joseph.According to Leg.All.III 242,'Joseph, however,being but a youth and lacking strength to contend (ἀγωνίσασθαι) with the Egyptian body and vanquish pleasure,runs away...' [65] Moreover,for the idea of a struggle in such a context,see T.Reub.5.After vs.1 tells us how bad(πονηραί)women are,we read in vs.2,'And whom she cannot overcome (καταγωνίσασθαι) by power,him she overcomes(καταγωνίζεται)by deceit.' On these grounds it is obvious that the motif of a 'struggle' in T.Joseph 2,2a belongs to the same kind of context.[66]

We turn next to the salvation described in T.Joseph 2,2b. Here,as in 1,4,the verb φυλάσσειν is used.We have seen that it occurs in connection with God's saving activity especially in the psalms(in individual thanksgivings as well as in individual laments).

The origin of φλογὸς καιομένης as it is used in 2,2b is very probably to be found in Dan.3 : εὐλογεῖτε,...τὸν κύριον...ὅτι... ἐρρύσατο ἡμᾶς ἐκ μέσου καιομένης φλογὸς καὶ ἐκ τοῦ πυρὸς ἐλυτρώσατο ἡμᾶς (vs.88 LXX).[67] Since the similarity is confined to the terminology alone,how can T.Joseph connect the expression 'burning flame' with the Egyptian woman ? The background of this is

in the wisdom-literature,where the sinner is described as a
burning flame (fire) in relation to the pious man;so,e.g.,
Sir.8,1o,'Kindle not the coals of the wicked lest thou be
burned with the flame of his fire(μὴ ἐμπυρισθῇς ἐν πυρὶ φλογὸς
αὐτοῦ)';cf.vs.3;28,22.Moreover,for God's deliverance of the
oppressed man from the 'flaming fire' of distress,see Sir.51,
2ff.,...καὶ ἐλυτρώσω με...ἐκ πλειόνων θλίψεων,ὧν ἔσχον,ἀπὸ πνιγμοῦ πυρᾶς
κυκλόθεν καὶ ἐκ μέσου πυρός... [68] Thus,whereas the expression φλογὸς
καιομένης in T.Joseph 2,2b comes from Dan.3 and the idea of the
sinner as a burning flame has its roots in the wisdom-literature,the style and the construction of 2,2b are typical of an
individual thanksgiving.

In T.Joseph 2,3,three terms describe the distress from
which Joseph is saved : ἐφυλακίσθην,ἐτυπτήθην,ἐμυκτηρίσθην. Three
facts are noteworthy.1).The first two verbs recur later on in
T.Joseph,but only in the second story about the selling of
Joseph - φυλακίζειν in 14,2 [69],and τύπτειν in (13,4;)13,9;14,
1f. [7o] For this reason it is clear that 2,3a has nothing to do
with the first story in T.Joseph. [71] 2).τύπτειν plays an important role in the martyr-traditions : the tyrant tries by force
to compel submission from the pious man (see,e.g.,IV Macc.6,8.
1o;9,12;The Acts of Euplus(Gr.rec.)2,2(ed.Musurillo)).
Although not certain,it is quite probable that this tradition
has influenced its use in T.Joseph. 3).An investigation of the
third verb (μυκτηρίζειν) [72] makes it clear that in vs.3 too
Joseph's distress and his salvation by God are meant.The idea
occurs frequently in the psalms.The pious man is mocked in his
oppression : Ps.22,7(21,8),'All who see me jeer at me (LXX,
ἐξεμυκτήρισάν με)...';see also 35,15(34,16);44,13(43,14);79(78),
4;8o,6(79,7);cf.Jer.2o,7.

Joseph is saved by God from these troubles : καὶ ἔδωκέ με
κύριος εἰς οἰκτιρμοὺς ἐνώπιον τοῦ δεσμοφύλακος (2,3b).This expression
is based on Gen.39,21 ,'But the Lord was with Joseph and kept
faith with him,so that he won the favour of the governor of
the Round Tower (LXX,καὶ ἔδωκεν αὐτῷ χάριν ἐναντίον τοῦ ἀρχιδεσμο-
φύλακος).' [73] Why do we find a different formulation in T.
Joseph 2,3b ? [74] This formulation is used especially in texts
which describe the salvation of the pious man (or the people
of Israel) from oppressions, -in particular in connection with
'being captive'.In I Ki.8,5o,Solomon prays,'Forgive thy people
their sins and transgressions against thee;put pity for them
in their captors' hearts (LXX,καὶ δώσεις αὐτοὺς εἰς οἰκτιρμοὺς
ἐνώπιον αἰχμαλωτευόντων αὐτούς)'.Ps.1o6(1o5),which narrates the
distress (θλίψεις) which the people of Israel suffered in the
past and from which it was saved,describes this salvation,
'he(=God) roused compassion for them in the hearts of all
their captors (vs.46. LXX,καὶ ἔδωκεν αὐτοὺς εἰς οἰκτιρμοὺς ἐναντίον
πάντων τῶν αἰχμαλωτισάντων αὐτούς)';II Chron.3o,9. [75]

In summary : T.Joseph 2,1-3 is not only closely linked
with 1,3(4)-7,but also belongs -qua style (although it has not
such an elegant style as we find in 1,3(4)-7),contents and
terminology- to an individual thanksgiving.Moreover,2,1-3,
like 1,3(4)-7,contains terms and expressions,some of which
recur only in the second story of the selling of Joseph
(ἐπίστευσέ μοι τὸν οἶκον αὐτοῦ in vs.1, φυλακίζειν and τύπτειν in vs.
3),whereas on the other hand vs.2 clearly refers to the first

story about the Egyptian woman,who is described as a πόρνη ,and
who -like the tyrant in the martyr-traditions- wants to bring
Joseph to transgress the law. So it has been proved that in
T.Joseph the individual thanksgiving does not end with 1,7,but
runs over into ch.2.

D. 2,4-6

Now it is possible to describe 2,4-6 more precisely than
has been done by Aschermann and Becker.Becker is of the opinion that '2,4-6 ist ebenfalls unter Aufnahme atl.Motive ge-
staltet und gut gegliedert... Im Gegensatz zu 1,4-7 ist es
nicht ausgeschlossen,dass der Verfasser hier einen ihm be-
kannten Psalm eingearbeitet hat.Josephs Leben lässt sich zwar
gut darin unterbringen,aber die Formulierungen sind so all-
gemein,dass die Aussagen grundsätzliche Gültigkeit erhalten..
..' [76] Because Becker (like Aschermann)has not seen that the
individual thanksgiving,far from concluding with 1,7,runs over
into ch.2,he has not noticed the real meaning and function of
these verses.The fact is that in an individual thanksgiving
it is quite normal for the speaker to conclude with some
general sentences in which he proclaims that God is faithful
and does not forsake the pious.Or,as Gunkel-Begrich say,'Ein
zweites Hauptstück des Dankliedes ist das Bekenntnis zu Jahve
als dem Retter aus der Not... Laut und fröhlich soll es er-
schallen : alle anderen,Götter und Menschen,helfen nicht.Jahve
allein ist getreu und hilft seinem Frommen ! Ihm allein traue
ich ! Das hat der Dankende an sich erfahren,und das sollen die
anderen Frommen von ihm lernen ! Aus seinem Beispiel sollen
sie den allgemeinen Satz bestätigt finden ! So spricht das
,,Bekenntnis" den geistigen Gehalt des Dankliedes in verhält-
nismässig abstrakter Form aus.,,Jahve hört auf seine Frommen,
wenn sie zu ihm schreien.'' ...Solche Verkündigung richtet
sich ihrer Natur nach an die übrigen und redet demnach von
Jahve gewöhnlich in der dritten Person : sie steht selbst-
verständlich an einer der wichtigsten Stellen des Gedichtes..
..: d.h. gewöhnlich am Schluss der Erzählung als das Ergebnis
der Erfahrungen des Dichters.' [77] Among the many texts which
are referred to in illustration of this are Ps.31,23(3o,24),
'...The Lord protects the faithful but pays the arrogant in
full', and 69,33(68,34),'for the Lord listens to the poor and
does not despise those bound to his service'.Thus it may be
concluded that T.Joseph 2,4-6 is the generalizing end of the
individual thanksgiving (which began with 1,3(4)).

Many of the terms in 2,4-6 occur frequently in the
psalms.[78] Besides the term 'God-fearing'(vs.4),a term so
general that it naturally occurs elsewhere(although it certainly has its place in the psalms),we find the idea that God does
not forsake(οὐκ ἐγκαταλείπειν) his pious ones.See Ps.9,1o(11),
'...for thou,Lord,dost not forsake (LXX, οὐκ ἐγκατέλιπες) those
who seek thee';37(36),28,'for the Lord is a lover of justice
and will not forsake (LXX, οὐκ ἐγκαταλείψει)his loyal servants..
..';94(93),14. [79] In 2,4 the distress is described in terms
that occur traditionally especially in the psalms : σκότος,
δεσμός,θλῖψις,ἀνάγκη. I have already discussed δεσμός in connection with T.Joseph 1,6. [80] θλῖψις is a fairly common term
which nevertheless is especially frequent in the Psalms.[81]

We find the term σκότος [82] in this sense almost exclusively in the Psalms.See,e.g.,Ps.54,6 LXX,φόβος καὶ τρόμος ἦλθεν ἐπ'ἐμέ,καὶ ἐκάλυψέν με σκότος [83];cf.143(142),3. [84] The term ἀνάγκη occurs in the same context : Ps.25(24),17,'Relieve the sorrows (LXX, αἱ θλίψεις) of my heart and bring me out of my distress (LXX, τῶν ἀναγκῶν) ';see also 31,7(3o,8);119(118),143;Esther 4,17(w) LXX; Job 5,19. [85] Finally,we note a text in which all four terms occur together : Ps.1o7(1o6),13f.,'So they cried to the Lord in their trouble (LXX,ἐν τῷ θλίβεσθαι αὐτοῦς) ,and he saved them from their distress (LXX, τῶν ἀναγκῶν) ;he brought them out of darkness (LXX, σκότους) ,dark as death,and broke their chains (LXX, τοὺς δεσμοῦς).'

T.Joseph 2,5 explains why God does not forsake those who fear him in their distress.'For God is not put to shame as a man,nor as the son of man is He afraid,nor as one that is earth-born is He weak or rejected' -a stylistically fine description of God's surpassing power,to be compared in style with Numb.23,19;Judith 8,16;Philo,Vita Mosis I 283 (see also I Sam.15,29;Philo,Vita Mosis I 173). The verbs here are often used to describe a man's situation in distress and oppression. We have seen that the pious and oppressed man is weak and ill. [86] Often he complains that God has rejected him;see,e.g., Ps.43(42),2;44,9.23(43,1o.24);6o,1.1o(59,3.12);74(73),1;77,7 (76,8);88,14(87,15). Often he complains that God has put him to shame;see,e.g.,Ps.44,9(43,1o);44,15(43,16);69(68),2o. He is urged not to be afraid,for God is with him;see,e.g.,Deut.1, 21;31,6.8;Jo.1,9;8,1;1o,25;cf.Ps.27(26),1;78(77),53;Sir.34,14; II Macc.15,8. God,however,is not as this weak and fearful man; he is powerful and does not forsake the pious ones in their distress.

Then we read in vs.6,'But in all places He is at hand,and in divers ways doth He comfort,(though)for a little space He departeth to try the inclination of the soul.' In connection with 1,6 we have seen that God's saving activity can be expressed by the term παρακαλεῖν. [87] God comforts man in his distress in divers ways and in all places he is at hand (παρίστασθαι). The verb παρίστασθαι is also used in connection with the salvation of the oppressed man;so,e.g.,Ps.1o9(1o8), 31,'For he stands at (LXX, παρέστη) the poor man's right side to save him from his adversaries.' Wisd.19,22 is especially important in this context : 'For in all things,O Lord,thou didst magnify thy people,and thou didst glorify them and not lightly esteem them;standing by their side in every time and place (καὶ οὐχ ὑπερεῖδὲς ἐν παντὶ καιρῷ καὶ τόπῳ παριστάμενος)'. [88] Just as this idea closes the song in Ps.1o9(1o8) and the whole book of Wisdom,in T.Joseph 2,6 it closes the individual thanksgiving : God is with his pious ones and comforts them. Vs.6c is a reply to the 'why' of the pious man's oppressions, and it clearly forms the transition to vs.7. If God is always with the pious man,where is he in times of distress ? And why is the pious man in distress ? The author of Ps.1o(9) asks God in his oppression,'Why stand so far off (LXX, ἀφέστηκας μακρόθεν),Lord,hiding thyself in time of need (LXX, ὑπερορᾷς [89] ἐν εὐκαιρίαις ἐν θλίβει)?' [90] The author of Ps.22(21) beseeches God,'Be not far from me,for trouble is near (LXX, μὴ ἀποστῆς ἀπ' ἐμοῦ,ὅτι θλῖψις ἐγγῦς),and I have no helper.' [91]

Indeed,in distress God is really 'absent'.But,as we read in T.Joseph 2,6,this absence is only for a short time(ἐν βραχεῖ).The pious man's distress is short-lived,and it is meant to test(δοκιμάζειν) him. The idea of a short time of sufferings and oppression occurs especially in those texts which speak about God's anger with,and his punishment of the people of Israel because of their trespasses;so,e.g.,in Is.57, 16f.,'I will not be always (LXX,οὐκ εἰς τὸν αἰῶνα) accusing,I will not continually (LXX,οὐδὲ διὰ παντός)nurse my wrath... For a time (LXX,βραχύ τι)I was angry at the guilt of Israel...';II Macc.7,32f.,'We are suffering for our own sins,and though our living God is angry for a little (βραχέως),in order to rebuke and chasten us,he will again be reconciled to his own serv- ants';see also vs.37,'...calling on God to show favour to our nation soon(ταχύ) ';see further 5,17 (βραχέως);Wisd.16,3(ἐπ'ὀλίγον) .5f.(οὐ μέχρι τέλους...πρὸς ὀλίγον).11(ὀξέως).After this short period of God's anger and punishment,which is meant as a chastisement to bring the people to repentance (see II Macc.7, 33,...χάριν ἐπιπλήξεως καὶ παιδείας...and Wisd.16,6, εἰς νουθεσίαν... εἰς ἀνάμνησιν ἐντολῆς νόμου σου),God has mercy on Israel and saves his people from distress (see Is.57,18f.(also παρακαλεῖν);II Macc.7,33.37;Wisd.16,7f.1off.(also ῥύεσθαι and σῴζειν)).

This idea of a short period of sufferings occurs also[92]in texts that deal with the sufferings of the righteous man.[92] After a short time of suffering,God will reward him in one way or another -during or after this earthly life;see II Macc.7, 36;I Peter 5,1o;II Clem.19,3;Pastor Hermae,Sim.7,6.We find this complex in T.Benj.5,4[93] too, ...καὶ ὁ δίκαιος προσευχόμενος πρὸς ὀλίγον ταπεινωθῇ,μετ'οὐ πολὺ φαιδρότερος ἀναφαίνεται... It is esp. the wisdom-literature,that tells us how God tests the right- eous man by making him suffer.If he goes through the trials, he is rewarded by God.I will'deal with these ideas more ex- tensively in my discussion of T.Joseph 2,7;for the moment,let me just point to the fact that the idea of a short time of sufferings could easily be connected with this complex of ideas,and the connection is also found in other places besides T.Joseph 2,6;see,e.g.,Wisd.3,5f.,in which it is said of the δικαίων ψυχαί (vs.1),'And having borne a little chastening,they shall receive great good;because God tested them,and found them worthy of himself.As gold in the furnace he proved them (καὶ ὀλίγα [94] παιδευθέντες μεγάλα εὐεργετηθήσονται,ὅτι ὁ θεὸς ἐπείρασεν αὐτοὺς καὶ εὗρεν αὐτοὺς ἀξίους ἑαυτοῦ ὡς χρυσὸν ἐν χωνευτηρίῳ ἐδοκίμασεν αὐτούς) ...';and I Peter 1,6f.,'This is cause for great joy,even though now you smart for a little while (ὀλίγον) ,if need be, under trials of many kinds(ἐν ποικίλοις πειρασμοῖς). Even gold passes(δοκιμαζομένου)through the assayer's fire,and more prec- ious than perishable gold is faith which has stood the test (τὸ δοκίμιον ὑμῶν τῆς πίστεως) ...'

In summary : T.Joseph 2,4-6 speaks in general terms about God's loyalty to the pious.We often find something like this at the end of an individual thanksgiving.Thus,T.Joseph 2,4-6 is the appropriate end of the individual thanksgiving,T.Joseph 1,3(4)-2,6. In 2,6c we find the motif of the righteous man's trial by God,which is the transition to vs.7.

E. 2,7

In vs.7 Joseph applies the idea of the righteous man's trial by God, generally formulated in T.Joseph 2,6, to his own oppression in the past, 'In ten [95] temptations (πειρασμοῖς) He showed [96] me approved (δόκιμον)...' The idea of a trial by God occurs in the O.T. quite frequently.[97] Especially in the wisdom-literature, however, it is connected with the idea of the (temporary) suffering of the pious from which God saves and rewards him, if the latter shows himself faithful; see, e.g., Sir.2,1-11; 33,1; Ps.66(65),1of.; Wisd.3,5f.(see I D); 11,9f.; I Cor.1o,13; II Cor.8,2; I Peter 1,6f.(see I D); 4,12; II Peter 2,9; Rev.2,1o; 3,1o; Pastor Hermae, Visio 4,3,4; Sim.7,1.

In Sir.2,1-11, just mentioned, the attitude of the pious man is described -as in T.Joseph 2,7('And in all of them I endured' : ...ἐμακροθύμησα)- by the verb μακροθυμεῖν ,'My son, when thou comest to serve the Lord, prepare thy soul for temptation. ..Accept whatsoever is brought upon thee, and be patient (μακρο-θύμησον) in disease and poverty'(Sir.2,1.4). The attitude of the pious man in times of suffering and oppression is that of patience, of μακροθυμία ; and patience is a μέγα φάρμακον (T.Joseph 2,7)[98], a remedy through which God saves one from distress.

In T.Joseph 2,7 ὑπομονή is parallel with this μακροθυμία ; it gives πολλὰ ἀγαθά [99]. It is not surprising that ὑπομονή (ὑπομένειν), a term originally used in the martyr-traditions (see, e.g., IV Macc.1,11; 5,23; 6,9, etc.; Ign., Smyrn.4,2; Mart.Polyc.2,2ff.; 3,1; 19,2; Mart.Carpi, Pamfili et Agathonicae 36; 4o (Gr.rec.; ed.Musu-rillo); The Martyrs of Lyons 1,7.2o.27.45 (ed.Musurillo)), should be used to describe the attitude of the righteous man in his distress, whether it is connected with the idea of a trial by God or not[100]. On these grounds it is to be expected that this combination of μακροθυμία and ὑπομονή should occur elsewhere too; so, e.g., II Tim.3,1of.; II Cor.6,4ff.[101] Job's attitude in his distress, is also characterized by both these terms in T. Job 26,4f.[102], where he asks his wife to remember the good things they received from God ...τὰ κακὰ πάλιν οὐχ ὑπομένομεν ; ἀλλὰ μακροθυμήσωμεν ἕως ἀν ὁ Κύριος σπλαγχνισθεὶς ἐλεήση ἡμᾶς ; see also 1,5 (and the variant in V); 4,6; 5,1; 27,7.[103]

Thus, when in T.Joseph we find that Joseph holds fast through his μακροθυμία and ὑπομονή in times of distress and oppression, it is the testing by God of Joseph as a pious man. In T.Joseph ὑπομονή is one of Joseph's most important qualities. The idea recurs in some very striking places : in 1o,1 (just after the first story), 'Ye see, therefore, my children, how great things patience (ἡ ὑπομονή) worketh...' [104]; and in 17,1 (just after the second story), 'Ye see, therefore, children, what great things I endured (ὑπέμεινα)...' Already on these grounds alone it is justifiable to consider both stories under the same motif, namely under Joseph's ὑπομονή. Moreover we also find a recurrence of Joseph's μακροθυμία ,in 18,3, 'For, behold, ye see[105] that out of my long-suffering (διὰ τὴν μακροθυμίαν) I took unto wife even the daughter of my masters'.[106]

This attitude of ὑπομονή, which is characteristic of the martyr, and of the pious and righteous man, who is closely related to the martyr, could easily be connected with the fig-ure of Joseph in T.Joseph. Joseph was traditionally one of the

righteous men who had been tested by God -like Abraham,Daniel
and many others;see I Macc.2,5lff.,'And call to mind the deeds
of the fathers which they did in their generations;that ye may
receive great glory and an everlasting name.Was not Abraham
found faithful in temptation(ἐν πειρασμῷ),and it was reckoned
unto him for righteousness ? Joseph,in the time of his
distress,kept the commandment,and became lord of Egypt...' [107]
Thus Joseph is one of the 'ancient pious fathers' who held out
in distress and were,therefore,rewarded by God;and,as we have
seen,because the attitude of the pious man in his oppression
could often be described by ὑπομονή,a connection between Joseph
and ὑπομονή could easily be made.Although in I Macc.2,5lff.
ὑπομονή is not explicitly mentioned[108],it is three times connected with Joseph in Josephus : in Ant.II 43,'Nay,he(=Joseph)
besought her(=the Egyptian woman) to govern her passions...,
while for his part,he would endure (ὑπομενεῖν) anything rather
than be obedient to this behest' [109];II 5o,'...he resisted her [110]
entreaties and yielded not to her threats,choosing to
suffer unjustly and to endure (ὑπομένειν) even the severest
penalty...';and II 69,'nay,it was for virtue's sake and for
sobriety that I was condemned to undergo (ὑπομένειν)a malefact-
or's fate...' Moreover,in Apoc.Pauli 47(Ti.p.65) we read,...
καὶ λέγει μοι εἷς ἐξ αὐτῶν,'Ιωσὴφ ὁ πραθεὶς ἐν Αἰγύπτῳ · ...οὐκ ἀπέδωκα
τοῖς ἀδελφοῖς μου,οῢ κατηράσαντό με. μακάριος γὰρ ὁ δυνάμενος ὑπομεῖναι
πειρασμόν... All this justifies the conclusion that T.Joseph 2,7
(and also 1o,1;17,1) exhibits a motif which was traditionally
connected with Joseph.

F. Summary

T.Joseph 1,3(4)-2,6 is an individual thanksgiving,in
which Joseph describes his salvation from distress and
oppression by God.It contains terms and expressions,of which
some occur only in the first story,others only in the second
story,others in both stories.Thus it may be concluded that
this individual thanksgiving is intended to be an introduction
to the whole of T.Joseph.[111] T.Joseph 2,6c introduces the idea
of the righteous man's testing by God.This links up with vs.7,
where this idea is applied to the actual life of Joseph.Jo-
seph's attitude is described in terms which occur frequently
in this kind of context,viz., μακροθυμία and ὑπομονή.The latter
one is traditionally connected with Joseph,and is a recurring
characteristic of Joseph elsewhere in T.Joseph,occurring
immediately after the first and immediately after the second
story. Thus once more it is clear that T.Joseph 1-2 is intended to be an introduction to the whole of T.Joseph.

G. Excursus :
T.Joseph 1,3(4)-2,6 : a late Jewish individual thanksgiving

Crüsemann,who deals extensively with the genre of the
individual thanksgiving in his book[112],remarks in his conclusions about the structure and the development of this sort of
psalm [113], '1.Konstitutives Formmerkmal der Dankpsalmen des
Einzelnen ist ein Reden in zwei Richtungen.Sie reden einmal
Jahwe direkt an(Du-Stil)und berichten zum anderen anderen
Menschen über sein Tun(Er-Stil). ...3. ...hat bei der Über-
eignung des Tieres...eine als Toda-Formel zu bezeichnende,

relativ feste Wendung ihren Sitz...7. ...so ist die Geschichte
der Gattung vor allem durch zwei Momente gekennzeichnet.Einmal
werden beide Grundteile der Gattung durch Aufnahme weiterer
Formelemente ausgebaut.Hauptsächlich die Verkündigung in der
Runde der Zuhörer ist dadurch betroffen.Hier dringen in star-
kem Masse Redeformen der Weisheit (Heilruf,Mahnwort,Sentenz),
...ein...Mit ihnen werden vom Beter aus dem Erlebten all-
gemeingültige Konsequenzen gezogen...8.Zum anderen wird die
strenge Bipolarität dadurch aufgelöst,dass der Adressat der
Rede mehrmals innerhalb des Psalms wechselt.hierbei kann die
Anrede oder der Bericht zum beherrschenden Stil des Psalms
werden...Diese Auflösung der Grundform wird mit einer gewissen
Ablösung von der ursprünglichen kultischen Situation zu er-
klären sein...9. ...dass...die Auflösung der Grundform im
Alten Testament nur zögernd und schrittweise und fast nirgends
bis zu einem völligen Bruch vollzogen wird...und erst im nach-
kanonischer Zeit wird aus dem Dankpsalm ein Gebet eines Einzelnen an seinen Gott...[114]

When we compare the structure of T.Joseph 1,3(4)-2,6 with
that of the canonical individual thanksgiving,we find some
differences.Most important,the 'Du-Stil' and the 'Toda-Formel'
are lacking in T.Joseph.Because of these differences the
following question might be raised : is it right to call T.
Joseph 1,3(4)-2,6 an individual thanksgiving ?

As we have seen,Crüsemann notices a development in this
type of psalm : other elements (an influence from the 'Weisheit' in particular) might be taken up,and either the 'Du-
Stil' or the 'Er-Stil' become prominent,the more so in later
(post-biblical) psalms. H.Ludin Jansen,in his book Die spätjüdische Psalmendichtung,ihr Entstehungskreis und ihr "Sitz im
Leben".Eine literaturgeschichtlich-soziologische Untersuchung,
[115] investigated especially these late Jewish psalms. He comes
to the following thesis :'Die spätjüdische Psalmendichtung
entstand in den Kreisen der ,,Weisen''...Man brauchte diese
Dichtungen zu erbaulichen und didaktischen Zwecken in der
Unterweisung...[116] On pp.28-35,he deals in particular with
(individual) thanksgivings,among which he reckons Ps.Sol.15;
Dan.2,2o-23;Ps.Sol.2;13 (and also Sir.51,1-12 : see p.65). In
his conclusion on p.35 he remarks ,'Kein alttestamentlicher
Dankpsalm hat auch nur annähernd so viele Weisheitsgedanken
aufgenommen als die Dichtungen,die wir bis jetzt behandelt
haben.Diese neuen Gedanken haben auch das Stilschema gesprengt
und die Ideen umgestaltet wie in keiner kanonischen Dichtung
dieser Art.'[117] Moreover,it is interesting that,whereas the
psalms in Ps.Sol.2;13;15 are poetic,Dan.2,2o-23 is in prose.
Concerning the use of prose or poetry in these late Jewish
psalms Jansen remarks ,'Da nun die Psalmen erbaulich-didak-
tischen Zwecken dienen sollten,wurde das frühere Schema der
Psalmen gesprengt...Wo nur erbaulich-didaktische Zwecke ver-
folgt wurden,wurde oft die Psalmenform aufgegeben;es war ja
leichter in Prosa zu schreiben.' [118]

From this the following conclusions can be reached : 1.
T.Joseph 1,3(4)-2,6 is an individual thanksgiving,but it is
in many respects different from an Old Testament individual
thanksgiving and belongs to a later development of this type
of psalm.We can find such a later development especially in

the non-canonical,late Jewish psalms; 2.Whereas in the Old
Testament thanksgiving elements of wisdom are already present,
they play an important,or rather prominent part in these later
psalms.This explains why T.Joseph 1,3(4)-2,6 is so strongly[119];
reminiscent of ideas which belong to the wisdom-literature
3.Moreover,many of these later psalms have a didactic function.[120] Undoubtedly,T.Joseph 1,3(4)-2,6 fulfils the same
function.This is made clear from the introduction(1,3) and its
transition to 2,7; 4.The change in style in T.Joseph 2,1-3
does not justify a sharp separation of this passage from the
previous and the following verses.

II.Joseph's attitude towards the Egyptian woman(T.J.3,1-1o,4)

A. Joseph's Praying,Fasting,Mourning and Humiliation

We have seen that T.Joseph 1,3(4)-2,6 is an individual
thanksgiving uttered by Joseph.It contains many terms that
come originally from the psalms,especially the genre of an
individual thanksgiving,but also from the genre of an individual lament.The following investigation of T.Joseph 3,1-1o,4
will argue that Joseph's attitude in his 'struggle' against
the Egyptian woman is the attitude we find especially in an
individual lament,where the poet complains of his distress
and oppression and beseeches God for salvation.

What is the attitude of the man who complains of his
distress,and prays for salvation ? 'Der Beter _fastet_ lange
Zeit,um die Gnade Gottes auf sich zu ziehen.Er trägt den
,,Sack'' des Sünders und bezeichnet sich mit Rücksicht darauf
als ,,schwarz''... Auf die Erde hingestreckt,in Sack und Asche
usw. klagt und fleht er'.[121] So we read in Ps.69,1off.(68,11
ff.),'I have broken my spirit with fasting (LXX,ἐν νηστείᾳ)... I
have made sackcloth (LXX, σάκκον) my clothing...I lift up this
prayer (LXX,τῇ προσευχῇ) to thee,O Lord...Rescue me (LXX, σῶσόν
με) from the mire,do not let me sink;let me be rescued from
the muddy depths (LXX,ῥυσθείην ἐκ τῶν μισούντων με καὶ ἐκ τοῦ βάθους
τῶν ὑδάτων)...';in Ps.1o9(1o8),24ff.,'My knees are weak with
fasting (LXX, ἀπὸ νηστείας)...Help me (LXX, βοήθησόν μοι),O Lord
my God;save me (LXX, σῶσόν με) ,by thy unfailing love...' When
Nehemiah hears the sad lot of those left behind in Jerusalem,
his reaction is as follows,'When I heard this news,I sat down
and wept;I mourned for some days,fasting and praying to the
God of heaven (LXX, ἔκλαυσα καὶ ἐπένθησα ἡμέρας καὶ ἤμην νηστεύων καὶ
προσευχόμενος ἐνώπιον θεοῦ τοῦ οὐρανοῦ)'.[122] When the threat of the
Assyrian armies is great,the reaction of the Israelites is as
follows (Judith 4,9-15),'And every man of Israel cried to God
with great earnestness...put sackcloth(σάκκους) upon their
loins...and cast ashes upon their heads,and spread out their
sackcloth (σάκκους) before the Lord;and they put sackcloth
(σάκκῳ) about the altar...And the Lord heard their voice,and
looked upon their affliction (τὴν θλῖψιν αὐτῶν): and the people
continued fasting (νηστεύων) many days in all Judaea and Jerusalem... had their loins girt about with sackcloth (σάκκους)...
and they cried unto the Lord with all their power,that he
would look upon (ἐπισκέψασθαι [123]) all the house of Israel for
good'; see (for the description of such a situation) also II
Chron.2o,3;I Macc.3,44ff.;II Macc.13,1off.;Syr.Bar.5,6f.;see

further Esther 4,16-17 LXX;Ezra 8,21ff.From the texts mentioned above it is clear that not only in the Psalms,but also
elsewhere the attitude of the man in distress is described in
these terms. Two other texts are important in this context :
Ps.6,'...all night long my pillow is wet with tears,I soak my
bed with weeping (LXX,ἐν δάκρυσίν μου)' [124] and '...for the Lord
has heard the sound of my weeping (LXX, τοῦ κλαυθμοῦ μου)' [125];
and Ps.34,13f.LXX, ἐγὼ δὲ ἐν τῷ αὐτοὺς παρενοχλεῖν μου ἐνεδυόμην
σάκκον καὶ ἐταπείνουν ἐν νηστείᾳ τὴν ψυχήν μου,καὶ ἡ προσευχή μου...ὡς
πενθῶν καὶ σκυθρωπάζων,οὕτως ἐταπεινούμην. [126]

So the attitude of the man in distress,that we find
especially as expressed in an individual lament [127],is as
follows : he prays (προσεύχεσθαι,δεῖσθαι),he fasts (νηστεύειν),he
weeps (πενθεῖν,δακρύειν,κλαίειν, etc.),he wears the σάκκος,and he
asks God to be saved (ῥύεσθαι,σῴζειν,λυτροῦν, etc. [128]) from
distress and from those who oppress him.It is just this
attitude that characterizes Joseph in the story about the
Egyptian woman : he prayed to God and asked to be saved and
delivered from the Egyptian woman : 3,3,'...and going into my
chamber,I prayed unto the Lord (προσηυχόμην κυρίῳ) ';4,3,'Owing to
all these things I lay upon the ground in sackcloth(ἐν σάκκῳ),
and besought God that the Lord would deliver me from the
Egyptian woman (ἐδεόμην τοῦ θεοῦ,ὅπως ῥύσεταί με ὁ κύριος ἐκ τῆς
Αἰγυπτίας)';4,8,'And I gave myself yet more to fasting and
prayer,that the Lord might deliver me from her (νηστείαν καὶ
προσευχήν,ὅπως ῥύσεταί με κύριος ἀπ'αὐτῆς)';7,4,'...I prayed unto
the Lord (προσευξάμενος κυρίῳ) ...';8,1,'...and I knelt(γόνυ
κλίνας) before the Lord all the day together with all the
night;and about dawn I rose up,weeping the while(δακρύων) and
praying for a release from the Egyptian woman (αἰτῶν λύτρωσιν ἀπὸ
τῆς Αἰγυπτίας) ';9,4,'...and listened to my voice as I prayed
(προσευχομένου)...'. [129] Several times we hear that Joseph fasted : 3,4,'And I fasted (ἐνήστευον) in those seven years...';3,
5,'...I drank no wine [130];nor for three days did I take my food
[131]';4,8,'And I gave myself yet more to fasting (νηστείαν) ...'
Joseph also put on sackcloth : 4,3,'Owing to all these
things I lay upon the ground in sackcloth(ἐν σάκκῳ)...' [132]

Finally,we read that Joseph wept : 3,6,'...and I wept
(ἔκλαιον) for the Egyptian woman of Memphis,for very unceasingly did she trouble me(ἐνόχλει μοι [133])...';3,9,'And when I
perceived it I sorrowed(ἐλυπήθην) unto death...and I lamented
(ἐπένθησα)for her many days...';6,3,'And when he (αὐτοῦ -b is
not correct) had gone out I wept(ἔκλαιον)...';8,1,'...and about
dawn I rose up,weeping the while(δακρύων)...' [134] We should
observe,however,that here two kinds of 'weeping' are mentioned,
viz.,weeping over one's own oppression(8,1) and weeping over
(the sins of) the other,the 'adversary'(3,6.9 and probably
also 6,3).Both kinds of weeping,which are closely related [135],
are characteristic of the one who complains in his distress.
For weeping over one's own oppression,see,e.g.,Ps.6,6(7),8(9).
[136];for weeping over the adversary,see,e.g.,Ps.34,14 LXX [137].
The motif of weeping especially over the sins of another
occurs elsewhere too.When Ezra hears that many Israelites have
married foreign women,he reacts as follows,'When I heard this
news,I rent my robe and mantle (LXX, καὶ ὡς ἤκουσα τὸν λόγον τοῦτον,
διέρρηξα τὰ ἱμάτιά μου)...I knelt down (LXX, κλίνω ἐπὶ τὰ γόνατά μου)
and spread out my hands to the Lord my God and said... While

Ezra was praying and making confession,prostrate in tears (LXX,
καὶ ὡς προσηῠξατο...κλαίων καὶ προσευχόμενος)before the house of God
... Then Ezra left his place...he neither ate bread nor drank
water,for he was mourning (LXX,ἐπένθει) for the offence committed by the exiles who had returned'(Ezra 9,3.5;1o,1.6)[138]. In
T.Joseph,when the Egyptian woman threatens to kill her husband,
Joseph's reaction is the same,'Ἐγὼ οὖν,ὡς ἤκουσα τοῦτο,διέρρηξα τὴν
στολήν μου...(5,2).

It is now clear that T.Joseph 3ff. attributes to Joseph
the attitude which is typical of the man who -in distress-
asks God for salvation. I shall now investigate these chapters
in greater detail,looking especially at Joseph's attitude in
his 'struggle' against the Egyptian woman[139],in order to
discover other elements which belong to the same context of a
man in distress.

First,the style in T.Joseph 3ff. is very striking.Several
times we find exclamatory sentences introduced by ποσάκις or
πόσα .'How often(ποσάκις)did the Egyptian woman threaten me
with death ! How often(ποσάκις)did she give me over to punishment...'(3,1);'How often(ποσάκις)did she flatter me with words
as a holy man...'(4,1);'How often(ποσάκις),though she were
sick,did she come down to me at unlooked-for times...'(9,4);
'Ye see,therefore,my children,how great things(πόσα)patience
worketh...'(1o,1);'Ye see,therefore,children,what great things
(πόσα)I endured...'(17,1).[140] Undoubtedly,this style is rhet-
orical.See,e.g.,Epict.IV 1,95,'I will become a friend of
Caesar;no one will wrong me if I am a companion of his.But,in
the first place,the number of things(πόσα)I must suffer and
endure in order to become his friend ! and the number of times
(ποσάκις),and the number of persons by whom(ὑπὸ πόσων)I must
first be robbed !'[141];cf.III 26,3.In the O.T./LXX the same
style is found,e.g.,Ps.78(77),4o;Job 13,23;Sir.2o,17;IV Macc.
15,22.It is,however,interesting that such a style can also
occur in an individual lament,making the lament more intense,
more moving : Ps.3,1(2),'Lord,how my enemies have multiplied !
(LXX, κῦριε,τί ἐπληθῦνθησαν οἱ θλίβοντές με ;)...'[142]

We have seen that threatening with death (see T.Joseph 3,
1)[143] is an action typical of the tyrant in the martyr-lit-
erature.[144] The following ...τιμωρίαις παραδοῦσα ἀνεκαλέσατό με ...
also belongs to this context : the tyrant compels the martyr
into submission through punishments;so,e.g.,IV Macc.4,24,'...
he(=Antiochus) beheld all his threats and penalties(τὰς ἑαυτοῦ
ἀπειλὰς καὶ τιμωρίας) utterly despised...';cf.5,1o.[145] From this
it may be concluded that some elements from the martyr-traditions are connected with the idea of the suffering of the
oppressed man (Joseph);we have seen the same for T.Joseph 2,
2[146] and the idea of ὑπομονή.[147]

In spite of the woman's alluring offer (3,2),Joseph did
not succumb to her;he remembered his father's words[148],he
entered his chamber[149],prayed and fasted (3,3f.).And when she
(or 'he',that is : his master) was away from home,he drank no
wine[150],and ate no food during three days,and gave it to the
poor and sick (3,5).Here we find the combination praying-
fasting-'giving alms',well-known in Judaism : see,e.g.,Tobit
12,8 BA,ἀγαθὸν προσευχὴ μετὰ νηστείας καὶ ἐλεημοσῦνης καὶ δικαιοσῦνης.
151

We read in 3,6 that Joseph 'sought the Lord early' :...
ὤρθριζον πρὸς κύριον ('and wept ...').[152] This expression appears
several times in the O.T.,again in connection with the situation of someone in distress.He rises early and prays to God
for salvation;so,e.g.,Ps.78(77),34f.,'When he(=God) struck
them,they began to seek him,they would turn and look eagerly
for God (LXX, ὤρθριζον πρὸς τὸν θεόν);they remembered that God was
their Creator (LXX,βοηθός),that God Most High was their deliv-
erer (LXX, λυτρωτῆς)';Job 8,5f.,'If only you will seek God be-
times (LXX, ὀρθριζε πρὸς κύριον)and plead for the favour of the
Almighty,if you are innocent and upright,then indeed will he
watch over you...';see also Ps.63,1(62,2);Sir.39,5;Hos.5,15;
Is.26,9.

In the beginning the Egyptian woman embraced Joseph as a
son,as Joseph was ignorant (cf. κἀγὼ ἠγνόουν [153]) concerning her
real intentions;later on,however,'she sought to draw[154] me
into fornication'(3,7f.).[155] Then,of course,he was no longer
ignorant (cf. νοήσας),and he saw through her guile and deceit,
and sorrowed unto death[156],and made attempts to turn her from
her evil lust (3,9f.).

Hereafter the Egyptian woman flattered Joseph as a 'holy
man',and praised his chastity openly before her husband...
βουλομένη καταμόνας ὑποσκελίσαι με (see 4,1f.).ὑποσκελίζειν is traditionally one of the actions which the enemies and adversaries
undertake against the oppressed man;so,e.g.,Ps.14o,4(139,5),
'Guard me (LXX, φύλαξόν με),O Lord,from wicked men;keep me safe
from violent men,who plan to thrust me out of the way (LXX,
ὑποσκελίσαι τὰ διαβήματά μου)';see also 37(36),31;cf.T.Dan 6,3.

Finally,after many other attempts,the Egyptian woman used
force : she held fast to his garment,but he fled away naked[157]
(8,2f.). Hereafter she accused him falsely[158], and he was cast
into prison (8,4).Then,he tells us,'When,therefore,I was in
fetters,the Egyptian was sick with grief,and she heard (ἐπ-
ηκροᾶτο) me,how I sang praises(ὕμνουν)unto the Lord being in the
house of darkness,and with glad voice rejoicing(χαίρων)glorif-
ied (ἐδόξαζον) my God only that I was delivered (ἀπηλλάγην)[159]
by a pretext from the Egyptian woman'(8,5).Joseph's action
here described is the usual action of the oppressed man after
his salvation : he praises and glorifies God who has saved him
from his distress.For this action,terms as δοξάζειν and ὑμνεῖν
[160] are used : δοξάζειν ,e.g.,in Ps.86(85),12; ὑμνεῖν in Ps.22,
22(21,23);7o,8 LXX.In fact an individual thanksgiving gives
expression to this praise of God,who has saved the oppressed
man from his distress,as he had requested in an individual
lament.[161]

The situation described in 8,5,however,is especially reminiscent of that of Shadrach,Meshach and Abed-nego in Dan.3
LXX.Because of their miraculous salvation from the fire they
praise God,...ὕμνουν καὶ ἐδόξαζον ... τὸν θεόν ...· ὑμνεῖτε ... ὅτι
ἐξείλετο ... καὶ ἔσωσεν ... ἐρρύσατο ... ἐλυτρώσατο ... (vss.51;88),
after which we read, καὶ ἐγένετο ἐν τῷ ἀκοῦσαι τὸν βασιλέα ὑμνούντων
αὐτῶν... (vs.91).Here is not only the combination ὑμνεῖν -
δοξάζειν [162] as a response following upon God's salvation[163],
but also the motif that the adversary,the one who causes the
distress,hears the hymn of praise.In Dan. it is the king,in
T.Joseph it is the Egyptian woman.[164]

Even when Joseph was in prison,the Egyptian woman did not give up her attempts,but Joseph did not succumb to her (9,1f.). And,as Joseph says,'...if a man liveth in chastity,and desireth also glory(δόξαν),and if the Most High knoweth that it is expedient for him,He bestoweth this also upon him,even as upon me.'(9,3).[165] The next two verses close the first story;they speak again of the woman's attempts to fulfil her desire.It is important to notice that the actions described here do not follow in time the actions narrated in the previous chapters.[166] If this is obvious for the action described in vs.5,then vs.4 too must be considered in the same way[167];it narrates again how often the Egyptian woman -sick and groaning[168]- came to Joseph ἐν ἀωρίᾳ[169],and heard him praying.This situation did not take place when Joseph was in prison,but had taken place many times in the history of Joseph and the Egyptian woman.[170] This being the case,Joseph's reaction is easier to understand: '...and understanding[171] her groanings (that is : 'understanding the reason of her groanings') I held my peace (ἐσιώπων). Different from his master[172],Joseph saw why the woman groaned and why she was sick.But he held his peace.[173] He did not reveal her evil intentions to anybody.[174] This characteristic will play an important role in the second story about the selling of Joseph (see III).

The story about the woman closes with a little sentence which -qua style (and terminology)- once more belongs to the genre of an individual thanksgiving : '...And the Lord guarded me (ἐφύλαξέ με)[175] from her devices.'(vs.5).

B. Joseph's σωφροσύνη

In T.Joseph 4,1f. the Egyptian woman praises Joseph's chastity (σωφροσύνη) openly before her husband.This characteristic of Joseph also occurs elsewhere in T.Joseph;so in 6,7, 'But that thou mayest learn that the wickedness of the ungodly hath no power over them that worship God in chastity(σωφροσύνη) ...';in 9,2f.,'...For God loveth him who in a den of darkness combines fasting with chastity (σωφροσύνη),rather than the man who in the chambers of the palace (b omits βασιλείων wrongly) combines luxury with licence (ἀκολασίας).And if a man liveth in chastity(σωφροσύνη) ...';and in 10,2f.[176] From this it is obvious that Joseph's σωφροσύνη plays an important role in the first story in T.Joseph.It is,however,a motif that is traditionally connected with Joseph;so in IV Macc.2,2f.,'This, certainly,is why we praise the virtuous (ὁ σώφρων)Joseph,because by his Reason,with a mental effort,he checked the carnal impulse.For he,a young man at the age when physical desire is strong,by his Reason quenched the impulse of his passions.' We find it in Philo too : De Jos.4o,'But while he was winning a high reputation in household affairs,his master's wife made him the object of her designs,which were prompted by licentious love (ἐξ ἔρωτος ἀκολάστου)... she made proposals of intercourse to him which he stoutly resisted and utterly refused to accept,so strong was the sense of decency and temperance (σωφροσύνην)which nature and the exercise of control had implanted in him';see also De Jos.57;87. Joseph's σωφροσύνη is also mentioned in Josephus,Ant. II 48,'Again,he might look not only for the enjoyment of those present privileges that were already his,by responding to her love,but for benefits yet greater,would he only submit;but for vengeance and hatred on her part,should he reject her suit and set more store on a reputation for chastity(τὴν τῆς σωφροσύνης δόκησιν) than on grat- ifying his mistress';see also Ant. II 5o;69. Finally,we find it in Jos.et As.4,9, καὶ ἔστιν Ἰωσὴφ ἀνὴρ θεοσεβὴς καὶ σώφρων...

Moreover,in Philo,De Jos.4o we heard that the Egyptian woman was carried away by an ἔρως ἀκόλαστος. The motif of the woman's ἀκολασία also occurs in T.Joseph 7,1,'But her heart was still set upon me with a view to lewdness(πρὸς ἀκολασίαν)...' ἀκολασία,however,is the antonym of σωφροσύνη,a contrast that we also find in T.Joseph 9,2;see further,e.g.,Arist.,Eth.Nic. 11o7 b 6;Thuc.3,37,3;Dio Chrys.23,6;Philo,Quod omnis 159;Praem. Poen.159f.;Spec.Leg.III 51;62;Vita Mosis II 55;Quis Heres 2o9; Agric.98;Mut.Nom.197;Just.,Apol.I 15,7.[177] From all this it is clear that the author of T.Joseph took up a traditional motif when he mentioned Joseph's σωφροσύνη.

C. Paraenesis : 1o,1-4

After the first story,Joseph addresses his sons in direct paraenesis ,'Ye see,therefore,my children,how great things patience worketh,and prayer with fasting (...πόσα κατεργάζεται [178] ἡ ὑπομονή,καὶ προσευχὴ μετὰ νηστείας) '(1o,1).Several times in this story we have found mention of prayer and fasting.Here,in 1o,1, they are connected with the idea of ὑπομονή,which we found in 2,7 but which does not occur in the first story itself.We find it again in the paraenesis directly after the second story , 'Ye see,therefore,children,what great things I endured (πόσα ὑπέμεινα) that I should not put my brethren to shame'(17,1).[179] Thus,its position immediately before the first story,together with its use in the paraenetic passages directly following each story,indicates that the author of T.Joseph intended to illustrate Joseph's ὑπομονή from both stories.

Joseph's attitude as the attitude of an oppressed man in distress -praying,weeping,fasting,wearing 'sackcloth'- is ultimately to be understood in the light of this idea of ὑπο- μονή.We find it again in 1o,2,'And ye,therefore,if ye follow after chastity and purity with patience and in humility of heart(...τὴν σωφροσύνην καὶ τὴν ἀγνείαν...ἐν ὑπομονῇ καὶ ταπεινώσει καρδίας)...' Here σωφροσύνη occurs too,as well as a new term, traditionally connected with it (see,e.g.,Philo,Vita Mosis II 137;I Clem.64,1;Ign.,Eph.1o,3),viz.,ἀγνεία.It is also a term that is used especially in connection with chastity (sexual purity);see,e.g.,Philo,Abr.98;Spec.Leg.II 56;Pastor Hermae, Mand.4,1,1. Parallel to ὑπομονή is another new term, ταπείνωσις καρδίας .Thus the correct attitude of man,as exemplified by Joseph,is patience and humility of heart.The virtue of humili- ty is a traditional motif often found in Jewish and Christian writings.The pious Jew and Christian humbles himself before God and men.[18o]

To return to the text of T.Joseph,God's response to the man who lives in this way is as follows :'...the Lord will dwell in you[181],because He loveth chastity[182].And wheresoever the Most High dwelleth,even though a man falleth into[183] envy [184],or slavery[185],or slander[186],or darkness[187],the Lord who

dwelleth in him,for the sake of his chastity not only deliver-
eth (ῥύεται) him from evil,but also exalteth and glorifieth
(ὑψοῖ καὶ δοξάζει) him even as me' (1o,2b-3). [188]

Besides God's saving activity described by the verb
ῥύεσθαι [189],another action of God is mentioned : he exalts (and
glorifies) : ὑψοῦν (and δοξάζειν).Both activities,which are
closely related,were mentioned in 1,7,...καὶ ἐρρύσατό με...καὶ
ὕψωσέ με . [190] A good attitude in distress and oppression results not only in God's salvation from distress,but also in
exaltation as a reward.In T.Joseph 9,3 we have seen the idea
of exaltation : 'And if a man liveth in chastity and desireth
also glory (δόξαν) ,and if the Most High knoweth that it is
expedient for him,He bestoweth this also upon him,even as upon
me.' But we find the idea of reward elsewhere too : 18,1,'If
ye also,therefore,walk in the commandments of the Lord,my
children,He will exalt(ὑψώσει) you there,and will bless you
with good things (ἐν ἀγαθοῖς) [191] for ever and ever';T.Sim.4,5,
'Beware,therefore,my children,of all jealousy and envy...,that
God may give you also grace and glory,and blessing (χάριν καὶ
δόξαν,καὶ εὐλογίαν) upon your heads,even as you saw in his (=
Joseph's) case' [192];T.Benj.4,1,'...Be followers of his (=
Joseph's - see IV C) compassion with a good mind,that ye also
may wear crowns of glory (στεφάνους δόξης)'.In this series of
texts two things are striking.In the first place,we find this
motif also in T.Joseph 18,1 (after the second story).Secondly,
every other time it occurs in the Testaments,it is connected
with Joseph.

Exaltation by God is a reward for the good and pious
attitude of a man in general,and of the oppressed man in
particular.In the latter case it is connected with God's 'saving' action. [193] The following examples illustrate this. Of the
pious man in general(cf.T.Sim.4,5;T.Benj.4,1),see,e.g.,Ps.37
(36),34,'Wait for the Lord and hold to his way;(he will keep
you safe from wicked men) and will raise you (LXX, καὶ ὑψώσει
σε) to be master of the land...';84,11(83,12),'...grace and
honour are his to give (LXX,χάριν καὶ δόξαν ῥώσει [194]).The Lord
will hold back no good thing (LXX,τὰ ἀγαθά [195]) from those whose
life is blameless';see also 88,2o LXX;149,4;Prov.18,1o;cf.Ps.
113(112),7;73(72),24;T.Job 43,16;I Clem.45,8;Pastor Hermae,
Visio 2,2,6.For στέφανος (cf.T.Benj.4,1),see,e.g.,I Cor.9,25;II
Tim.4,8;James 1,12;I Peter 5,4;Rev.2,1o;cf.T.Job 4o,3.

This idea of exaltation and reward (usually described by
such terms as ὑψοῦν,δοξάζειν,εὐλογεῖν,δόξα,εὐλογία) occurs specifically in connection with the oppressed man,who is saved by God
because of his pious attitude.For examples,see : II Sam.22,49,
'(God) who dost snatch me from my foes and set me over (LXX,
ὑψώσεις με)my enemies,thou dost deliver me (LXX,ῥύση με) from
violent men';Ps.9,14 LXX,'Have pity on me,O Lord;look upon my
affliction ἐκ τῶν ἐχθρῶν μου,ὁ ὑψῶν με from the gates of death';
Ps.91(9o),14f.,'Because his love is set on me,I will deliver
(LXX, ῥύσομαι) him;...I will be with him in time of trouble
(LXX, ἐν θλίψει);I will rescue him and bring him to honour (LXX,
δοξάσω αὐτόν) ';see further 18,48(17,49);Is.63,9. In the first
instance this idea of 'exaltation' differs little from that of
'salvation' and is not directly concerned with reaching a
'higher status';but,because of the similar use of ὑψοῦν and the

combination ὑφοῦν - δοξάζειν [196] ,both ideas could easily be connected,as we can see especially in T.Joseph 18,1f.

It is not accidental that in the Testaments this idea of exaltation and reward occurs only in connection with Joseph. In these writings,Joseph is the person par excellence who - after a time of distress in which he kept faithful to God - is saved from his oppression and exalted and honoured : he becomes 'king' of Egypt.The reason for this is found in the fact that in the O.T./LXX the same pattern is connected with Joseph. The motif of the 'exaltation' of the slave Joseph to 'king' of Egypt,which has its roots in the Genesis-story,occurs in Ps. lo5(lo4),17ff.[197] Moreover,in I Macc.2,53 Joseph's 'exaltation is described as a reward by God because of Joseph's faithfulness throughout his troubles.And finally,we read in Wisd.lo, 13f.,'When a righteous man(=Joseph) was sold,wisdom[198] forsook him not[199] ,but from sin she delivered(ἐρρύσατο)him;she went down with him into a dungeon,and in bonds[200] she left him not, till she brought him the sceptre of a kingdom(σκῆπτρα βασιλείας), and authority over those that dealt tyrannously with him;she showed them also to be false that had accused him,and gave him eternal glory (δόξαν αἰώνιον) '.[201]

The condition for this exaltation by God is,as we have seen,that one remains faithful to him and does his commandments.A characteristic of this attitude is humility,ταπείνωσις . We have found this in T.Joseph lo,2.Its place in the context, however,can be understood more clearly now : the pious man humbles himself;hereafter he will be exalted by God (see,e.g., Matt.23,12;Luke 14,11;18,14;James 4,lo;I Peter 5,6).More important,however,is the fact that this self-humiliation stands over against self-exaltation,which can be described also by the verb ὑφοῦν .Over against the pious,God-fearing man who humiliates himself,and is exalted by God afterwards (ὑφοῦν) stands the sinner who exalts himself(ὑφοῦν).Because Joseph is the one who possesses ὑπομονή,who wants to be completely dependent on God,and who humbles himself,after which he is saved and exalted by God,he stands over against the sinner who exalts himself.Joseph does not exalt himself.And it is precisely when this theme is reached that the second story about the selling of Joseph begins.

D. Summary

Joseph's attitude towards the Egyptian woman is the attitude of the oppressed man who asks God for salvation from his distress.Joseph's fasting,weeping and wearing sackcloth proved to belong to this kind of context.Joseph is not primarily the 'Tugendheld';his praying and fasting are not the decisive weapons in his struggle against the woman.[202] Joseph is like the oppressed man in an individual lament : he beseeches God through prayers,fasting,etc. for salvation,and after he has been saved he praises God.From all this it has become clear that T.Joseph 1-2 in which we find an individual thanksgiving,is closely connected with 3,1-lo,4. Other characteristics of Joseph are his silence(σιωπᾶν)[203] and his σωφροσύνη ;the latter is a motif which is traditionally connected with Joseph.[204]

In the paraenesis after the first story (lo,1-4) we have
found not only terms which occur in the previous story,but
others such as ἀγνεία and ταπείνωσις καρδίας,and the important
idea of ὑπομονή,which also occurs just before the first story
and in the paraenetic passage directly after the second story.
Finally,the motif of the pious man's exaltation(ὑφοῦν) is
applied to Joseph.

III. Joseph's attitude towards his brothers (T.J.lo,5-18,4)

A.

In the previous section I have discussed the motifs of
man's exaltation(ὑφοῦν) by God and of the pious man's humility-
his self-humiliation(ταπείνωσις),which stands over against
self-exaltation,an idea which can also be described by the
verb ὑφοῦν.[205] Therefore,it is not surprising that directly
after the motif of exaltation by God (lo,3) we find that of
man's self-exaltation (lo,5).Both are described by the verb
ὑφοῦν. Elsewhere in T.Joseph both these motifs occur together,
but now in reversed order : 17,8-18,1,'And I exalted not myself (οὐχ ὕφωσα ἐμαυτόν) among them(=Joseph's brothers) in
arrogance (ἐν ἀλαζονείᾳ) because of my worldly glory(τὴν κοσμικὴν
δόξαν μου),but I was among them as one of the least (τῶν ἐλαχίστ-
ων).If ye also,therefore,walk in the commandments of the Lord,
my children,He will exalt (ὑφώσει) you there...' Hence I conclude that it is not permissible to separate the first story
from the second one,especially with respect to Joseph's attitude.[206] I have made such a separation only because the
stories deal with two different situations.

Just as Joseph refrained from exalting himself among his
brothers,when he had reached a position of honour in Egypt
(17,8),so also he refrained from exalting himself among them
when he was still with his father (before being sold).In spite
of the fact that his father loved him,'...I did not exalt myself (οὐχ ὑφούμην) in my heart' (lo,5ab).Although he was still
young then,he already feared God.[207] For,'I knew that all
things would pass away(τὰ πάντα παρελεύσεται), and I took the
measure of myself(ἐμέτρουν ἐμαυτόν) and I honoured my brothers'
(lo,5c-6a).Joseph humbled himself,and he did not exalt himself
among his brothers -in spite of Jacob's love for him and in
spite of the δόξα he had in Egypt;for he knew that everything
would pass away,and that his δόξα in Egypt was worldly.He did
not exalt himself - for he feared God.

What is the background to these ideas ? In the first
place,self-exaltation (described by the verb ὑφοῦν)is,on the
one hand,traditionally connected with the activity of for-
getting God and being disobedient to him.On the other hand,it
is for the most part the result of having much power,wealth,
glory,etc.[208];see,e.g.,Deut.8,12ff.,'When you have plenty to
eat and live in fine houses of your own building,when your
herds and flocks increase,and your silver and gold and all
your possessions increase too,do not become proud and forget
the Lord your God (LXX,μή...ὑφωθῇς τῇ καρδίᾳ καὶ ἐπιλάθῃ κυρίου τοῦ
θεοῦ σου)...' [209];II Chron.26,16,'But when he(=Uzziah) grew
powerful his pride led to his own undoing (LXX,ὑφώθη ἡ καρδία
αὐτοῦ τοῦ καταφθεῖραι): he offended against the Lord his God...';

Deut.17,19f.;Judith 9,7;Ps.131(13o);Prov.18,1off.LXX;Ezek.28,
2ff.;Dan.5,1f.LXX;5,22f.;Hos.13,6;Ps.Sol.1,4ff.;Par.Jer.6,21
(23).

Secondly,the δόξα,in which or because of which one exalts
oneself,is perishable.It is a worldly δόξα (T.Joseph 17,8) and
everything in this world (wealth,power, δόξα ,and also the man
who possesses it) is perishable (T.Joseph 1o,5). For examples
of this traditional emphasis,see,e.g.,Sir.11,4ff.,'Glory not
(μὴ καυχήσῃ) in the putting on of raiment,and exalt not thyself
in the day of honour (δόξης) ... many powerful have suffered
great abasement,and also honourable (ἔνδοξοι) been delivered up
into the hands of others';Wisd.5,8f.,'What did our arrogancy
profit us ? And what good have riches and vaunting (ἀλαζονείας
[210]) brought us ? Those things all passed away (παρῆλθεν ἐκεῖνα
πάντα) as a shadow...';T.Job 33,3f. ἐμοῦ ὁ θρόνος ἐν τῷ ὑπερκοσμίῳ
[211] ἐστίν,καὶ ἡ τούτου δόξα...ὁ κόσμος [211] ὅλος παρελεύσεται [212] καὶ ἡ
δόξα αὐτοῦ φθαρήσεται... ;see also Job 19,9;Ps.49,16f.(48,17f.);
Prov.18,1off.LXX;Sir.44,6ff.;Is.3,8 LXX;14,11;16,14;28,1ff.;
4o,6;Jer.13,18;Ps.Sol.2,5.19ff.;Or.Sib.8,75ff.;Syr.Bar.82f.;
Philo,Spec.Leg.I 311;Acta Thomae 135.

Joseph's attitude towards his brethren is not characterized by self-exaltation.[213] He was one of the least[214] among
his brothers.He took the measure of himself[215] and honoured
(ἐτίμων) his brothers (1o,6a);he feared,had respect for,them.
[216] The most important consequence of this attitude was his
silence when he was sold : '...when I was being sold,I
refrained from telling (ἐσιώπων ...μὴ εἰπεῖν) my race to the
Ishmaelites,that I am the son of Jacob,a great man and a
mighty' (1o,6). And this is characteristic of Joseph's attitude in the story about his being sold : he held his peace for
the sake of his brethren,and did not say that he was Jacob's
son,and therefore,an ἐλεύθερος.This 'silence' is the expression
of the honour of his brothers and the contrary of self-exalt-
ation.That indeed the honouring of the brothers (besides the
fear of God) is the central theme,is also obvious from 11,1,
'Do ye also,therefore,have the fear of God[217] in all your
works before the eyes (ἐν πάσῃ πράξει ὑμῶν πρὸ ὀφθαλμῶν... -b is not
correct),and honour(τιμᾶτε) your brethren.For everyone who doeth
the law of the Lord,shall be loved by Him.' [218]

In the story about the selling of Joseph[219] Joseph did
not tell anybody about his real status,but passed himself off
as a slave.When he was interrogated,'...I said that I was
their home-born slave,that I might not put my brethren to
shame (ἵνα μὴ αἰσχύνω τοὺς ἀδελφούς μου)' (11,2).Even when he was
threatened until death,he kept saying that he was a slave (11,
3).Here again,in this story threatening with death plays a
role;Joseph is,as it were,the martyr who,in spite of everything,is faithful[220] -to the love and the respect for his
brothers.When he was interrogated and even punished and beaten
by Pentephres,he kept saying that he was a slave and no free
man,he kept 'holding his peace','... τιμωρεῖς [221] ...ὡς δὲ οὐκ
ἤλλαξα λόγον τυπτόμενος[222] ...' (14,1f.).When the Ishmaelites,
after their return[223],said to Joseph that they had heard that
he was the son of a great man[224]in Canaan,and that his father
mourned for him (15,1f.),his reaction was the same,'and again
I desired to weep,but I restrained myself[225], ἵνα μὴ αἰσχύνω τοὺς

ἀδελφούς μου.And I said I know not,I am a slave' (15,3). One
other incident involves Joseph's silence:Pentephres' wife
wanted to buy Joseph 'at any price'.Finally one of her eunuchs
bought him for her at the price of eighty pieces of gold,
though he claimed that he had paid a hundred pieces of gold.
Joseph's reaction was the same,'And though I saw (this) I held
my peace,lest the eunuch should be unmasked (ἐσιώπησα,ἵνα μὴ
ἐτασθῇ ὁ εὐνοῦχος)' ^{226} (16,6).

Thus,being silent,hiding the truth,is the central
characteristic of Joseph's attitude in this story.What its
meaning is,we can discover from the paraenesis which directly
follows the story,'Ye see,therefore,children,what great things
I endured that I should not put my brethren to shame(πόσα
ὑπέμεινα,ἵνα μὴ καταισχύνω τοὺς ἀδελφούς μου)'(17,1).Joseph was
silent because he had ὑπομονή ;and,conversely,'enduring'
implied being silent and not telling his real status - for the
sake of his brothers. ^{227} He respected them and did not exalt
himself.On the contrary,he endured injustice and humiliated
himself. ^{228} This feature of silence occurred once in the first
story ^{229} ,when he was silent and endured injustice for the sake
of the Egyptian woman.

Our author's use of this motif of Joseph's silence may be
traced to a tradition which is also found in Philo.We read in
De Jos.246ff.,'...They(=his brothers) praised also the pre-
eminent self-restraint of his modest reticence(τὴν ὑπερβάλλουσαν
μετ'αἰδοῦς καρτερίαν).He had passed through all these vicissi-
tudes,yet neither while in slavery did he denounce his
brothers for selling him nor when he was haled to prison did
he in his despondency disclose any secret,nor during his long
stay there make any revelations of the usual kind,since
prisoners are apt to descant upon their personal misfortunes
...though he had a suitable opportunity for disclosing the
facts,did he say a word about his own high lineage...(...οὔτε
δουλεύων βλάσφημον οὐδὲν εἶπε κατὰ τῶν ἀδελφῶν ὡς πεπρακότων οὔτ'...
ἐξελάληρέ τι τῶν ἀπορρήτων...οὐδ'ἐφθέγξατό τι περὶ τῆς ἰδίας εὐγενείας...
..)'. ^{230} It is important that Philo connects Joseph's silence
with his καρτερία ,since this word has its place in the martyr-
terminology and is a synonym of ὑπομονή (see,e.g.,IV Macc.15,
30;Philo,Cher.78).Later too the true history of Joseph's being
sold by his brothers is kept secret , 'In fact the story of
their conspiracy and selling of him to slavery was so completely unknown and remained so secret...'(De Jos.250).When
he wanted to make himself known to his brethren,Joseph sent
away all the Egyptians who were present ^{231} ,'So then,overcome
by family affection,he hastened to conclude his reconciliation.
And that no reproach might attach to the brothers (ὑπὲρ τοῦ
μηδὲν ὄνειδος προσβαλεῖν τοῖς ἀδελφοῖς) for their action,he judged
it best that no Egyptian should be present at the first recognition' (De Jos.237).Joseph does not reveal his brothers'
deed,lest one should attach ὄνειδος to them.This motif in Philo
is the same as that described by ἵνα μὴ αἰσχύνω τοὺς ἀδελφούς μου
in T.Joseph. ^{232} Philo and T.Joseph differ in that the latter
connects the motif much more obviously with Joseph's silence
before his kingship. ^{233}

The same motif occurs in Josephus. When Joseph makes himself known to his brothers,he says,'And for your part,I would

have you too forget the past and rejoice that that old im-
prudence has resulted in such an end,rather than be afflicted
with shame (ἢ δυσφορεῖν αἰσχυνομένους) for your faults...' (Ant. II
163).Here,however,different from T.Joseph (and Philo),this
idea is not introduced in connection with Joseph's silence,
though Josephus knows of this too : 'Joseph,on his side,com-
mitting his cause entirely to God,sought neither to defend himself nor yet to render a strict account of what had passed,but
silently underwent his bonds and confinement (τὰ δεσμὰ δὲ καὶ τὴν
ἀνάγκην σιγῶν ὑπῆλθεν),confident that God,who knew the cause of
his calamity and the truth,would prove stronger than those who
had bound him...' (Ant. II 60).Joseph's silence is here connected with his confidence that God will save him.[234] This connection is not explicit in T.Joseph,but it is possibly in the
background -in the first story,where God's saving
activity is emphasized.

In T.Joseph,however,Joseph's silence is not merely an
expression of enduring injustice (connected or not with his
confidence in God),but it is -more positively- connected with
his brotherly love,and,in general,with his love to others.It
is interesting that in T.Benj.5,4f. the attitude of keeping
silent as an expression of enduring injustice is described as
characteristic of the righteous and pious man in general[235],
'For if any one does violence to a holy man,he repenteth;for
the holy man is merciful to his reviler,and holdeth his peace
(καὶ σιωπᾷ).And if any one betrayeth a righteous soul,and the
righteous man be humbled for a little -praying (all the time)-
not long after[236] he appeareth more glorious,even as was
Joseph my brother.' So,when the righteous man is done wrong,
he holds his peace and has mercy on the one who does not treat
him well;he prays (for him ?[237]),and is rewarded afterwards :
'he appeareth more glorious'. Such an idea occurs also in the
final paraenetic passage in T.Joseph,'And if any one seeketh
to do evil unto you,do well unto him,and pray for him[238],and
ye shall be redeemed of the Lord from all evil(καὶ ἀπὸ παντὸς
κακοῦ λυτρωθήσεσθε διὰ κυρίου)' (18,2). Here we also find the
idea of salvation from all distress,a motif that often occurs
in T.Joseph 1,3-1o,4.In 18,2 this motif is connected especially with the attitude towards the neighbour,and in particular towards the evil-doer.

Summing up - the author of T.Joseph has connected the
traditional motif of Joseph's silence on the one hand with his
ὑπομονή [239] and on the other hand -more positively- with his
attitude towards his brothers[240] and towards others (the
Egyptian woman,the eunuch).

In the paraenesis following the story about the selling
of Joseph,Joseph exhorts his sons to love one another and to
hide each other's faults,'Do ye also,therefore,love one another (ἀγαπᾶτε ἀλλήλους) ,and with long-suffering[241] hide ye one
another's faults (συγκρύπτετε ἀλλήλων τὰ ἐλαττώματα) .For God
delighteth in the unity of brethren (τέρπεται γὰρ ὁ θεὸς ἐπὶ ὁμο-
νοίᾳ ἀδελφῶν [242]),and in the purpose of a heart that takes
pleasure in love(ἀγάπην)' (17,2f.).This was also Joseph's
attitude when Jacob and his sons had settled in Egypt.He did
not reproach his brothers for anything,but comforted them and
loved them after Jacob's death even more,...καὶ οὐκ ὠνείδισα,ἀλλὰ
καὶ παρεκάλεσα αὐτούς...ἠγάπησα αὐτούς... (17,4f.).[243] Finally,Joseph

also translated this love towards his brothers into action,so that,'Their children were my children,and my children as their servants;their life was my life,and all their suffering was my suffering,and all their sickness was my infirmity.My land was their land;their counsel was my counsel(ἡ βουλὴ αὐτῶν,βουλή μου. b is not correct)' (17,5ff.).[244]

In summary[245]: according to the second story Joseph does not exalt himself among his brothers,but honours and loves them.Hence,he holds his peace and does not reveal his social status.As in the first story,here too Joseph's situation is sometimes described in terms which are often used in the martyr-stories.His attitude can best be characterized by the term ὑπομονή/ὑπομένειν,which,though it does not occur in the story itself,is found in the paraenetic passage which directly follows the story (exactly as in the case of the first story and of the following paraenesis).Here,in the paraenesis,he exhorts his sons to love one another,to hide one another's faults,to do well to the evil-doer (in distress) and to pray for him.After that,they will be saved and rewarded by God.

B.

It is now possible to give a brief description of Joseph 's attitude in T.Joseph. T.Joseph 1,3(4)-2,6 has the style of an individual thanksgiving,in which Joseph as the oppressed man gives thanks to God for his salvation.We find references to both the first and the second stories.Joseph's distress is described as a trial by God,in which his ὑπομονή (and μακροθυμία) becomes evident.This term ὑπομονή occurs in contexts of central importance in T.Joseph;thus it is the key to Joseph's attitude in the two stories following on ch.1-2.

In the first story,Joseph's attitude is that of the man who asks God for salvation -an attitude which we can find especially in an individual lament.His praying,fasting,weeping, etc. belong to this context.After his salvation he praises God and glorifies him who has saved him from his distress (i.e., the Egyptian woman).Moreover,we found here the traditional motif of Joseph's σωφροσύνη . At the end of the story the motif of his silence occurs. In the paraenesis directly after the first story,ὑπομονή is mentioned and connected with ταπείνωσις καρδίας . We also found here the idea of exaltation and reward by God.

This exaltation,described by the verb ὑψοῦν(and δοξάζειν) stands over against the self-exaltation (also described by ὑψοῦν),with which the second story begins.In this story Joseph's attitude is characterized especially by his silence and is connected,on the one hand,with ὑπομονή/ὑπομένειν ,which is -here also- not mentioned in the story itself,but in the paraenetic passage directly following on the story,and,on the other hand,with his attitude towards his brothers.In the paraenesis immediately after the second story,in addition to exhortations to brotherly love,to hiding one another's faults and to doing good to evil-doers,we find the term ὑπομένειν once more,as well as the ideas of salvation and exaltation by God.

Finally,in both stories,which -as we have seen- belong indissolubly together,traces of the martyr-traditions can be found.

IV. Joseph as an example of ethics.
The paraenetic passages in the Testaments of the XII Patriarchs
(except T.Joseph)

A.Joseph's attitude towards the Egyptian woman: T.Reub.4,8-1o

The warning against πορνεία is central in Reuben's paraenesis to his sons.According to T.Reub.4,6, πορνεία 'deceiveth
the mind and understanding' and 'leadeth down young men into
Hades before their time (κατάγει νεανίσκους εἰς ᾅδην,οὐκ ἐν καιρῷ
αὐτῶν[246])'. The connection between death and πορνεία (cf.also
vs.7,...καὶ γὰρ <u>πολλοὺς ἀπώλεσεν</u> ἡ πορνεία...) comes from the wisdom-
literature,and in particular from Prov.5 and 7,where the
terminology is the same.[247] Finally we read that πορνεία '...
bringeth reproach[248] upon him and derision with Beliar and the
sons of men' (4,7).At this point Joseph is introduced as an
example of good behaviour (4,8-1o).[249] 'For because Joseph
guarded himself from every woman[250] and purged his thoughts
from all fornication[251],he found favour in the sight of the
Lord and men[252]' (vs.8).Then,in vs.9,we hear about the
Egyptian woman's attempts to bring Joseph to πορνεία ,'For the
Egyptian woman[253] did many things unto him,and summoned magic-
ians (μάγους) ,and offered him love potions(φάρμακα)...' This
motif is often connected with πόρνη - πορνεία[254];the actions
here described undoubtedly allude to the same event as in T.
Joseph 6.[255] Whatever the woman did,'...the inclination of his
soul admitted[256] no evil desire(ἐπιθυμίαν πονηράν) ' (vs.9). The
expression ἐπιθυμία πονηρά occurs elsewhere in the Testaments
only in T.Joseph 3,1o and 7,8,and in both places in connection
with πορνεία .[257]

Because of Joseph's good and pious attitude,'the God of
my fathers delivered him from every visible and hidden death
(ὁ θεὸς τῶν πατέρων μου ἐρρύσατο αὐτὸν ἀπὸ παντὸς ὁρατοῦ καὶ κεκρυμμένου
θανάτου) ' (vs.1o).God's deliverance of Joseph is described by
the verb ῥύεσθαι also in T.Joseph[258],and the wording here in
T.Reub. represents a stereotyped formulation that occurs
elsewhere in the Testaments : T.Sim.2,8,...ὁ θεὸς αὐτοῦ καὶ ὁ θεὸς
τῶν πατέρων αὐτοῦ...ἐρρύσατο αὐτὸν ἐκ τῶν χειρῶν μου ;and T.Gad 2,5,
...ὁ θεὸς τῶν πατέρων μου ἐρρύσατο ἐκ τῶν χειρῶν μου...[259] Since
death is a serious threat for the oppressed man in the psalms
[260],we find God's deliverance (ῥύεσθαι) of him from death there
also;see,e.g.,Ps.56,13(55,14),'for thou hast rescued me from
death (LXX,ὅτι ἐρρύσω τὴν ψυχήν μου ἐκ θανάτου) ...';see also 33(32),
19.[261] The visible death referred to in T.Reub.4,1o probably
means death as a consequence of overt action by others,whereas
hidden death probably refers to the food prepared by the
Egyptian woman.[262]

<u>In summary</u> : in Reuben's exhortation concerning πορνεία,
Joseph is introduced as an example of virtue : he held aloof
from πορνεία -in spite of all the attempts of the Egyptian
woman.Therefore God saved him from death.The situation and the
terminology are strongly reminiscent of T.Joseph,and especially of the first story.T.Reub.4,1o is -in thought and,at
least for the first part,also in terminology- a stereotyped
formulation in connection with Joseph in the Testaments.

B. Joseph's attitude towards his brothers

1. T.Zeb.8,4f.

When Zebulun relates to his sons the story of the selling of Joseph,he describes how,when the brothers wanted to kill Joseph and Joseph pleaded for mercy,he had pity on Joseph and cried together with him.In ch.5 Zebulun exhorts his sons,'I bid you to keep the commands of the Lord,and to show mercy to your neighbour,and to have compassion towards all(ποιεῖν ἔλεος ἐπὶ τὸν πλησίον καὶ εὐσπλαγχνίαν πρὸς πάντας ἔχειν)...' (vs.1).[263] This was Zebulun's attitude towards Joseph[264],but also towards other people who were in troubles and in distress.[265] The beginning of ch.8 contains the same exhortation (in almost the same terminology)[266], ...ἔχετε εὐσπλαγχνίαν κατὰ παντὸς ἀνθρώπου ἐν ἐλέει...(vs.1).

Zebulun then puts forward Joseph as an example.The introduction ὅτε γὰρ κατήλθομεν εἰς Αἴγυπτον(vs.4) is a stereotyped formulation for this purpose (see also T.Sim.4,3,καὶ ὅτε κατέβημεν εἰς Αἴγυπτον).[267] Zebulun describes Joseph's attitude towards his brothers in Egypt,and Zebulun's sons are exhorted to take up the same attitude,'...Joseph bore no malice (οὐκ ἐμνησικάκησεν) against us,but when he saw me,he had compassion (ἐσπλαγχνίσθη).To whom taking heed[268],do ye also,my children, approve yourselves without malice (ἀμνησίκακοι γίνεσθε) ,and love (ἀγαπᾶτε) one another,and do not reckon (μὴ λογίζεσθε) ,each one of you,the evil of his brother' (vss.4f.).The same attitude of Joseph is mentioned in T.Sim.4,4,...εὔσπλαγχνος καὶ ἐλεήμων,οὐκ ἐμνησικάκησε...ἀλλὰ καὶ ἠγάπησε...It is noteworthy that,although the words σπλαγχνίζεσθαι,εὐσπλαγχνία,εὔσπλαγχνος and ἐλεεῖν,ἔλεος, ἐλεήμων are frequently used in the Testaments,this is not the case with μνησικακεῖν,(ἀ)μνησίκακος.These words occur only twice in the Testaments,and both times in connection with Joseph (T.Sim.4,4;T.Zeb.8,4ff.).The reason for this is that this connection already occurs in Gen.'When their father was dead Joseph's brothers were afraid and said : 'What if Joseph should bear a grudge against us (LXX, Μήποτε μνησικακήσῃ ἡμῖν Ιωσηφ)and pay us out for all the harm that we did to him ?' ' (Gen.5o,15).Then they said to Joseph,'In his last words to us before he died,your father gave us this message for you : "I ask you to forgive your brothers' crime and wickedness (LXX, Ἄφες αὐτοῖς τὴν ἀδικίαν καὶ τὴν ἁμαρτίαν αὐτῶν)..." ' (Gen.5o,16f.).

This act of remission,which characterizes Joseph's attitude here and which is precisely the act of οὐ μνησικακεῖν (an expression which occurs also in T.Zeb.8,4),is also mentioned in T.Zeb.8.There,however,in Zebulun's paraenesis to his sons, he uses a different expression,...μὴ λογίζεσθε ἕκαστος τὴν κακίαν τοῦ ἀδελφοῦ αὐτοῦ (vs.5).[269] A few examples may illustrate this: Ps.32(31),1f.,'Happy the man whose disobedience is forgiven (LXX, ἀφέθησαν αἱ ἀνομίαι),whose sin is put away ! Happy is a man when the Lord lays no guilt to his account (LXX,οὐ μὴ λογίσηται κύριος ἁμαρτίαν)...'[270].In I Clem.6o,1f.,God is addressed,'... Ο "merciful and compassionate" (ἐλεῆμον καὶ οἰκτίρμον)[271],forgive us (ἄφες ἡμῖν) our iniquities and unrighteousness,and transgressions,and shortcomings.Reckon not every sin(μὴ λογίσῃ πᾶσαν ἁμαρτίαν) of thy servants and handmaids...' The connection here between this act of God and his mercy(ἐλεῆμων)also occurs in

T.Zeb.9,7,'...for He is merciful and compassionate,and He setteth not down in account evil to the sons of men(ὅτι ἐλεήμων ἐστὶ καὶ εὔσπλαγχνος,μὴ λογιζόμενος κακίαν τοῖς υἱοῖς τῶν ἀνθρώπων)..'[272]

Thus it is clear how Joseph's ἀμνησικακία and willingness to forgive his brothers (ideas present in the Gen.-story) could be connected with such terms as εὔσπλαγχνος (σπλαγχνίζεσθαι, εὐσπλαγχνία) and ἐλεήμων (ἐλεεῖν,ἔλεος).Moreover,whereas the terms εὔσπλαγχνος,etc.,and ἐλεήμων,etc.,traditionally belong together [273],we find elsewhere μνησικακεῖν,etc.,on the one hand,in connection with ἐλεεῖν,etc.,and,on the other hand,in connection with σπλαγχνίζεσθαι,etc.So,e.g.,Zech.7,9f.,'These are the words of the Lord of Hosts : Administer true justice,show loyalty and compassion (LXX, ἔλεος καὶ οἰκτιρμόν) to one another,do not oppress the orphan and the widow,the alien and the poor,do not contrive any evil (LXX,μὴ μνησικακείτω ἐν ταῖς καρδίαις ὑμῶν)one against another' (see for the combination ἐλεεῖν,etc., - μνησικακεῖν,etc., further Prov.21,24ff.;I Clem.2,4f.);Pastor Hermae, Mand.9,2f.,'...you shall know his(=God's) great mercifulness (εὐσπλαγχνίαν),that he will not desert you,but will fulfil the petition of your soul.For God is not as men who bear malice (μνησικακοῦντες),but is himself without malice (ἀμνησίκακος) and has mercy (σπλαγχνίζεται) on that which he made.'

   In summary : in an exhortation concerning ἔλεος and εὐσπλαγχνία,Zebulun cites Joseph as an example (8,4f.).He did not bear malice against his brethren in Egypt.The term μνησικακεῖν is taken from the Gen.-story.The willingness to forgive,which also occurs in Gen. in connection with Joseph,recurs (worded differently) in 8,5. Because of this,and since μνησικακεῖν,etc., can be connected with both ἐλεεῖν,etc.,and σπλαγχνίζεσθαι,etc., a combination of these three terms was natural.This combination occurs also in T.Sim.4,4.Finally,the willingness to forgive,together with love to one another,to which Zebulun exhorts his sons with reference to the example of Joseph,is in accordance with Joseph's own paraenesis to his sons in T. Joseph 17,2 (after the second story) and with his attitude towards his brothers,especially in Egypt (T.Joseph 17,4ff.)[274].

2. T.Sim.4,3-6;5,1a

   Over against Zebulun's attitude towards Joseph(ἔλεος,εὐσπλαγχνία) stands Simeon's attitude which is characterized as ζῆλος (T.Sim.2,6f.) and φθόνος (T.Sim.2,13f.;cf.ch.3).[275] According to T.Sim.2,Simeon wanted to kill Joseph,but God 'delivered him out of Simeon's hands'.[276] After a warning against φθόνος (3,1),and a description of the bad consequences of envy and the method of getting rid of it (3,2-6),we hear that Simeon wept even more than the other brothers,since he was αἴτιος τῆς πράσεως Ἰωσήφ (4,2).Therefore he did not grieve when he was bound as a spy by Joseph in Egypt,for he knew that he was suffering justly (4,3).[277] But,'Joseph was a good man (ἀνὴρ ἀγαθός),and had the spirit of God within him[278]:being compassionate and pitiful,he bore no malice against me (εὐσπλαγχνος καὶ ἐλεήμων,οὐκ ἐμνησικάκησέ μοι);but even loved(ἠγάπησε) me even as the rest of his brethren' (4,4).Here Joseph is called a 'good man',an epithet used elsewhere in the Testaments in connection with Joseph (T.Dan 1,4;T.Benj.3,1 -on which see IV C).

In T.Sim.4,4,Simeon calls Joseph εὐσπλαγχνος and ἐλεήμων, and explains that Joseph bore no malice against(οὐκ ἐμνησικάκησε) him. Joseph's attitude here is the same as was found in T.Zeb. 8,4.Moreover,Joseph even loved(ἠγάπησε) Simeon,as his other brothers.As we have seen,Joseph's love for his brothers is also mentioned in T.Joseph 17,5,...ἠγάπησα αὐτούς...[279] Moreover, in T.Joseph 17,4 we are told that Joseph did not reproach his brothers,...οὐκ ὠνείδισα. It is striking that both of these verbs also occur in T.Sim.4,6,'All his days he reproached us not (οὐκ ὠνείδισεν ἡμᾶς) concerning this thing,but loved us (ἠγάπησεν ἡμᾶς) as his own soul and beyond his own sons...' This last sentence is strongly reminiscent of T.Joseph 17,7.Simeon also tells how Joseph helped his brothers with all kinds of gifts (cf.T.Joseph 17,5f.) in T.Sim.4,6,ἐρρύξασεν ἡμᾶς,καὶ πλοῦτον καὶ κτήνη καὶ καρποὺς πᾶσιν ἡμῖν ἐχαρίσατο.[280] It is evident that a close relationship exists between T.Sim.4,4.6(esp.vs.6) and T.Joseph 17,4-7 -in terminology as well as in contents.

Referring to the example of Joseph[281] Simeon exhorts his sons to beware of ζῆλος and φθόνος ,through which he himself was blinded in his attitude towards Joseph,to walk ἐν ἀπλότητι ψυχῆς[282] καὶ ἐν ἀγαθῇ καρδίᾳ (4,5;cf.vs.7),and to love one another (4,7).If they do this,they will be rewarded by God,even as Joseph was[283] (cf.T.Joseph 9,3;1o,3;18,1).[284] Then Simeon describes the harmful effect of φθόνος on the man who is possessed by it (T.Sim.4,8f.).One can even see when a person is seized with this πνεῦμα τοῦ φθόνου (connected with ζῆλος);his appearance makes it immediately clear.[285] Therefore Joseph was 'comely in appearance,and goodly to look upon[286],because no wickedness dwelt in him' (5,1a).Since man's external appearance corresponds with his internal character,and Joseph had a good appearance,the conclusion is obvious : in Joseph dwelt no wickedness (οὐκ ἐνοίκησεν ἐν αὐτῷ οὐδὲν πονηρόν)[287],an idea closely related with Joseph's epithet (in the Testaments) ἀνὴρ ἀγαθός .

<u>In summary</u> : in Simeon's exhortation concerning φθόνος and ζῆλος ,Joseph is held up as an example.He is the ἀνὴρ ἀγαθός. No wickedness dwelt in him;he was εὐσπλαγχνος and ἐλεήμων and bore no malice against his brethren.He loved them and did not reproach them,but gave them many gifts. Simeon's sons are exhorted to beware of φθόνος and ζῆλος ,and to love one another so that they may be rewarded by God. Joseph's attitude here is closely related to that described in T.Joseph 17,4-7,and it is strongly reminiscent of T.Zeb.8,4f.

3. Excursus : T.Dan 1,4-9 and T.Gad

In T.Dan and in T.Gad,Joseph is mentioned only in the biographical material and is not cited in the paraenesis as an example of ethics.Hence,I may confine the discussion of these two Testaments to a few remarks.[288]

a.T.Dan 1,4-9. In this passage three things are important for the subject under discussion : 1.Joseph's epithet : he is called 'the true and good man' (see IV C); 2.Dan's attitude towards Joseph : it is characterized by ζῆλος and ἀλαζονεία ,with which θυμός and the desire to kill Joseph are connected; 3.the recurrent idea,that God saves Joseph (vs.9).[289]

b.T.Gad. According to ch.1f.,Joseph brought a bad report of the sons of Zilpah and Bilhah to his father.This is undoubtedly intended to give an explanation of Gen.37,2.[290] The act provoked Gad's hatred of Joseph[291].He wanted to kill Joseph,but God saved him (2,5) and punished Gad (5,6-11). In the paraenesis,Gad warns against μῖσος ,through which he himself was blinded in his attitude towards Joseph.Over against the hatred,love is mentioned;so,e.g.,6,3,'love ye,therefore, one another from the heart;and if a man sin against thee,cast forth the poison of hate and speak peaceably to him...' Now Joseph's role in T.Gad becomes clear.Joseph is the one who sinned only a little (cf.4,6 : ἐν ὀλίγῳ) against his brothers. Gad's reaction to Joseph's sin was,however,completely wrong. He hated him,whereas he should have spoken to him peaceably (cf.ch.6).[292] So from the example of his wrong attitude (hatred and envy) towards Joseph,who sinned against him,Gad makes clear what the right attitude (especially love and forgiveness) is towards the sinner.[293] Because the biographical material in T.Gad describes Joseph's attitude towards his brothers as (a little) sin,Joseph cannot be introduced as an example of ethics in the paraenesis !

C. Joseph as an ἀνὴρ ἀγαθός : T.Benj.3ff.

At the very beginning of his exhortations to his sons, Benjamin introduces Joseph as an example of ethics[294],'Do ye also,therefore,my children,love the Lord God of Heaven,and keep His commandments,following the example of the good and holy man (τὸν ἀγαθὸν καὶ ὅσιον ἄνδρα) Joseph' [295] (3,1). As we have seen[296],Joseph is called ἀνὴρ ἀγαθός elsewhere in the Testaments : T.Sim.4,4 (ἀνὴρ ἀγαθός);T.Dan 1,4 (ἀνδρὸς ἀληθινοῦ[297] καὶ ἀγαθοῦ). It is especially in T.Benj. that the figure of the ἀνὴρ ἀγαθός plays an important role (see 4,1f.;6,1).The origin of this expression,which occurs in the O.T./LXX several times[298],is undoubtedly in the wisdom-literature.Here 'ἀνὴρ ἀγαθός' is one of the expressions used to describe the good,wise and righteous man as the counterpart of the sinner,the fool,the wicked;see,e.g.,Prov.13,22,'A good man (ἀγαθὸς ἀνήρ) leaves an inheritance to his descendants,but the sinner's hoard passes to the righteous (δικαίοις)'[299];14,14,'The renegade reaps the fruit of his conduct,a good man (ἀνὴρ ἀγαθός) the fruit of his own achievements'[300];see further 3o,23 LXX;Sir.29,14. In the Testaments it is Joseph who is considered as this ἀνὴρ ἀγαθός.

In the paraenesis to his sons Benjamin gives a description of the ἀνὴρ ἀγαθός or ἀνὴρ ὅσιος [301],using the example of Joseph.[302] It is,however,obvious that not everything that Benjamin says about the good and holy man refers to Joseph. Rather,the figure of Joseph is only the peg,on which Benjamin hangs his speculations on the good and holy man.The expression διάνοια ἀγαθή ,which is another important motif in T.Benj.,is closely connected with that of 'the good man'.[303]

In 3,3 Benjamin exhorts his sons to fear God and to love their neighbour.He continues,'...and even though the spirits of Beliar ask for you to be delivered up to every evil of tribulation[304],yet shall no evil of tribulation have dominion over you (κατακυριεύσῃ ὑμῶν),even as it had not over Joseph my brother' (3,3).After pointing out how many dangers Joseph was exposed to in his lifetime and how he was saved by God ('How many[305] men wished to slay him[306],and God ἐσκέπασεν αὐτόν' -vs. 4a),Benjamin takes up the idea expressed in vs.3 and specifies it in vss.4b-5,'For he that feareth God[307] and loveth his neighbour[308]' : a) 'cannot be smitten[309] by the spirit of the air[310] of Beliar --- σχεπαζόμενος ὑπὸ τοῦ φόβου τοῦ θεοῦ' and b) 'cannot be ruled over[311] by the device of men or beasts --- βοηθούμενος ὑπὸ τῆς (τοῦ κυρίου)[312] ἀγάπης,ἧς ἔχει πρὸς τὸν πλησίον.' In 5,2 we find a related idea,'If ye do well,even the unclean spirits will flee(φεύξεται)from you,and the very beasts will dread you and flee from you(φεύξεται...φοβηθέντες).' This idea occurs also elsewhere in the Testaments : see T.Iss.7,7;T. Napht.8,4.6. The idea is sometimes connected with God's help to the righteous man :'...since you have with you the God of heaven...'(T.Iss.7,7).[313]

This complex of ideas is to be traced originally to the O.T.: Job 5,19ff.,'You may meet disaster six times,and he will save you;seven times,and no harm shall touch you.In time of famine he will save you from death,in battle from the sword... and when violence comes you need not fear.You will laugh at violence and starvation and have no need to fear wild beasts (ἀπὸ δὲ θηρίων ἀγρίων οὐ μὴ φοβηθῇς),after which LXX continues, θῆρες γὰρ ἄγριοι εἰρηνεύσουσίν σοι.[314]

So in T.Benj.3,3-5 Benjamin says that the man who fears God and loves his neighbour (and thus does well) cannot be 'overcome' either through the θλῖψις which comes from Beliar and his spirits or through that which comes from men and beasts.On the contrary,he is saved[315],even as Joseph was saved by God.Although God's saving activity is described by a different verb (σκεπάζειν),the idea of Joseph's salvation is the same as we have so often found it in T.Joseph.[316]

As an example of Joseph's brotherly love,Benjamin tells how Joseph asked Jacob[317],'that he would pray for our brethren that the Lord would not set down in account[318] whatever evil they had devised regarding him[319]' (3,6).

In 3,1,Benjamin exhorted his sons to follow the good and holy man Joseph.Almost the same exhortation is found in 4,1[320], 'See ye,children,the end of the good man (τοῦ ἀγαθοῦ ἀνδρὸς τὸ τέλος)? Be followers (μιμήσασθε) of his compassion(εὐσπλαγχνίαν) with a good mind,that ye also may wear crowns of glory (στεφάνους δόξης).' Although Joseph is not mentioned,he is undoubtedly meant by the 'good man'.We may deduce this : a)from the use of μιμεῖσθαι which also occurred in 3,1;b)from the occurrence of εὐσπλαγχνία which,as we have seen[321],is one of Joseph's virtues; c)especially from the occurrence of the idea of God's reward[322] which we find elsewhere in the Testaments exclusively in connection with Joseph.[323]

Benjamin goes on to say that the good man has no 'dark eye'[324];'for he showeth mercy to all men (ἐλεᾷ γὰρ πάντας)[325], even though they be sinners,even though they devise with evil intent concerning him.So by doing good(ὁ ἀγαθοποιῶν)he over- cometh evil[326],being shielded by the good;and he loveth the righteous (τοὺς δὲ δικαίους ἀγαπᾷ)as his own soul.' (4,2f.).It is striking that here the good man is characterized by qualities which originally belong to God.In the LXX it is God who has

mercy on all men (see Wisd.11,23f., ἐλεεῖς δὲ πάντας...ἀγαπᾶς γὰρ
τὰ ὄντα πάντα...;cf.15,1f.;Sir.18,13)[327].We also find in the O.
T. the idea that God loves the righteous;see Ps.146(145),8
(LXX, ...κύριος ἀγαπᾷ δικαίους);cf.Prov.15,9.

What is especially important in the next two verses (4,
4f.)[328](also because of 5,1) is the good man's attitude towards the wicked man,the sinner : 'him that rejecteth the Most
High he admonisheth and turneth back(νουθετῶν ἐπιστρέφει)'.In 5,1
we read among other things,'the profligate will reverence you
and turn unto good (ἐπιστρέψουσιν εἰς ἀγαθόν)'. This idea that the
wicked man or the sinner is 'turned unto good' by the pious
man's attitude,is a traditional motif[329].It is,however,very
important that we also find it in connection with Joseph :
T.Joseph 6,6.8,'...I have kept it to convict thee (εἰς ἔλεγχόν
σου),if haply thou mayest see it and repent(μετανοήσεις)... I
raised her up and admonished her(ἐνουθέτησα)'[330],and in particular in Philo,De Jos.8off.,esp.86f.,'...they (=the fellow-
prisoners) were rebuked(ἐνουθετοῦντο)by his wise words and
doctrines of philosophy,while the conduct of their teacher
effected more than any words.For by setting before them his
life of temperance and every virtue...he converted (ἐπέστρεφε)
even those who seemed to be quite incurable,who as the long-
standing distempers of their soul abated reproached themselves
for their past and repented(μετανοοῦσι)with such utterances as
these...' Similarly we read in T.Benj.5,1,'...and the covetous
will not only cease from their passion ,but even give the
objects of their covetousness to them that are afflicted.'

Moreover,the attitude of the wicked man also changes towards the good man (or the man who has a good mind) himself :
'...wicked men will be at peace with you (εἰρηνεύσουσιν ὑμῖν) '
(5,1).[331] From T.Gad 6,6,e.g.,it is obvious that both ideas
are closely connected,'...For he who denieth may repent (μετανοεῖ)so as not again to wrong thee[332];yea,he may also honour
thee and fear and be at peace (φοβηθήσεται καὶ εἰρηνεύσει)'. The
origin of the idea that the wicked man will be at peace with
the 'good man' is,in my opinion,to be found in the wisdom-
literature;see,e.g.,Sir.6,5f.,'Gentle speech multiplieth
friends(πληθυνεῖ φίλους αὐτοῦ)...let those that are at peace with
thee (οἱ εἰρηνεύοντές σοι) be many...';see further Prov.15,28a
LXX;cf.Job 5,19ff.LXX (see above).[333]

Not only do the wicked change their attitude towards the
good man,but even the unclean spirits and wild beasts[334] flee
(φεύξεται -φοβηθέντες).[335] And even 'darkness fleeth away from
him' (5,2f.).

Ch.5,4f. describes the attitude of the good man(ἀνὴρ ὅσιος/
δίκαιος) towards the one who does wrong to him,'For if any one
does violence to a holy man,he repenteth;for the holy man is
merciful to(ἐλεεῖ) his reviler,and holdeth his peace (σιωπᾷ)'
(vs.4). In oppression the pious man's attitude is characterized by ἔλεος [336] and by 'being silent',qualities characteristic of Joseph.[337] In vs.5 Joseph is explicitly mentioned,
'And if any one betrayeth a righteous soul,and the righteous
man be humbled(ταπεινωθῇ) for a little -praying (all the time)-
not long after[338] he appeareth more glorious,even as was
Joseph my brother.' Already in the O.T. we find the idea of

'humiliation' by others (enemies) in connection with Joseph :
Ps.lo5(lo4),18,'he(=Joseph) was kept a prisoner (LXX,ἐταπείνωσαν)
with fetters on his feet...'[339] T.Benj.5,5 also mentions the
idea of a reward -found in the Testaments exclusively in connection with Joseph.[340] So in these verses (vss.4f.) some
characteristics of Joseph are transferred to the portrait of
the good,pious and righteous man,which is central in T.Benj.

In summary[341] : Benjamin exhorts his sons to imitate the
ἀνὴρ ἀγαθὸς καὶ ὅσιος Joseph.He cites the example of Joseph in
the description of his ideal of the good and pious man.He
mentions φόβος θεοῦ and love to one another. εὐσπλαγχνία and ἔλεος
also play an important role,and even the keeping of silence is
mentioned.The consequences of such an attitude are that God
will save in times of oppression,that he will shield the good
man and reward him,that the wicked men and the sinners will
repent,and that Beliar,his spirits,the wild beasts and the
wicked deeds of men will have no power over him. In conclusion,
T.Benj. uses some elements in connection with Joseph which can
be found in T.Joseph (in the first and the second story/the
paraenesis after the first and the second story),and other
elements which can be found either in other Testaments (apart
from T.Joseph) or both in other Testaments and in T.Joseph.

D. Joseph as a wise man ? T.Levi 13

In the first verse of T.Levi 13,Levi exhorts his sons to
fear the Lord with their whole heart and to walk in simplicity
[342] according to his [343] law.[344] Here,in the very first verse,
the word νόμος occurs;it is the central term in the next three
verses : 'And do ye also teach your children letters[345],that
they may have understanding(σύνεσιν)all their life,reading
unceasingly the law (τὸν νόμον) of God.For every one that
knoweth the law (γνώσεται νόμον)of God shall be honoured... and
many men shall desire to serve him,and to hear the law (νόμον)
from his mouth.'

We must first of all ask ourselves why specifically does
this passage occur in T.Levi.The answer must be : because Levi
and the Levites are very closely related to the law of God and
have of old a special function to perform with regard to it.
In the Testaments themselves it is Levi who knows the law,and
who is taught the law by Isaac : T.Reub.6,8,'Therefore I
command you to hearken to Levi,because he shall know the law
of the Lord(γνώσεται νόμον κυρίου)...';T.Levi 9,6f.,'And Isaac
called me continually to put me in remembrance of the Law of
the Lord... And he taught me the law of priesthood,of sacri-
fices...' In the O.T. the Levites read and teach(διδάσκειν) the
law,while the people of Israel listen(ἀκούειν): see,e.g.,Deut.
31,9ff.;I Esdras 9,4o-55 LXX;Neh.8,3ff.;9,3f.

In T.Levi 13 this function has clearly changed : here,the
'Levite' is the wise man,the σοφός,who reads the law and so
gets wisdom in his life;through his knowledge of the law and
(connected with it) the fear of God,he gets wisdom and walks
in righteousness.As a result of this,he is honoured and
people desire to hear the law from his mouth.In addition to
verses 2-4 quoted above,one should also notice vs.5, ποιήσατε
δικαιοσύνην... and vs.7,σοφίαν[346] κτήσασθε ἐν φόβῳ θεοῦ...

The origin of the idea of the σοφός as it is described here,is to be found especially in the wisdom-literature.See Sir.15,1ff.,'For he that feareth the Lord(ὁ φοβούμενος κύριον) doeth this,and he that taketh hold of the law(τοῦ νόμου)findeth her(=wisdom)... she will feed him with the bread of under-standing(συνέσεως),and will give him the waters of knowledge (σοφίας) to drink... and she will exalt him above his neighbour, and will open his mouth in the midst of the assembly.Joy and gladness shall he find...';Prov.9,1o-1oa LXX;2,2ff.;for the combination νόμος - σοφία/σύνεσις,see further Deut.4,6ff.;Ps.37 (36),3of.(also δικαίου);Sir.24,23ff.;cf.6,37 (;Syr.Bar.44,14; 46,3f.;77,16);other important texts are Sir.1,4ff.;21,11.17; 25,9;33(36),1ff.;37,23ff.;39,1-11;44,1o-15;45,1ff. For the idea that the people listen to the wise man's wisdom -express-ed by the verb ἀκούειν (cf.T.Levi 13,4)- see,e.g.,I Ki.4,29ff. (5,9ff.);cf.Sir.25,9.[347]

In Sir.15,1ff.(quoted above) we have also found the idea that the wise man will find joy and gladness and will be praised.This well-known motif (see further Sir.37,23f.;39,9 ff.;44,1o-15) also occurs in T.Levi 13,3f.,'For every one that knoweth the law of God shall be honoured,and shall not be a stranger whithersoever he goeth.Yes,many friends shall he gain more than his parents[348],and many men shall desire to serve him[349]...'

After the sons of Levi have been exhorted to 'work righteousness' (vss.5f.)[350],they are urged to gain wisdom : σοφίαν κτήσασθε[351]...(vs.7);for,'if there be a leading into captivity,and cities and lands be destroyed,and gold and silver and every possession[352] perish,the wisdom of the wise nobody can take away(τοῦ σοφοῦ τὴν σοφίαν οὐδεὶς δύναται ἀφελέσθαι), save the blindness of ungodliness,and the maiming (that comes) of sin.'(vs.7). The background of this idea is in Greek-hellenistic philosophy;thus,Plut.,Mor.475E[353],'...Fortune,in fact,can encompass us with sickness,take away(ἀφελέσθαι)our possessions,slander us to people or despot;but she cannot make the good and valiant and high-souled man base or cowardly, mean,ignoble,or envious,nor can she deprive us of that dis-position,the constant presence of which is of more help in facing life than is a pilot in facing the sea'[354];and Mor.6o7 EF[355],'...And yet for a plant one region is more favourable than another for thriving and growth,but from a man no place can take away happiness,as none can take away virtue or wis-dom (ἀνθρώπου δὲ οὐδεὶς ἀφαιρεῖται τόπος εὐδαιμονίαν,ὥσπερ οὐδὲ ἀρετὴν οὐδὲ φρόνησιν); nay,Anaxagoras in prison was busied with squaring the circle,and Socrates,when he drank the hemlock,engaged in philosophy...'

What wisdom really means for the wise man,we learn from T.Levi 13,8,'for even among enemies it (=σοφία) shall be a glory[356] to him,and in a strange country a fatherland,and in the midst of foes shall prove a friend.' Finally we read in vs.9,'If he (ὁ σοφός) teaches and does those things (i.e.,if he reads the law of God,has the fear of God,does justice,gains wisdom and teaches to live according to the law and so to get wisdom and fear of God[357]),he shall be enthroned with a king, as was also Joseph our brother.' The idea that the wise man will be σύνθρονος βασιλέως through his wisdom,comes undoubtedly from the wisdom-literature;see Wisd.6,2of.,'So then desire of wisdom promoteth to a kingdom.If therefore ye delight in thrones and sceptres,ye princes of people,honour wisdom,that ye may reign for ever.' It is with reference to this idea that Joseph is mentioned in T.Levi 13.

But are we allowed to conclude that T.Levi 13 depicts Joseph as a wise man,a σοφός ? It is,of course,possible that this text really does see him as a σοφός.Besides the idea of kingship,to which wisdom leads the wise man,reference to a stay in a foreign country (see vs.8) can also be applied to Joseph. Moreover,the idea that the wise man stands firm,even when he loses everything,is easily connected with the history of Joseph;for we have seen in T.Joseph that Joseph shows ὑπομονή in all his oppressions,as Job in T.Job : see T. Job 4,4ff.,...ἐπιφέρει δέ σοι πληγὰς πολλάς,ἀφαιρεῖταί σου τὰ ὑπάρχοντα, τὰ παιδία σου ἀναιρήσει. ἀλλ'ἐὰν ὑπομεύνῃς...;cf.37,3ff. Moreover,the expression ἀνὴρ ἀγαθός which plays a prominent role in the wisdom-literature where it is connected with the σοφός[358],could have contributed to identification of Joseph with the σοφός. Finally,wisdom is traditionally connected with Joseph,especially because of his explanation of dreams;so already in Gen. 41,39,'...Since a god has made all this known to you,there is no one so shrewd and intelligent as you (LXX, φρονιμώτερος καὶ συνετώτερός σου)';cf.vs.33;further Ps.lo5(lo4),22,'to correct (LXX, παιδεῦσαι)[359] his officers at will and teach his counsellors wisdom (LXX,σοφίσαι)'[360];Philo,De Jos.lo6,where the Egyptian king says among other things,'My soul has a prophetic inkling that my dreams will not for ever remain veiled in obscurity,for in this youth there are signs and indications of wisdom (σοφίας) ...';Jos.,Ant.II 87,'Marvelling at the discernment and wisdom (φρόνησιν...σοφίαν) of Joseph,the king asked him...';cf.II 9.

    In summary : in Levi's exhortation to his sons,we find that the traditional relationship of Levi and the Levites to the law of God is reaffirmed,but the nature of it has changed. Here the ideal of the wise man,the σοφός,who knows the law,who has the fear of God and who gets σύνεσις and σοφία,is the central theme.Through his wisdom he makes many friends and the people desire to serve him and to hear the law from his mouth. He stands firm,whatever catastrophy may touch him.Wherever he is,he has σοφία as a friend (and a fatherland) with him.He achieves even a king's throne. On this point Joseph is introduced as an example.But is Joseph to be considered as a σοφός in this text ? He was in distress,he lost everything,he was in a foreign country,and yet he became 'king'.Because of this, because elsewhere in the Testaments Joseph is called ἀνὴρ ἀγαθός (an expression which in the wisdom-literature is parallel to σοφός) and because wisdom is traditionally connected with Joseph,it is possible that in T.Levi 13 Joseph is to be considered as a σοφός .But in the other Testaments we do not find a trace of this idea.[361]

V. Conclusions

I. Joseph's attitude in T.Joseph

1. T.Joseph 1-2 is an introduction to the whole of T.Joseph.

   a. 1,3(4)-2,6 is an individual thanksgiving in which Joseph
      describes his salvation from distress by God. It is
      different from an Old Testament individual thanksgiving,
      and it belongs to a later development of this type of
      psalm. Moreover, this explains why it contains so many
      reminiscences of ideas which belong to the wisdom-
      literature. Its function is didactic-ethical.

   b. 2,6c-7 : 1. God tests the pious man (Joseph) with
                 affliction.
              2. Joseph's attitude is characterized by ὑπομονή
                 (and μακροθυμία) ; his attitude in the follow-
                 ing two stories must be understood in the
                 light of this.

   c. in 1-2 terms and expressions are used which occur either
      in the first story, or in the second story, or in both
      stories.

2. Both stories in T.Joseph (3,1-1o,4 and 1o,5-18,4) are
   intended to illustrate Joseph's ὑπομονή and his self-
   humiliation in oppression (hence the occasional use of
   terms from the martyr-traditions), followed by his salvation and exaltation/reward by God. Both stories belong
   indissolubly together.

   a. T.Joseph 3,1-1o,4 : Joseph's attitude towards the
      Egyptian woman is the attitude of the man in oppression,
      who complains of his distress and asks God for salvation
      -it is characterized especially by praying, weeping,
      fasting and wearing sackcloth. After his salvation he
      praises God and gives thanks to him. This attitude is in
      particular characteristic of the man in distress as
      described in an individual lament. Other characteristics
      of Joseph in this story are his σωφροσύνη and his 'keeping
      silence'.
      In the paraenesis at the end of the first story we find
      besides ὑπομονή (and praying, fasting, σωφροσύνη, etc.) and
      the idea of salvation by God, also the idea of exaltation
      /reward by God, which is the consequence of self-humili-
      ation, and which stands over against self-exaltation, a
      theme with which the second story begins.

   b. T.Joseph 1o,5-18,4 : Joseph's attitude towards his
      brothers : he does not exalt himself; he honours his
      brethren; therefore he holds his peace and does not tell
      his social status.
      In the paraenesis at the end of the second story we find
      again, besides ὑπομένειν and the exhortation to brotherly
      love and forgiveness (also illustrated by Joseph's
      attitude towards his brothers in Egypt), the ideas of
      salvation and exaltation/reward by God.

II. Joseph as an example of ethics in the paraenetic passages
   in the other Testaments

   1. The idea of Joseph's salvation and exaltation/reward by
      God occurs several times in other Testaments -sometimes
      in stereotyped formulae; ὑπομονή ,however,is not mentioned.

   2. Joseph's attitude towards the Egyptian woman (in general
      terms) occurs in T.Reub.4,8-1o (in a paraenesis about
      πορνεία).

   3. Joseph's attitude towards his brothers in Egypt is
      characterized by such terms as οὐ μνησικακεῖν,εὐσπλαγχνία,ἔλεος,
      ἀγάπη ,and forgiveness.He is described in this way in the
      paraenetic passages in T.Zeb. as well as in T.Sim.

   4. In T.Benj.3ff. Joseph serves as a model of the ἀνὴρ ἀγαθός,
      an expression which occurs also elsewhere in the Testa-
      ments with reference to Joseph. Important characteristics
      include : φόβος θεοῦ,ἀγάπη,εὐσπλαγχνία,ἔλεος,'keeping silence'
      in oppression.The ideas of salvation from (protection in)
      oppression and of exaltation/reward by God play an
      important role.T.Benj. contains terms and expressions
      which are found either in T.Joseph,or in other Testaments,
      or both in T.Joseph and other Testaments.

   5. In T.Levi 13 Joseph is possibly considered as a wise man
      (σοφός) .We do not,however,find this idea elsewhere in the
      Testaments,so that it is not an important feature of the
      portrait of Joseph in the Testaments at all.

Harm W. Hollander
Westminster and Cheshunt
Colleges
Cambridge,England
(Theologisch Instituut
Rapenburg 59
Leiden,The Netherlands)

NOTES

1. This article has been composed during a one year's stay in Cambridge,England.I should like to thank the Netherlands Organisation for the Advancement of Pure Research (Z.W.O.),The Hague,The Netherlands,and the Dullerts-stichting,Arnhem,The Netherlands,for providing grants to make this possible. I should also like to thank Dr.F.C. Lindars and Dr.J.C.O'Neill,who were so kind to correct my English. This article forms a part of a doctoral dissertation on the ethics of the Testaments of the Twelve Patriarchs which is in preparation under the supervision of Prof.dr.M.de Jonge,Leiden,The Netherlands.

2. For this reason I shall deal only very briefly with the motifs which appear in the first story about Joseph and the Egyptian woman in T.Joseph;the biographical account of the selling of Joseph in T.Joseph;T.Joseph 18,3f.;T. Sim.2;T.Zeb.1-5;T.Dan 1,4-9;T.Gad 1-3;5f. For the same reason I shall deal neither with T.Napht.5-7 (for these chapters,see esp. Th.Korteweg,'The meaning of Naphtali's visions',in Studies on the Testaments of the Twelve Patriarchs.Text and Interpretation,ed.by M.de Jonge, Leiden 1975,ch.XVI),nor with T.Reub.1,2;6,7;T.Sim.1,1; 8,3f.;T.Levi 12,7;T.Jud.12,11;25,1f.;T.Napht.1,8;T.Benj. 1,4;2;1o,1. Moreover,T.Joseph 19f. will be excluded from discussion.

3. On the whole the text followed is that of the new edition (shortly to be issued) prepared at Leiden under the guidance of M.de Jonge,with the cooperation of H.J.de Jonge, Th.Korteweg and the present writer. This new text follows in broad outline the text of MS b,published in M.de Jonge,Testamenta XII Patriarcharum (Ps.V.T. 1),Leiden 197o.The cases where the new text differs from b (except in cases of orthographical variants) will be noted explicitly. The translation of passages of the Testaments given in this article are taken from R.H.Charles,The Testaments of the Twelve Patriarchs,London 19o8,and,if this is not possible (because Charles follows a different text),the translation is my own.

4. The theme of Jacob's love towards Joseph (cf.Gen.37,3f.) plays an important role in the Testaments : see T.Joseph 1o,5; T.Sim.2,6; T.Dan 1,5; T.Gad 1,5. It determines the brothers' attitude (jealousy) towards Joseph for the greater part.

5. See T.Sim.,passim. Cf. also T.Dan 2,5 and T.Gad 3,3;4,5, passages in which envy is closely connected with hate,a passion which already in Gen. characterizes the brothers' attitude towards Joseph (see 37,4.8). It is also important to note that we find the brothers' φθόνος (an idea not found in Gen.) in Philo,De Jos.5(connected with μῖσος) and in Jos.,Ant.II 1o(connected with μῖσος);13;27. See also IV B2.

6. Already a theme in Gen.37. See also T.Joseph 1,4; T.Sim. 2,7.11;3,3; T.Zeb.1,7;2;4,2.11;T.Dan 1,4.7ff.; T.Gad 2, 1f.4;6,2.

7. Cf.T.Reub.4,1o : 'every visible and hidden death'. 'Visible death' most likely means the overt threatening with death (esp.by the brothers),whereas 'hidden death' refers to the food prepared by the Egyptian woman (see

T.Reub.4,9 and T.Joseph 6).

8. See further T.Benj.3,4,'How many men wished to slay him ...'

9. Cf.also T.Asher 5,4. For T.Joseph 1,3 (esp.concerning its relation to the following verses),see I B.

1o. Diss.Berlin 1955 (typescript). For the discussion of T. Joseph 1-2,see pp.77-82;136-14o.

11. (AGJU VIII),Leiden 197o. For the discussion of this passage,see pp.23o-234.

12. Op.cit.,p.229;243.

13. Op.cit.,pp.232f. See esp. p.233 n.5.

14. I find it a real contempt of textual criticism to omit (in the text) ἐν δεσμοῖς,καὶ ἔλυσέ με (vs.6),which can be found in all MSS (except d),as Aschermann,op.cit.,p.77 n.2 and Becker,op.cit.,p.232(see esp.n.2) do,because in their opinion it is a dittography and disturbs the structure; Charles too thought that it was an interpolat- ion,and put it between brackets in his edition : see R.H. Charles,The Greek Versions of the Testaments of the Twelve Patriarchs,Oxford 19o8,p.183. Obviously,it forms the transition to vs.7 : thematically,it is parallel to the previous sentences; formally,it goes with what follows,for it is the first of four sentences in which there is no name for God,who is the subject of the second verb. For the structure of 1,4-7,see esp. Ascher- mann,op.cit.,pp.78f. and Becker,op.cit.,pp.231f.

15. Although vs.4 has the verb in the third person, it describes the situation from the point of view of the first person (see με...με...με...).

16. I follow the terminology used among others by Gunkel (see H.Gunkel-J.Begrich,Einleitung in die Psalmen.Die Gattung- en der religiösen Lyrik Israels, Göttingen 1933) and prefer the term 'individual thanksgiving'('Danklied') to the one used by Aschermann and Becker ('Lobpsalm'). Cf. also F.Crüsemann,Studien zur Formgeschichte von Hymnus und Danklied in Israel (WMANT 32), Neukirchen 1969,p. 21o n.1,'Der Gunkelsche Terminus ,,Danklied(er) des Einzelnen''(Einleitung S.265ff) soll gegenüber Wester- manns Umbenennung in ,,Berichtender Lobpsalm des Einzel- nen''(Loben Gottes S.76ff) zunächst beibehalten werden.'

17. LXX,... καὶ ὁ κύριος ἀντελάβετό μου. I shall frequently give the LXX-reading beside the translation of the Hebrew text,because I am of the opinion that the Testaments as a whole were written originally in Greek and that the author of the Testaments (T.Joseph) used the LXX (see also M.de Jonge,The Testaments of the Twelve Patriarchs. A Study of their Text,Composition and Origin, Assen 1953, p.118). Naturally,I am aware of the possibility of a Greek translation of an original Hebrew document, and with respect to this particular problem it will be use- ful to quote the LXX-reading.
The translations of Old and New Testament texts are taken from the New English Bible; I shall also follow the verse divisions in the N.E.B. (which -in the case of a number of Psalms- differ from the verse divisions in the Hebrew text); in the cases in which a special LXX-reading is quoted, this will be mentioned ; in this case the trans- lation given is my own. The translation of passages

in apocryphal and pseudepigraphical writings(except those of the Testaments) are taken from R.H.Charles, The Apocrypha and Pseudepigrapha of the Old Testament in English I,II,Oxford 1913. The text and translation of passages in the Apostolic Fathers are taken from The Apostolic Fathers I,II, ed.by Kirsopp Lake (Loeb ed.).

18. LXX,...καὶ ἐγένετο κύριος ἀντιστήριγμά μου.

19. LXX, ἐταπεινώθην,καὶ ἔσωσέν με. See further Ps.34,4(33,5);1o7 (1o6),13;12o(119),1;Ezra 8,23;Jonah 2,2(3).

2o. LXX,...καὶ ἀνήγαγέν με ἐκ λάκκου ταλαιπωρίας. See T.Joseph 1,4.

21. In individual thanksgivings God can also be addressed directly;then,of course,the second person is used. See esp.Crüsemann,op.cit.,pp.21o-284(passim).

22. See further Gunkel-Begrich,op.cit.,p.268, where it is said with regard to the description of the speaker's lot we find in an individual thanksgiving : 'Sie richtet sich gewöhnlich an die Gäste der Feier...Daher erklärt es sich, dass von Jahve in diesen Zusammenhängen in dritter Person gesprochen wird.'

23. See the concordance(Hatch-Redpath) on the Old Testament (particularly on the Psalms),s.v.these words. σωτήρ (1,6) is also a term which often occurs in this context.

24. See above, and esp.n.2o.

25. In the story about Joseph in Gen. neither ἀνάγειν nor χαλᾶν is used (in the LXX).

26. See also Ps.71(7o),2o, '...and lift me (LXX, ἀνήγαγές με) again from earth's watery depths'; Ps.3o,3(29,4),...ἀνήγαγες...τὴν ψυχήν μου,ἔσωσάς με ἀπὸ τῶν καταβαινόντων εἰς λάκκον.

27. These terms,however, are found neither always nor exclusively in an individual thanksgiving. Some of them also occur in other kinds of psalms, esp.in an individual lament. See below.

28. λιμός occurs in the same context in T.Joseph 1,5. For the combination λιμός-διατρέφειν see also Judith 5,1o.

29. The idea that God comforts people in their distress (θλίψεις) is also found in II Cor.1,4;T.Sol. D 4,11. Other important texts, in which the term θλῖψις,however, does not occur, are Is.4o,11;49,13;51,3.12;57,18;66,13;Bar.4, 3o;II Cor.7,6;cf.Matt.5,4. See also T.Joseph 2,6.

3o. 'You may meet disaster six times, and he will save you; seven times, and no harm shall touch you. In time of famine he will save you from death, in battle from the sword (LXX, ἐν λιμῷ ῥύσεταί σε ἐκ θανάτου,ἐν πολέμῳ δὲ ἐκ χειρὸς σιδήρου λύσει σε)'. Cf.Acts 2,24;Ign.,Philad.8,1. In Ps.1o5 (1o4),2o the verb λύειν is also used in connection with Joseph; but here the subject is not God ,but the Egyptian king, 'Then the king sent and set him free (LXX, ἔλυσεν αὐτόν)...'

31. For ἐλευθεροῦν with God as subject (vs.5) see also II Macc. 1,27. For ὑψοῦν in this context (vs.7) see also II Sam.22, 49;I Chron.17,17 LXX. See further,among others, Ps.9,13 (14);18,48(17,49);27(26),5;Is.63,9, and see II C. The expression ἡ κραταιὰ αὐτοῦ χείρ (1,5) is used esp. in connection with the salvation of the people of Israel from Egypt by God : see,e.g.,Ex.13,3.9.14.16;Deut.5,15;6,21;7, 8.19;9,26;26,8;Jer.39,21;Bar.2,11;Dan.9,15 Th;Ps.136(135), 12;Neh.1,1o. See further I Clem.6o,3 where this formula also occurs in connection with God's saving activity.

32. Gunkel-Begrich,op.cit.,pp.269f.
33. See esp. αὐτοὶ ἤθελόν με ἀνελεῖν. See also above.
34. See also,among others,Ps.33(32),19;87,7 LXX;1o7(1o6),1o.
    14.18;Job 5,2o;Sir.51,6.9. The attitude of the adversar-
    ies towards the oppressed man can also be characterized
    by μῖσος ; so,e.g.,Ps.35(34),19;1o9(1o8),3.5 (see T.Joseph
    1,4).
35. Namely ἐμίσησαν and λάκκον. For ἀνελεῖν and ἐχάλασαν see
    above.
36. For ἐπράθην εἰς δοῦλον see Ps.1o5(1o4),17;cf.Wisd.1o,13;
    Philo,De Jos.27o. For πιπράσκειν see also T.Joseph 1o,6;
    for δοῦλος see also T.Joseph 11,2f.;13,6ff.;15,2f. For
    αἰχμαλωσία see also T.Joseph 14,3 (αἰχμάλωτον). It is remark-
    able that these terms in 1,5 only occur in the second
    story about the selling of Joseph in T.Joseph. See also
    below.
37. Exceptions may be ἐν φυλακῇ and ἐν δεσμοῖς in vs.6; but the
    terms themselves do not occur in the Genesis-story about
    Joseph (LXX).
38. See above and n.28.
39. See also vs.17(t). Cf.Lament.3,28.
4o. See also Matt.25,36.39.43f. In this text ἐπισκέπτεσθαι and
    φυλακή also occur,while the style characteristic of T.
    Joseph 1,4-7 is also used here. But in Matt. it is not
    God who saves;therefore,only the contents (the terminolo-
    gy) of both texts agree;see Aschermann,op.cit.,pp.137ff.
41. Cf.Is.49,9. For the combination δεσμός - φυλακή see Is.42,
    6f.,'I,the Lord,have called you(=the Lord's servant) with
    righteous purpose...I have formed you,and appointed you..
    ..to open eyes that are blind,to bring captives out of
    prison (LXX, ἐκ δεσμῶν),out of the dungeons (LXX, ἐξ οἴκου
    φυλακῆς) where they lie in darkness.' In Wisd.1o,14 δεσμός
    is used in connection with Joseph : 'And in bonds (ἐν
    δεσμοῖς) she(=wisdom) left him not...' See further,of
    course,T.Joseph 2,4;9,1(δεσμός) and 8,4(φυλακή).
42. βασιλεῖ διαβολὴ γλώσσης ἀδίκου... In the Psalms ἐνδιαβάλλειν
    occurs as an activity of the adversaries towards the
    pious man in his oppression : 38,2o(37,21);71(7o),13;1o9
    (1o8),4.2o.29.
43. See Gunkel-Begrich,op.cit.,pp.282f.,'Beide Gattungen sind
    einander in manchem ähnlich...:beide enthalten eine
    Schilderung der Not,die in den Klagepsalmen gegenwärtig
    ist,in den Dankliedern aber der Vergangenheit angehört :
    beide reden von der Errettung,die in jenen als Gewissheit
    der Erhörung vorweggenommen wird,in diesen aber bereits
    geschehen ist...Ähnliche Bilder und Ausdrücke finden sich
    in beiden;dieselben Verhältnisse werden überall vorausge-
    setzt...Hinzu kommt,dass beide Gattungen auch beieinander
    Anleihen zu machen pflegen.'
44. Against Becker,who attacks Aschermann because he 'aller-
    dings T Jos 1,3 nicht stark genug abhebt,sondern mit in
    das Gedicht einbezieht.' (op.cit.,p.231 n.3). See also I
    G.
45. λάκκος : 9,2; φυλακή : 8,4; δεσμός : 9,1; ῥύεσθαι : 4,3.8;1o,3;
    φθόνος : 1o,3.
46. οἱ ἀδελφοί : 1o,5f.;11,1f.;15,3;17,1(.3).4; πιπράσκειν : 1o,6;
    δοῦλος : 11,2f.;13,6ff.;15,2f.(17,7); αἰχμαλωσία : cf.14,3
    (αἰχμάλωτος).
47. ὑφοῦν : 1o,3(.5;17,8);18,1; θάνατος : 3,1(.9);6,5;11,3(17,5).

48. The grammatical subject,however,is Photimar,and not God himself. See T.Joseph 11,6,'And the Lord gave me favour in the eyes of the merchant, and he entrusted unto me his house.'

49. See II C.

5o. See I A. Moreover,I think it not permissible to separate poetry from prose in this kind of literature in such a way as Aschermann and Becker do. If one wanted to use these categories,one would have to admit that 2,3a,in which three verbs Aor.Pass. occur,is also poetic (see Deut.32,15;cf.Hebr.11,37,a verse which is very well constructed),so that a sharp distinction(1,4-7:poetry;2,1-3: prose) is in any case wrong. See also I G.

51. This expression is not found in connection with Joseph in Josephus or Philo either. For the construction(which, although not unusual,is not so frequent),see for instance I Macc.8,16;IV Macc.4,7;Xen.,Memor.4,4,17.

52. ἐπείγουσαν - b is not correct.

53. Cf.T.Joseph 3,8.

54. Vs.1o; LXX, εἶδος ἔχουσα πορνικόν. See also the following words : ἢ ποιεῖ νέων ἐξίπτασθαι καρδίας.

55. See T.Joseph 8,2;this word does not occur in the Genesis-story about Joseph.

56. Other texts,in which ἀναιδής occurs in such a context, are Sir.23,6;26,11. See further K.Berger,'Materialien zu Form und Überlieferungsgeschichte neutestamentlicher Gleichnisse,N.T. XV(1973),p.35 n.4, where the author rightly says that ἀναιδής is probably originally erotic.

57. In vs.2 it is not said that the woman wants to act lawlessly,but that she wants to bring Joseph to commit a lawless action.

58. Quoted according to the edition and translation of Colson-Whitaker (Loeb ed.),as for all the other Philo quotations in this article.

59. See also Philo,Somn.II 124.

6o. See also Philo,De Jos.68 ,'...I will fear none of the tyrant's menaces, even though he threaten me with death (κἂν θάνατον ἀπειλῇ)...'

61. See,e.g.,IV Macc.11,2o;15,29;16,16;17,11.13f. Cf.Philo, Flacc.48;Spec.Leg.I 57;79;Vita Mosis I 3o7;Mart.Polyc.19, 2;The Acts of Euplus(Gr.rec.)2,2(ed.Musurillo);The Martyrs of Lyons 1,4o(ed.Musurillo).

62. Cf.Wisd.4,1f.;Sir.4,28.

63. See also Becker,op.cit.,p.233.

64. See,e.g.,Mut.Nom.81;Migr.Abr.2oo;Leg.All.II 1o8;Abr.48.

65. That in this text Joseph is described negatively, as almost everywhere in Philo,except in De Jos.,is not directly important for what is argued here.

66. Therefore,its use is not primarily influenced by the martyr-traditions,although it is not always possible-as in the case of IV Macc.-to make a sharp distinction between both kinds of context.

67. Cf.I Macc.2,59;III Macc.6,6.

68. See also IV Macc.18,14f. For Sir.51,1ff. as an individual thanksgiving see also I G.

69. For φυλακίζειν see also I Clem.45,4.

7o. In 14,2 both words are found together.

71. M.de Jonge,The Testaments...,p.1o2 as well as Becker,op.

<u>cit.</u>,p.233 have not noticed this;they both wrongly try to connect vs.3a with the first story about the Egyptian woman.

72. In T.Joseph this word occurs only here.
73. Cf.39,4;T.Joseph 11,6.
74. I am of the opinion that the author used the LXX,and not the MT. See n.17.
75. For the same expression see also Neh.1,11. Moreover,from a comparison of the translations of Dan.1,9 by LXX and Th it is evident that the alteration in T.Joseph 2,3b from Gen.39,21 could be made very easily;it is,however,not permissible to conclude from this that in T.Joseph 2,3b one has to do only with a translation-variant of the MT.
76. <u>Op.cit.</u>,pp.233ff.
77. <u>Op.cit.</u>,p.272.
78. For the division of these verses see Becker,<u>op.cit.</u>,pp. 233f.
79. See also among others II Macc.6,16;Bel et Dr.38;I Clem. 11,1;Pastor Hermae,Sim.2,9.
80. See I B.
81. See the concordance,s.v. θλῖψις.
82. See also T.Joseph 8,5;9,1f.
83. See also θλῖψις in vs.4.
84. For this use of σκότος see also Is.42,7;49,9.
85. Cf.II Cor.6,4(;12,10). Here,however,the idea of God's salvation of the pious man from his distress is not present;its background is rather to be found in popular moral philosophy.
86. See I B.
87. See I B.
88. See further Wisd.10,11,in which wisdom plays this role, and II Tim.4,17. Both these texts also deal with the idea of salvation of the oppressed,which is expressed among others by the term ῥύεσθαι.
89. See Wisd.19,22,in which ὑπερορᾶν stands over against παρίστασθαι (see above).
90. Ps.10,1(9,22).
91. Vs.11(12). See further Ps.35(34),22;38,21(37,22);I Sam. 28,15f.
92. Of course,the idea of a chastisement and punishment by God because of sins is absent here.
93. <u>b</u> is not correct.
94. It does not matter very much that the term ὀλίγα does not directly imply a time limit. See also The Martyrdom of the Saintly Dasius 4,4(ed.Musurillo), 'Better for me to endure a few tortures and penalties (ὀλίγας ὑπομεῖναι βασάνους καὶ τιμωρίας) for the name of our Lord Jesus Christ, and then after death I shall inherit eternal life to-gether with all the saints';The martyrdom of Saints Agape,Irene,and Chione at Saloniki 2,4(ed.Musurillo), ... διὰ πυρὸς προσκαίρου...τόν...τῆς δόξης στέφανον... For this idea of a short period of sufferings,see also K.Berger,<u>Die Amen-Worte Jesu.Eine Untersuchung zum Problem der Legi-timation in apokalyptischer Rede</u> (<u>BZNW</u> 39),Berlin 1970, pp.164f.Nr.4.
95. See Becker,<u>op.cit.</u>,p.234 n.6,'Nach Jub 19,8 bestand Abraham...10 Versuchungen (vgl.17,17;18,1ff.;19,2f.) ebenso Aboth 5,4 (Aboth 5,1ff. finden sich weitere Bei-

spiele für die Beliebtheit der Zahl zehn als abgerundete
Zahl der Fülle).Nach Jub 39,8 dauerten Josephs Versuchungen ein Jahr,sieben Jahre nach TJos 3,4.Hiobs Versuchungen erstrecken sich nach THiob 16ff. über Jahrzehnte.'

96. ἀνέδειξε. For such a construction see also Dan.1,2oLXX.

97. See,e.g.,Gen.22,1;Ex.16,4;2o,2o;Deut.8,2;13,3;Ju.2,22;3,
1.4;II Chron.32,31.

98. For such a use of the term φάρμακον see also Sir.6,16;
Philo,Agric.98;Ign.,Eph.2o,2.

99. See T.Joseph 18,1,'If ye also,therefore,walk in the
commandments of the Lord,my children,He will exalt you
there,and will bless you with good things(ἐν ἀγαθοῖς) for
ever and ever',and see also the next verse. See further
n.loo.

loo. Connected with the idea of a trial: e.g.,Ps.Sol.16,14f.;
Rom.5,3f.;James 1,2ff.12ff.;Did.16,5;cf.Hebr.12,1ff.
Without explicit mention of a trial: see,e.g.,Rom.12,12;
II Cor.1,6;II Thess.1,4;II Tim.2,9f.;Hebr.lo,32f.36;Rev.
1,9;II Clem.11,4f.(here also τὰ ἀγαθά -see above,and n.
99);17,7;Pastor Hermae,Visio 2,2,7.

lol. See further I Cor.13,4ff.;Col.1,11;James 5,7ff.;I Clem.
62,2;64,1;Barn.2,2;Ign.,Polyc.6,2;Ign.,Eph.3,1.

lo2. See moreover James 5,11,...τὴν ὑπομονὴν Ἰὼβ ἠκούσατε...

lo3. Ed.Brock.See also ed.Kraft.

lo4. It also plays a part in the direct paraenesis of Joseph
to his sons: see vs.2.

lo5. One should also notice the use of ὁρᾶτε in these three
texts(lo,1;17,1;18,3).

lo6. Besides ὑπομονή (see n.lo4), μακροθυμία also plays a role
in the direct paraenesis of Joseph to his sons: see 17,2.

lo7. Many other'fathers' are mentioned here. For such series
of pious men see further Sir.44ff.;IV Macc.18,11ff.;
Judith 8,26ff.;Hebr.11;I Clem.45,4ff.(here also in connection with ὑπομονή).

lo8. It does occur,however,in I Clem.45,4ff.(see n.lo7);but
in this text Joseph is not mentioned.

lo9. Text and translation according to the edition of Marcus-
Thackeray (Loeb ed.),as also the other Josephus quotations in this article.

llo. ἀπειλαῖς. See T.Joseph 3,1.

111. And so it is not only connected with the first story
(see also I A).

112. See n.16.

113. See pp.282-284. The underlining is mine.

114. Namely in I QH and Sir.51LXX.

115. SNVAO II.Hist.Filos.Klasse 1937,Nr.3,Oslo 1937.

116. Op.cit.,p.55.

117. See also p.5o,'In den Dankpsalmen(sc.of the late Jewish
period) spielte die Belehrung die vorherrschende Rolle,
oder ein Weisheitmotiv füllte die ganze Dichtung aus'.

118. Op.cit.,pp.131f.

119. This is,of course,also due to the genre of a 'testament'.

12o. Cf.Jansen,op.cit.,p.132,'Seid bussfertig und demütig,
willig zu leiden,seid geduldig und glaubt an Gottes Güte
und Fürsorge trotz aller Widerwärtigkeiten:das ist das
Leitmotiv all dieser erbaulichen Gebete(i.e.the ',,lite-
rarische" spätjüdische Psalmen und Prosagebete')...'

121. Gunkel-Begrich,op.cit.,p.179;cf.p.231.

122. Neh.1,4.Cf.Dan.9,3,'Then I(=Daniel) turned to the Lord

God in earnest prayer and supplication with fasting and sackcloth (LXX, προσευχήν...ἐν νηστείαις καὶ σάκκῳ) and ashes.'

123. Cf.T.Joseph 1,6.
124. Vs.6(7).
125. Vs.8(9).
126. See further II Sam.12,16ff.;I Ki.21(2o),27;I Clem.55,6.
127. Naturally,we find such a description not only in laments, for it is the attitude of the pious Jew in general who is in distress and wants to be saved from his troubles by God.
128. For these terms and the idea of salvation by God,see I.
129. 3,7b is not important here.
13o. (ἐὰν δὲ ἀπεδήμει,) οἶνον οὐκ ἔπινον -b is not correct.
131. On this verse see also above.See further 9,2.
132. On this verse see also above.
133. Cf.Ps.34,13 LXX(see above).See further Jos.et As.7,3.
134. On this verse see also above.
135. Therefore it is sometimes very difficult to decide which kind of weeping is meant.
136. See above.Cf.Ps.114,8 LXX.
137. See above.
138. Cf.T.Levi 2,3f.
139. See Introduction and n.2.For the motifs used in this story see M.Braun,History and Romance in Graeco-Oriental Literature,Oxford 1938,pp.44-95;De Jonge,The Testaments.. ..,pp.1o2ff.;Becker,op.cit.,pp.234ff.
14o. See also T.Benj.3,4,'How many (πόσοι) men wished to slay him(=Joseph),and God shielded him !...' Cf.T.Joseph 9,1, πολλάκις...
141. Text and translation according to the edition of W.A. Oldfather (Loeb ed.).
142. See Gunkel-Begrich,op.cit.,pp.216f.,'Gern verstärkt man die Wirksamkeit der Klage...verrät die leidenschaftliche Aufwallung des Betenden.Sie wird am deutlichsten fassbar in der bezeichnenden Umbildung der Schilderung zur Form der Frage.Statt der einfachen Schilderung ,,viel sind meiner Feinde" heisst es hier ,,wie viele sind meiner Gegner...' See also n.14o.
143. See also T.Joseph 11,3.
144. See I C.
145. For ἀπειλή,see further The Martyrdom of the Saintly Dasius 9,2(ed.Musurillo);Ep.Phileae(A)3(ed.Musurillo);for τιμωρία, see further The Martyrdom of the Saintly Dasius 4,4;11,1.
146. Esp. in connection with the use of παρανομεῖν. See I C.
147. See I E.
148. See for this De Jonge,The Testaments...,pp.157f. n.3o9. b is not correct. 'πατέρων' should be omitted.
149. εἰσερχόμενος εἰς τὸ ταμιεῖον. Undoubtedly from Gen.43,3o.
15o. See above and n.13o.
151. See W.Bousset-H.Gressmann,Die Religion des Judentums im späthellenistischen Zeitalter (HbNT 21),Tübingen 1966, pp.179ff.
152. Cf.8,1.
153. Cf.14,4,'For she wished to see me out of desire of sin, but I was ignorant(καὶ ἡγνόουν) concerning all these things.' This is again a clear proof that both stories belong together,and that it is impossible to consider the one as secondary with respect to the other.
154. ἐφελκύσατο. Cf.8,2,'...forcibly dragging(ἐφελκομένη)me to

have connection with her.' See for this use of ἐφέλκεσθαι
also Ep.Jer.43.
155. It is clear that T.Joseph 3ff. -in any case 3f.- is not
intended to give a description of a series of events
which follow one after the other (in time);see also below.
156. ἐ λυπήθην ἕως θανάτου. Cf.Sir.37,2;Jonah 4,9.
157. γυμνὸς ἔφυγον. Cf.Mark 14,52. This combination does not
occur in the Gen.-story.
158. ἐσυκοφάντησε. Cf.1o,3. See also Philo,De Jos.27o,'Of these
years he(=Joseph) spent seventeen up to adolescence in
his father's house,thirteen in painful misfortunes,the
victim of conspiracy,sold into slavery,falsely accused
(πιπρασκόμενος,δουλεύων,συκοφαντούμενος),chained in a prison..'
This motif is also found in connection with the adversaries of the oppressed man in the psalms;see,e.g.,Ps.119
(118),122.134,'...let not the proud oppress me (LXX, μὴ
συκοφαντησάτωσάν με ὑπερήφανοι)..Set me free from man's
oppression (LXX, λύτρωσαί με ἀπὸ συκοφαντίας ἀνθρώπων)...'
159. Cf.9,1,... λυτρώσω...καὶ ἀπαλλάξω. For the use of ἀπαλλάσσειν
in such a context see IV Macc.9,16,'...Consent to eat,
that so you may be released(ἀπαλλαγῆς) from your tortures..
..';cf.T.Job 25,1o.
16o. Others too,as for instance αἰνεῖν. For χαίρειν -also used
in T.Joseph 8,5- see among others Is.66,14;Hab.3,18;Zech.
1o,7;cf.I Peter 4,13.
161. See also Gunkel-Begrich,op.cit.,pp.248f.
162. For this combination see also Is.25,1;42,1o;T.Sol.1,8;
Dan.3,56 LXX;Johannis Liber de Dormitione Mariae 25 (Ti.
p.1o2);cf.Ps.22,22f.(21,23f.).
163. See also the use of ὅτι ;see namely T.Joseph 8,5 where it
is used too.
164. T.Joseph 8,5,...ἐπηκροᾶτό μου,πῶς ὕμνουν κύριον...Although it
is true that the verb ἐπακροᾶσθαι does not occur in the LXX
and the N.T. except in Acts 16,25 where Paul and Silas
' προσευχόμενοι ὕμνουν τὸν θεόν' in prison,the situation
described here is quite different: in the first place
they praise God not after their salvation;in the second
place we do not find here the combination ὑμνεῖν-δοξάζειν,
but ὑμνεῖν-προσεύχεσθαι ; in the third place it is not their
adversary who hears them singing,but their fellow-prison-
ers (against De Jonge,The Testaments...,p.1o6;158 n.32o).
165. On this verse see II C.
166. See also n.155.
167. See the introducing word ποσάκις ,which in my opinion
clearly tends in this direction (see above).
168. Cf. ἀσθενοῦσα...τοὺς στεναγμοὺς αυτῆς. See also 7,1f.;8,5.
169. Cf.3,6;8,1.
17o. Praying was one of Joseph's actions in his 'struggle'
against the woman.Nowhere do we read that he prayed in
prison.On the contrary,there he praised and glorified God
(see above);against De Jonge,The Testaments...,p.1o6.
171. συνιών. Cf.3,9 (νοήσας...ἔγνων).
172. See 7,1f.
173. This must not be connected with the beginning of vs.4 in
such a way as to mean that,when Joseph heard the woman
(in prison),he stopped praying (against De Jonge,The
Testaments...,p.1o6).
174. Cf.also 5,2f.

175. Cf.1,4;2,2.See also I B and C. For the first part of this verse see IV A and n.249.
176. For these verses see II C.
177. Both of these terms come from the Greek world,and are originally neither Jewish nor Old Testament.
178. For such a use of κατεργάζεται see James 1,3;Pastor Hermae, Visio 2,3,1.
179. See also I E.
18o. With regard to the Testaments,see T.Reub.6,1o;T.Jud.19, 2;T.Gad 5,3. See further among others II Chron.33,12.23; Ps.34,13f.LXX;Sir.2,17;7,17;Is.58,3;Ps.Sol.3,8;Matt.18, 4;I Clem.53,2;55,6;Barn.3,1. For this idea of 'humility' see below.
181. κύριος κατοικήσει ἐν ὑμῖν (1o,2;cf.vs.3). For this expression see T.Zeb.8,2;T.Dan 5,1;T.Benj.6,4;cf.Barn.16,8ff.;Ign., Philad.8,1;Pastor Hermae,Mand.3,1;1o,1,6.
182. Cf.9,2. See also Ps.83,12 LXX.
183. ... κἄν τις περιπέσῃ... For such a use of περιπίπτειν see T. Dan 4,5(in my opinion the correct text here is as follows: ἐὰν ζημίᾳ,ἐὰν ἀπωλείᾳ τινὶ περιπέσητε...);Dan.2,9 LXX; II Macc.6,13;9,21;1o,4;James 1,2;I Clem.51,2;cf.Acta Joannis 111(2o)v.1.
184. Cf.1,3.7;see I A and B.
185. Cf.1,5;see I B and n.36.
186. Cf.8,4;see II A and esp.n.158.
187. ἡ σκοτίᾳ (b omits it because of hmt.).Cf.2,4;see I D.
188. This is motivated by vs.4,'For in every way the man is held fast (συνέχεται),whether in deed,or in word,or in thought.' That is to say,the man in whom God dwells,is held fast by it completely,and does not give up his σωφροσύνη,so that he is saved and exalted by God.He does not sin,when God dwells in him,but keeps his σωφροσύνη. Cf.Job 31,23 LXX,φόβος γὰρ κυρίου συνέσχεν με,καὶ ἀπὸ τοῦ λήμματος αὐτοῦ οὐχ ὑποίσω, and see T.Joseph 1o,5, ...εἶχον τὸν φόβον τοῦ θεοῦ ἐν τῇ διανοίᾳ μου.
189. Cf.1,7;see I B.
19o. See I B and esp.n.31.
191. Cf.2,7,καὶ πολλὰ ἀγαθὰ δίδωσιν ἡ ὑπομονή. See I E.
192. Cf.also Gen.49,25f.;Deut.33,13ff.
193. Hence it is often found in the Psalms.
194. See esp.T.Sim.4,5.
195. See esp.T.Joseph 18,1;see also n.191.
196. For this combination(T.Joseph 1o,3),see also Ps.36,2o LXX;Is.4,2;cf.Ps.149,4f.
197. Cf.A.Weiser,Die Knechtsgleichnisse der synoptischen Evangelien (STANT 29),München 1971,p.185,'In den Psalmen und auch im Midrasch lebt die Erzählung von der Erhöhung des Sklaven Josef,zum Teil wiedergegeben mit den gleichen Formulierungen,fort...'
198. It does not make much difference that in this text Joseph is saved and exalted by σοφία.
199. οὐκ ἐγκατέλιπεν.Cf.T.Joseph 2,4.
2oo. ἐν δεσμοῖς. Cf.T.Joseph 1,6;2,4.
2o1. Cf.Deut.33,13ff.
2o2. Against among others Becker,op.cit.,pp.229ff.;K.H. Rengstorf,'Herkunft und Sinn der Patriarchen-Reden in den Testamenten der zwölf Patriarchen',in La Littérature Juive entre Tenach et Mischna.Quelques problèmes, sous

la rédaction de W.C.van Unnik,Leiden 1974,pp.4of. Moreover,in T.Sim.2,13;3,4 too praying,weeping and fasting
are the characteristics of the man in distress(c.q.
Simeon) who asks God for salvation(c.q.for healing);see
also T.Reub.1,8-1o.

2o3. For σιωπᾶν see the next section.

2o4. Hence it is not correct to emphasize this particular
characteristic of Joseph,and to subordinate to it his
fasting and praying,etc.(see also n.2o2).

2o5. See also T.Reub.6,5.1o;cf.Ps.131(13o),1f.;Dan.5,22f.

2o6. See also I A.

2o7. Cf.I Ki.18,12;Ps.71(7o),5;Eccl.12,1;Did.4,9;Barn.19,5.On
the whole the time of youth is seen as a time in which
one easily falls into -particularly sexual- sins;see,e.g.,
T.Reub.1,6;2,9;T.Jud.11,1(over against 1,4);and further
among others Prov.7,1o LXX;22,15;Plut.,Mor.45oF;496F-497
A. See also IV A and n.247. It is,however,striking that
in T.Joseph 1o,5 νήπιος is used.

2o8. The investigation concerning man's self-exaltation is
partly based on material collected by Dr.K.Berger and the
present author on the idea of καυχᾶσθαι in Paul. It is
hoped that the conclusions of this study may be published
in the future.

2o9. Cf.Philo,Virt.161ff.

21o. Cf.T.Joseph 17,8. ἀλαζονεία is one of the words which occur
regularly in the context of 'self-exaltation'.

211. Cf.T.Joseph 17,8.

212. For such a use of παρέρχεσθαι see besides the texts
mentioned(T.Joseph 1o,5 and Wisd.5,9) further : Wisd.2,
4;T.Job 33,8;34,4;43,7;James 1,1o;Acta Thomae 88 (;cf.
Matt.24,35;Mark 13,31;Luke 21,33;II Peter 3,1o;Did.1o,6).

213. See also the Apocryphal Story of Joseph in Coptic,trsl.
by J.Zandee (in Vig.Chr.15(1961),pp.193-213),p.18,36f.,
'...Joseph went to his brothers and he humiliated himself for them all'.

214. T.Joseph 17,8. Cf.I Cor.15,9;Eph.3,8.

215. ἐμέτρουν ἐμαυτόν . This expression belongs also to the context of self-exaltation and boasting. See,e.g.,Ign.,
Trall.4,1,'I have many thoughts in God,ἀλλ'ἐμαυτὸν μετρῶ,
ἵνα μὴ ἐν καυχήσει ἀπόλωμαι...'

216. ...διὰ τὸν φόβον αὐτῶν (1o,6). For the combination τιμᾶν -
φοβεῖσθαι,see further Levit.19,32;Prov.3,7.9;7,1a LXX;I
Peter 2,17.

217. Cf.1o,5.

218. Cf.9,2;1o,2.

219. See Introduction and n.2. It is,however,very important
that (as has been argued above) in this story many terms
and expressions are used which have already occurred in
the first two chapters of T.Joseph : so ἐπίστευσέ μοι τὸν
οἶκον αὐτοῦ (11,6;cf.2,1); φυλακισθῆναι (14,2;cf.2,3);τύπτειν
(13,(4.)9;14,1f.;cf.2,3);δοῦλος (11,2f.;13,6ff.;15,2f.(;17,7);
cf.1,5;see,however, δουλεία in 1o,3).On the other hand
there are some terms which occur in both stories : so
ἀπειλεῖν 'until death' (11,3;cf.3,1); τιμωρεῖν (14,1;cf.3,1,
τιμωρία); ἡγνόουν (14,4;cf.3,8); for σιωπᾶν see below.

22o. Cf.3,1. See I C; II A.

221. Cf.3,1. See II A.

222. Cf.2,3. See I C.

223. See 11,5.

224. ἀνδρὸς μεγάλου. Cf.1o,6;15,5.
225. Cf.Gen.42,24 and esp.43,3of.
226. ἐτασθῇ is undoubtedly original. Cf.Esther 2,23 LXX,ὁ δὲ
     βασιλεὺς ἥτασεν τοὺς δύο εὐνούχους καὶ ἐκρέμασεν αὐτούς...
227. And one time(16,5f.) for the sake of an eunuch.
228. Cf.1o,2, ἐν ὑπομονῇ καὶ ταπεινώσει καρδίας. See above,and also
     II C and D.
229. 9,4. See II A.
23o. See also the following.
231. Cf.Gen.45,1.
232. αἰσχύνη (αἰσχύνειν,καταισχύνειν) and ὄνειδος (ὀνειδισμός,ὀνειδίζειν)
     are often parallel: see,e.g.,T.Levi 15,2;Is.3o,5;54,4;
     Jer.15,9.
233. Also Joseph himself does not reproach (ὀνειδίζειν) his
     brothers (during his kingship) : T.Joseph 17,4;T.Sim.4,
     6. See below.
234. The same idea also occurs in Ps.38,13ff.(37,14ff.);cf.
     Is.53,7.
235. Cf.n.234. See also K.Berger, 'Die königlichen Messias-
     traditionen des Neuen Testaments',NTSt 2o(1973/74),p.16
     n.58,'...und die Weisheitsschrift aus der Kairoer Geniza
     fol.2b,2ff.:'Der Weg der Gerechten und Demütigen ist,
     sich schweigend beiseite zu halten,zu ertragen ohne Auf-
     hören die Angriffe der Toren und sich nicht den Heuch-
     lern anzuschliessen.' ' For Jesus'silence,as it is
     described in the passion-narratives(and in I Peter 2,22
     f.) see among others G.Schneider,Verleugnung,Verspottung
     und Verhör Jesu nach Lukas 22,54-71.Studien zur luka-
     nischen Darstellung der Passion (STANT 22),München 1969,
     esp.p.33 n.56;p.68(no.23). Silence as an expression of
     enduring injustice is a known motif in the martyr-trad-
     itions : see,e.g.,The Martyrs of Lyons 1,2o(ed.Musurillo)
     'Sanctus,too,withstood(ὑπομένων) all the indignities that
     men heaped on him with extraordinary,superhuman strength.
     These wicked men hoped that the severity and persistence
     of the tortures would make him say something that he
     should not;but he resisted them with such determination
     ὥστε μηδὲ τὸ ἴδιον κατειπεῖν ὄνομα μήτε ἔθνους μήτε πόλεως ὅθεν ἦν
     μήτε εἰ δοῦλος ἢ ἐλεύθερος εἴη...' (see also the following
     verses);The Martyrdom of Saint Irenaeus Bishop of Sir-
     mium 3,3(ed.Musurillo);see also The Martyrdom of Pionius
     the Presbyter and his Companions 18,1o(ed.Musurillo);
     The Martyrdom of Saint Conon 2,7;6,2(ed.Musurillo).
     Finally,reference may be made to Plut.,Mor.487C,'Thus it
     was with Cato:he so won over his elder brother Caepio by
     obedience and gentleness and silence(σιωπῇ)from his
     earliest childhood that finally,by the time they both
     were men,he had so subdued him and filled him with so
     great a respect for himself...'(text and translation
     from Plutarch's Moralia,ed./trsl. by W.C.Helmbold,Loeb
     ed.vol.VI).
236. b is not correct;read: ...μετ'οὐ πολύ...
237. It is not clear whether the righteous man prays for
     salvation from his distress or prays for the evil-doer;
     the latter is quite possible.
238. εὔχεσθε ὑπὲρ αὐτοῦ. Cf.T.Gad 7,1;Matt.5,44 and others.This
     motif is also found in the martyr-traditions:see,e.g.,
     The Martyrs of Lyons 2,5(ed.Musurillo). See also n.237.

239. Cf. καρτερία in Philo.See above.

240. The same connection is also found in Philo;but there
Joseph's silence is referred to esp.after his enthrone-
ment.See above.

241. ἐν μακροθυμίᾳ (read the singular,against b).For this term
see I E.

242. Cf.Sir.25,1,'Three things hath my soul desired,and they
are lovely in the sight of God and men:the concord of
brethren(ὁμόνοια ἀδελφῶν),and the friendship of neighbours,
and a husband and wife suited to each other.' For such a
use of τέρπεται see Wisd.1,13,'Because God made not
death;neither delighteth he when the living perish(οὐδὲ
τέρπεται ἐπ᾽ἀπωλείᾳ ζώντων).'

243. Whereas ἠγάπησα refers to ἀγαπᾶτε (vs.2) and ἀγάπην (vs.3),
οὐκ ὠνείδισα takes up συγκρύπτετε ἀλλήλων τὰ ἐλαττώματα (vs.2).
This stands out more clearly,when one compares Prov.17,9
(LXX, ὃς κρύπτει ἀδικήματα,ζητεῖ φιλίαν· ὃς δὲ μισεῖ κρύπτειν,
διίστησιν φίλους καὶ οἰκείους) with Sir.22,2ο(...καὶ ὁ ὀνειδίζων
φίλον διαλύσει φιλίαν). For παρεκάλεσα see Gen.5ο,21,where
Joseph 'comforts' his brothers,when they are afraid of
his vengeance after Jacob's death,'...Thus he comforted
them(παρεκάλεσεν αὐτοὺς) and set their minds at rest.'

244. Cf.T.Sim.4,6;see Gen.47,11f.;5ο,21.

245. For 17,8;18,1-3 see above and I E;II C. 18,4(cf.T.Sim.5,
1;T.Napht.1,7f.;Gen.39,6) and ch.19-2ο are not important
for this subject (see Introduction and n.2).

246. Cf.T.Jud.16,3, ...ἀπολέσθαι οὐκ ἐν καιρῷ ὑμῶν.

247. See Prov.5,5 (LXX, τῆς γὰρ ἀφροσύνης οἱ πόδες κατάγουσιν τοὺς
χρωμένους αὐτῇ μετὰ θανάτου εἰς τὸν ᾅδην..);7,27 (LXX,ὁδοὶ ᾅδου
ὁ οἶκος αὐτῆς κατάγουσαι εἰς τὰ ταμεῖα τοῦ θανάτου);5,23 (LXX,
...καὶ ἀπώλετο δι᾽ἀφροσύνην);7,26 (LXX, πολλοὺς γὰρ τρώσασα κατα-
βέβληκεν καὶ ἀναρίθμητοί εἰσιν οὓς πεφόνευκεν);cf.6,32;Sir.9,6.
9. For the combination πορνεία - πλανᾶν (T.Reub.4,6;cf.5,3;
T.Jud.17,1;T.Benj.6,3) see also Prov.7,21 (LXX, ἀπεπλάνη-
σεν δὲ αὐτόν...);Sir.9,8, ...ἐν κάλλει γυναικὸς πολλοὶ ἐπλανήθη-
σαν... For the idea that esp.young people become easily
victims of a πόρνη,see,e.g.,Prov.7,1ο LXX,...ἣ ποιεῖ νέων
ἐξίπτασθαι καρδίας ;Philo,Spec.Leg.III 51;Virt.39f.;and see
also n.2ο7.

248. ὄνειδος αὐτῶν ποιεῖ. Cf.6,3. This idea also occurs in the
wisdom-literature : Prov.6,32f.,'So one who commits
adultery is a senseless fool...he will get nothing but
blows and contumely and will never live down the dis-
grace(LXX, τὸ δὲ ὄνειδος αὐτοῦ οὐκ ἐξαλειφθήσεται εἰς τὸν αἰῶνα)';
cf.Sir.23,26.

249. In ch.5 the well-known motif of κόσμησις occurs,through
which women try to seduce men,and which is also found in
T.Joseph 9,5.

250. ἐφύλαξεν ἑαυτὸν Ἰωσὴφ ἀπὸ πάσης γυναικός. Cf.Prov.6,24,'to
keep you from the wife of another man(LXX,τοῦ διαφυλάσσειν
σε ἀπὸ γυναικὸς ὑπάνδρου)...'

251. τὰς ἐννοίας ἐκαθάρισεν (b is not correct)ἀπὸ πάσης πορνείας.Cf.
T.Benj.8,2,'He that hath a pure mind(διάνοιαν καθαράν) in
love,looketh not after a woman with a view to fornicat-
ion(εἰς πορνείαν) ...';T.Reub.6,1;T.Joseph 4,6.

252. εὗρεν χάριν ἐνώπιον κυρίου καὶ ἀνθρώπων. For this expression,
which stands over against 'it bringeth reproach upon him
and derision with Beliar and the sons of men'(vs.7),see

also T.Sim.5,2;cf.Prov.3,3f.(cf.II Cor.8,21;Polyc.,Phil.
6,1);Sir.45,1;Luke 2,52. With regard to Joseph,see T.
Joseph 11,6;12,3;cf.Gen.39,4.21;5o,4;Acts 7,1o.

253. ἡ Αἰγυπτία. Cf.T.Joseph 3,1.6;4,3;8,1.5;16,5.

254. So already in II Ki.9,22 LXX, ...ἔτι αἱ πορνεῖαι Ιεζαβελ τῆς
μητρός σου καὶ τὰ φάρμακα αὐτῆς τὰ πολλά (cf.Rev.9,21);Nahum
3,4 LXX. For the combination μάγοι - φαρμακοί see Dan.2,2;
cf.Did.2,2;5,1;Barn.2o,1.

255. See vs.1, καὶ ἀποστέλλει μοι βρῶμα ἐν γοητείᾳ πεφυραμένον. For
γοητεία in this connection see,e.g.,Plut.,Mor.139A;256C.

256. ἐδέξατο. Cf.Sir.51,26,...καὶ ἐπιδεξάσθω ἡ ψυχὴ ὑμῶν παιδείαν...

257. See also Pastor Hermae,Visio 1,1,8;1,2,4;Mand.12,2,2.
Without direct connection with the idea of πορνεία,the
expression ἐπιθυμία πονηρά also occurs elsewhere in Pastor
Hermae : Visio 3,8,4;Mand.8,5;12,1,1ff.;12,2,4f.;Sim.5,
1,5;5,3,6;6,2,1;9,25,2.

258. See 1,7;4,3.8;1o,3.

259. See esp. the stereotyped formulation of the subject God
in T.Reub.4,1o;T.Sim.2,8 and T.Gad 2,5.

26o. See I B.

261. For the construction ῥύεσθαι - ἐκ χειρῶν...which is found
in T.Sim.2,8;T.Gad 2,5,see Ps.31,15(3o,16),'...rescue me
from my enemies(LXX, ῥῦσαί με ἐκ χειρὸς ἐχθρῶν μου)...';71
(7o),4;82(81),4;97(96),1o;Wisd.2,18;Esther 4,17(z) LXX.

262. See I A and esp.n.6,7 and 8.Cf.T.Joseph 6,5, ...ἐπλήρωσας
αὐτὸ θανάτου...and 6,6,(God) ...ἀπεκάλυψέ μοι τὴν κακίαν σου...

263. Cf.vs.3, ἔχετε οὖν ἔλεος ἐν σπλάγχνοις ὑμῶν...

264. See 2,4ff.;4,2;cf.5,2.

265. See ch.6-7. For the whole of T.Zeb.,and esp.for the
problem of the longer and the shorter text in T.Zeb.,
reference may be made to M.de Jonge,'Textual criticism
and the analysis of the composition of the Testament of
Zebulun',in Studies on the Testaments of the Twelve
Patriarchs.Text and Interpretation,ed.by M.de Jonge,
Leiden 1975 (ch.X),in which he argues that the longer
text must be original.

266. See also 7,2f.

267. Cf.T.Joseph 17,4,καὶ ὅτε ἦλθον οἱ ἀδελφοί μου εἰς Αἴγυπτον...
For T.Sim.4,3,see also IV B2.

268. εἰς ὃν ἐμβλέποντες. Cf.Sir.2,1o, ἐμβλέψατε εἰς ἀρχαίας γενεάς.
See also T.Sim.4,5, ...ἐννοῶντες τὸν πατράδελφον ὑμῶν (see IV
B2) and T.Benj.3,1, ...μιμούμενοι τὸν ἀγαθὸν καὶ ὅσιον ἄνδρα
Ἰωσίφ (see IV C).

269. See also T.Joseph 17,2, ...συγκρύπτετε ἀλλήλων τὰ ἐλαττώματα.
See III A.

27o. Cf.Rom.4,7f.;I Clem.5o,6.

271. Well-known epithets of God;see,e.g.,T.Jud.19,3;Ex.34,6;
II Chron.3o,9;Neh.9,17;Ps.86(85),15;1o3(1o2),8;111(11o),
4;145(144),8;Sir.2,11;Joel 2,13;Jonah 4,2.

272. For the expression 'not setting down in account evil to
...',see also T.Benj.3,6(see IV C);II Sam.19,2o R(LXX);
II Cor.5,19;Apoc.Sedr.16.

273. See,e.g.,Apoc.Mosis 27;T.Job 26,5;Apoc.Sedr.5;13(here in
connection with the remission of sins);14f.;II Clem.1,7;
Polyc.,Phil.6,1;Pastor Hermae,Visio 1,3,2;cf.Prov.12,1o;
17,5 LXX;Luke 1,77f.(here in connection with the remission of sins). In the Testaments this combination occurs
very often;see T.Sim.4,4;T.Zeb.,passim ;T.Benj.4.

274. Moreover,Joseph's μακροθυμία ,as it is found in this context in T.Joseph 17,2(cf.2,7;18,3) and his ἀμνησικακία ,as
it is found in Gen.5o;T.Sim.4,4;T.Zeb.8,4 are only different words for the same thing. See,e.g.,Pastor Hermae,
Mand.8,1o, ... μακρόθυμον εἶναι,μνησικακίαν μὴ ἔχειν ...and I
Clem.62,2, ...μακροθυμίᾳ...ἀμνησικάκως...

275. For the attitude of ζῆλος towards Joseph,cf.Gen.37,11
(LXX, ...ἐζήλωσαν...);see also Jos.,Ant.II 1o. In Gen. the
attitude of φθόνος towards Joseph is not found;but it
occurs in Jos.,Ant.II 1o;13;27;Philo,De Jos.5. Cf.T.Dan
2,5;T.Gad 3,3;4,5;T.Joseph 1,3(.7);1o,3.See I A and n.5.

276. Vs.8. For this formulation (see T.Gad 2,5;cf.T.Dan 1,9),
see IV A and esp.n.261. For the expression ἀποστέλλειν τὸν
ἄγγελον αὐτοῦ ,mostly used in connection with man's salvation by God,see II Chron.32,21f.;II Macc.15,22f.;Dan.3,95
LXX;6,23 Th;Acts 12,11;cf.Gen.48,16;Ps.34,7(33,8). See
also T.Joseph 6,6f.

277. See esp. the formulation ὅτε κατέβημεν εἰς Αἴγυπτον ;see IV
B1 and n.267. For ἔδησέ με ὡς κατάσκοπον,see Gen.42,24 and
42,9.11.14.16.31.34.

278. ἔχων πνεῦμα θεοῦ ἐν ἑαυτῷ ,which comes from Gen.41,38. Cf.
T.Benj.8,2.

279. Cf.T.Joseph 17,2f.;T.Zeb.8,5. See III A.

280. It is interesting that the subject of the verbs δοξάζειν
and χαρίζεσθαι is often a monarch;in such cases both
these verbs have to do with gifts the monarch grants to
some people;so δοξάζειν in Esther 3,1;6,6ff.;Dan.1,2o
LXX;2,6;I Macc.2,18;1o,65.88;11,42.51;14,39;so χαρίζεσθαι
in Esther 8,7;II Macc.1,35;IV Macc.11,12;cf.II Macc.4,
32.

281. See also ἐννοῶντες τὸν πατράδελφον ὑμῶν. Cf.T.Zeb.8,5;T.Benj.
3,1.

282. Discussion of ἀπλότης ,which is one of the central themes
in the Testaments,is outside the scope of this article.

283. 4,5,'...that God may give you also grace and glory,and
blessing upon your heads,even as ye saw in his(=Joseph
's) case.'

284. See also T.Joseph 1,7;T.Benj.4,1. See II C.

285. ...ὡς πνεῦμα πονηρὸν καὶ ἰοβόλον ἔχων,οὕτως φαίνεται τοῖς ἀνθρώποις
(vs.9).See also 5,1b,ἐκ γὰρ ταραχῆς τοῦ πνεύματος τὸ πρόσωπον
δηλοῖ. Cf.T.Sim.4,1f.(and also T.Joseph 7,1f.).

286. ὡραῖος τῷ εἴδει καὶ καλὸς τῇ ὄψει.See Gen.39,6 LXX,καλὸς τῷ
εἴδει καὶ ὡραῖος τῇ ὄψει... Cf.T.Napht.1,7f.;T.Joseph 18,4.

287. For such a use of ἐνοικεῖν see,e.g.,Rom.7,17.2o;cf.7,18;
cf.also Wisd.1,4.

288. See also Introduction and n.2.

289. For vs.8 see T.Gad 2,2;for (οὐδὲ ἔασε) τὸ ἀνόμημα τοῦτο
ποιῆσαι... (vs.9) see T.Zeb.1,7;4,12;T.Gad 2,5.

29o. See De Jonge,The Testaments...,pp.98f.

291. For the brothers' μῖσος towards Joseph,see T.Joseph 1,4;
Gen.37,4.8;Jos.,Ant.II 1o;Philo,De Jos.5.

292. Cf.T.Zeb.2,3, Εἰ δὲ καὶ ἥμαρτον,ἐν παιδείᾳ παιδεύσατέ με... See
also the Apocryphal Story of Joseph in Coptic(see n.213)
p.18,38f.,'saying(to them),"Forgive me my dreams..." '

293. See also Levit.19,15-18.

294. Ch.2 will not be discussed.Here -in particular from vs.
3 onwards- we have to do with three different texts," β "
;c;and A. The A-text is not without interest (cf.De

Jonge,The Testaments...,p.3o,'It has taken the leitmotiv
of T.Jos.X 5 - XVII 1,Joseph's attempts to spare his
brothers,and has developed this to almost ridiculous
extremes'),but it is (probably) secondary.See De Jonge,
The Testaments...,pp.29f.

295. μιμούμενοι...'Ιωσήφ. Cf.T.Sim.4,5;T.Zeb.8,5.See also T.
Benj.4,1,...μιμήσασθε...τὴν εὐσπλαγχνίαν αὐτοῦ(= τοῦ ἀγαθοῦ
ἀνδρός) ;see below.

296. See IV B2 and 3.

297. For such a use of ἀληθινός,see Job 1,1 LXX,'There lived
in the land of Uz a man named Job, καὶ ἦν ὁ ἄνθρωπος ἐκεῖνος
ἀληθινός,ἄμεμπτος...' (see also 1,8;2,3;8,6).

298. See,e.g.,I Sam.9,2;II Sam.18,27;Tobit 9,6 S;II Macc.15,
12;IV Macc.4,1;cf.Luke 23,5o;Acts 11,24.

299. See the context,in which also σοφός,ἄφρων,ἀσεβής,εὐσεβής,
ἄδικος occur.

3oo. See the context,in which also ἄκακος,πανοῦργος,σοφός,ἄφρων,
φρόνιμος occur.

3o1. For the expression ἀνὴρ ὅσιος which occurs in T.Benj.3,1
in connection with Joseph,see also 5,4;Deut.33,8;cf.T.
Joseph 4,1,...ὡς ἁγίῳ ἀνδρί.

3o2. ἀνὴρ ἀγαθός also occurs in 4,1(cf.vs.2);6,1; ἀνὴρ ὅσιος
also occurs in 5,4.

3o3. So already in 3,2.

3o4. καὶ ἐὰν τὰ πνεύματα τοῦ Βελίαρ εἰς πᾶσαν πονηρίαν θλίψεως ἐξαιτή-
σωνται ὑμᾶς... Cf.T.Job 2o,2,καὶ ἀπελθὼν (subj.:Satan) ᾐτήσατο
τὸ σῶμά μου παρὰ τοῦ Κυρίου ἵνα ἐπενέγκη μοι πληγήν ;16,1f.v.1.,
...ὁ διάβολος...ἐξῃτήσατο κατ'ἐμοῦ τὸν πόλεμον παρὰ τῷ θεῷ (V);
Luke 22,31. See for the construction esp.Esther 8,12(n)
LXX,τόν τε ἡμέτερον σωτῆρα...Μαρδοχαῖον καί...Εσθηρ...αἰτησάμενος
(subj.:Haman) εἰς ἀπώλειαν.

3o5. πόσοι. This is strongly reminiscent of the use of πόσος
and ποσάκις in T.Joseph. See II A.

3o6. ἠθέλησαν ἀνελεῖν αὐτόν. The threat of death proved to be
used very often in connection with Joseph.See I A and
esp.n.6,7 and 8.

3o7. See vs.3,'Fear ye the Lord...'

3o8. See vs.3,'...and love your neighbour...'

3o9. οὐ δύναται πληγῆναι.

3lo. τοῦ ἀερίου πνεύματος τοῦ Βελίαρ. Cf.T.Sol.16,3,...ὁ Βεελζεβοὺλ
ὁ τῶν ἀερίων καὶ ἐπιγείων καὶ καταχθονίων πνευμάτων δεσπότης... ;
18,3;22,1;cf.Eph.2,2.

311. οὐ δύναται κυριευθῆναι. See vs.3,...κατακυριεύσῃ...

312. Although the text given here is textcritically beyond
doubt,it is quite possible that τοῦ κυρίου was originally
a gloss:it clearly disturbs the context,whereas on the
other hand it could easily be put into the text by a
scribe who did not understand the context,as a parallel
to τοῦ φόβου τοῦ θεοῦ(vs.4).It is interesting that MS d
(and c) omits it.

313. Cf.T.Napht.8,6,'...and the Lord shall hate him.'

314. Cf.T.Benj.5,1, ...οἱ πονηροὶ ἄνθρωποι εἰρηνεύσουσιν ὑμῖν...(see
below). For the same complex of ideas,see also Ps.lo6
(lo5),41f.

315. 5,2 expresses the same theme;it also occurs in 4,3,'...
even though they devise with evil intent concerning him.
So by doing good he overcometh evil,being shielded
(σκεπαζόμενος) by the good...'

316. σκεπαζόμενος ,used in T.Benj.3,4,is parallel to βοηθούμενος, used in 3,5. σκεπάζειν as an action of God is very often parallel to other verbs which express an action of 'saving',as βοηθεῖν,ῥύεσθαι,σῴζειν,etc. See,e.g.,Ex.12,27;I Sam. 26,24 LXX;Judith 8,15;Ps.17(16),7f.;27(26),5;64,1f.(63, 2f.);91(9o),14;Ps.Sol.13,1ff.;cf.Ex.15,2;Judith 9,11;Ps. 71(7o),4ff.;Sir.51,2f.;III Macc.6,6ff. The fact that it is said that man is shielded by the fear of God(T.Benj. 3,4) or by the good(T.Benj.4,3;cf.3,5,'helped by the love...'),does not make much difference.In the first place,in T.Benj.3,4 in the example of Joseph,God himself is subject of σκεπάζειν. In the second place,the pious and God-fearing men are the very people who are shielded by him;see,e.g.,Ps.31,19f.(3o,2of.);61,4f.(6o,5f.).

317. b cannot be correct.The text now constituted(see n.3) reads : καὶ γὰρ ἐδεήθη τοῦ πατρὸς ἡμῶν Ἰωσήφ,ἵνα... According to the next verse(...ὦ τέκνον Ἰωσήφ)the subject of ἐδεήθη must be Joseph.See also below, n.32o.

318. ἵνα μὴ λογίσηται αὐτοῖς ὁ κύριος. See IV B1.

319. εἴ τι ἐνεθυμήθησαν πονηρὸν περὶ αὐτοῦ. See T.Sim.2,14, ἔγνων γάρ,ὅτι πονηρὸν πρᾶγμα ἐνεθυμήθην ἐνώπιον κυρίου . Cf. for such an expression Wisd.3,14;Matt.9,4;cf.T.Job 49,1.

32o. The last two verses of ch.3 do not fit in the context. One expects that Jacob would pray to God and would ask forgiveness for his sons(Joseph's brothers).And indeed, vs.7 begins with καὶ οὕτως ἐβόα Ἰακώβ (it is interesting that in the O.T. βοᾶν is often used as a description of calling on and praying to God,and so it can often be parallel to προσεύχεσθαι/εὔχεσθαι -as in T.Benj.3,6f.:see Ex.8,8.12(8,4.8);I Sam.7,5.8f.;II Chron.32,2o;Jonah 2, 1f.(2,2f.);moreover,in these texts God is asked for salvation,whether for one's own salvation-II Chron.32, 2o;Jonah 2,1f.(2,2f.),or for another's sake (περί)-Ex.8, 8.12(8,4.8);I Sam.7,5.8f.). But instead of the prayer we expect,we read :'O child Joseph,thou hast prevailed over the bowels of thy father Jacob.' And then,'he embraced him,and kissed him for two hours...'(περιλαβὼν αὐτόν,... κατεφίλει. Cf.Gen.46,29.For the combination περιλαμβάνειν - (κατα-)φιλεῖν see Gen.29,13;33,4;48,1o).
Not only vs.7,but also vs.8 does not fit in the context. With regard to this verse Charles(in his Translation,p. 2o2) and Becker(in Die Testamente der zwölf Patriarchen (JSHRZ III 1),Gütersloh 1974,pp.132f.) think that 'concerning the Lamb of God and Saviour of the world' and 'in the blood of the covenant,for the salvation of the Gentiles and of Israel,and shall destroy Beliar and his servants' are Christian additions to the originally Jewish 'In thee shall be fulfilled the prophesy of heaven,that a blameless one shall be delivered up for lawless men,and a sinless one shall die for ungodly men'; so both scholars mentioned above hold in fact the A-text to be original.Charles remarks among other things , 'The idea of vicarious suffering and propitiation was not unfamiliar to pre-Christian Judaism,and especially with regard to the martyrs under Antiochus Epiphanes...' (Becker seems to agree with Charles). Charles' remark is,of course,right,but nowhere do we read that the martyr dies as a blameless and sinless

man for lawless and ungodly men.Moreover,it is alto-
gether unlikely that ἀμνὸς belongs to the Christian
addition but ἄμωμος belongs to the (original) Jewish text,
as in T.Joseph 19,8 the expression ἀμνὸς ἄμωμος (cf.I
Peter 1,19) occurs.Therefore I conclude that T.Benj.3,8
cannot be divided into Christian and Jewish phrases.This
verse is either wholly Christian or wholly Jewish.And
this question can only be solved on the basis of a
thorough investigation of related passages in the Testa-
ments.This,however,would be far beyond the scope of the
subject.
On these grounds it is likely that both these verses are
additions to the original text of T.Benj.The textcritic-
al difficulties of vs.6(see also n.317) make this all
the more probable.Moreover,vs.8 has (almost) nothing to
do with the figure of Joseph:Joseph has not died for the
sake of others.

321. See IV B1 and 2.
322. στεφάνους δόξης.It is obvious that by 'τὸ τέλος' also this
reward (δόξα) is meant.Moreover,see Philo,De Jos.122,
where Philo referring to Joseph's exaltation remarks,
τοιαῦτα τῶν εὐσεβῶν τὰ τέλη... (cf.246).
323. See II C.
324. Cf.3,2,'...he that hath his mind right,seeth all things
rightly(πάντα βλέπει ὀρθῶς)';see also T.Dan 2,4,'For the
spirit of anger encompasseth him with the nets of deceit,
and blindeth his natural eyes (τυφλοῖ τοὺς φυσικοὺς ὀφθαλμοὺς
αὐτοῦ),(and) through lying darkeneth(σκοτοῖ) his mind,
and giveth him its own peculiar vision';T.Gad 5,7,'For
true repentance after a godly sort...driveth away the
darkness (τὸ σκότος),and enlighteneth the eyes (φωτίζει τοὺς
ὀφθαλμοὺς)...';cf.T.Jud.13,6;14,1.
325. Cf.T.Zeb.7,2;8,1.See also T.Benj.4,4;5,4.
326. See above.Cf.5,2;T.Joseph 18,2.
327. See also Rom.11,32.
328. Since vss.4 and 5 have not so much to do with the figure
of Joseph as such(see also above),it is not necessary
to discuss them in detail.
329. See,e.g.,II Clem.17,2,'Let us then help one another,and
bring back those that are weak in goodness,that we may
all be saved,and convert and exhort one another (ἐπι-
στρέψωμεν ἀλλήλους καὶ νουθετήσωμεν)';Pastor Hermae,Visio 1,
3,1f.;Mand.8,1o;cf.Clem.Hom.18,19,3.
33o. Here,however,the woman's repentance is not brought about
by Joseph's pious attitude as such,but by the miracle
that Joseph as a pious man did.Without any doubt a
(temporary) repentance on the part of the woman is
meant . We hear that she wept (ἔκλαυσε),a reaction connected with the act of repentance (see,e.g.,T.Reub.1,
9f.;T.Sim.2,13).Moreover,she promised to behave better
(vs.9),while also δέ in 7,1 points to the fact that in
ch.6 a (temporary) repentance is meant.
331. See also '...will reverence you...' in the same verse.
332. Undoubtedly,the statement 'For if any one does violence
to a holy man,he repenteth(μετανοεῖ)' in T.Benj.5,4 has
the same meaning.
333. For T.Levi 13,4,see IV D and n.348.
334. See also above.

335. See,besides the texts mentioned above,also T.Dan 5,1;
James 4,7;Pastor Hermae,Mand.11,14;12,2,4;12,4,7;12,5,2.
336. For ἐλεεῖν see also above.
337. On Joseph's silence,see II A;III A. On Joseph's mercy
and compassion,see IV B1 and 2.
338. See n.236.
339. For the idea of 'humiliation' (ταπεινοῦν)by others,see
further also Ps.38,8(37,9);94(93),5;1o6(1o5),42;116(114),
6;116,1o(115,1);142,6(141,7);cf.9,13(14);25(24),18;31,7
(3o,8);Lament.1,3.7.9.This idea of 'humiliation' by
others is,however,not the same as the idea of 'self-
humiliation',although both these ideas are related.
34o. See esp. II C.
341. In ch.6 the description of the good man(cf.vs.1,... τοῦ
ἀγαθοῦ ἀνδρός ...) is continued.But because in my opinion
it is not directly concerned with Joseph himself,it is
not necessary to discuss this chapter(as well as the
rest of T.Benj.);see also Introduction and n.2. In my
dissertation(see n.1) I hope to return to the subject
of the 'good man'.
342. ἐν ἁπλότητι. See n.282.
343. b is not correct.Read : αὐτοῦ.
344. See 19,2;cf.T.Reub.3,8;T.Joseph 4,5.
345. διδάξατε...γράμματα. Cf.Dan.1,4.
346. It is obvious that σύνεσις (vs.2) and σοφία (vs.7) mean the
same thing;see,e.g.,T.Zeb.6,1;Ex.35,31.35;I Chron.22,12;
II Chron.1,1off.;Judith 8,29;Job 28,2o;Ps.49,3(48,4);
Prov.24,3;cf.Dan.1,4;Prov.16,21;17,24;Sir.3,29;18,27ff.;
47,14. See also below.
347. For T.Levi 13,2bc reference may be made esp. to Sir.,
prol.1ff.,...τοῦ νόμου καὶ τῶν προφητῶν...καὶ ὡς οὐ μόνον αὐτοὺς
τοὺς ἀναγινώσκοντας δέον ἐστὶν ἐπιστήμονας γίνεσθαι... (cf.Deut.
17,19).
348. Cf.T.Benj.5,1(see IV C).In T.Levi 13 it is the wise man
who -through his wisdom,his knowledge of the law and his
fear of God- makes many friends.
349. Cf.Sir.1o,25.See also Philo,Leg.All.III 192ff.
35o. For these verses,cf.Job 4,8;Prov.11,21 LXX;22,8;Sir.7,1
ff.;Hos.8,7;1o,12;Gr.Apoc.Bar.15,2;II Cor.9,6;Gal.6,7ff.
351. Cf.Prov.4,4f.;17,16;Sir.51,25.
352. κτῆσις. Cf. ...σοφίαν κτήσασθε...in the same verse.
353. Text and translation from Plutarch's Moralia,ed./trsl.
by W.C.Helmbold (Loeb ed.,vol.VI).
354. Cf.476A, ἡ δὲ τοῦ φρονίμου διάθεσις...
355. Text and translation from Plutarch's Moralia,ed./trsl.
by Ph.H.de Lacy and B.Einarson (Loeb ed.,vol.VII).
356. λαμπρά. Cf.Wisd.6,12, λαμπρὰ καὶ ἀμάραντός ἐστιν ἡ σοφία...
357. ἐὰν διδάσκῃ ταῦτα...This,however,is different from what has
been said in vs.2(διδάξατε...γράμματα).In vs.9 it has to do
with instruction in the law and in wisdom,which flows
from it,in short with teaching the people to walk
according to the law of God (see also καὶ πράττῃ in the
same verse).
358. On Joseph as the good man in the Testaments,see IV C.
359. For the idea that the wise man teaches (παιδεύειν) see,e.
g.,Sir.37,23, ἀνὴρ σοφὸς τὸν ἑαυτοῦ λαὸν παιδεύσει...
36o. Cf.also Wisd.1o,13f.,where it is σοφία which saves Joseph
from his oppressions and ...ἤνεγκεν αὐτῷ σκῆπτρα βασιλείας.

361. Hence it is an overstatement to say that Joseph is '...
für die Testamente...der Typus des Weisen'(Rengstorf,<u>art.</u>
<u>cit.</u>,p.43).
Intentionally I have omitted a discussion on the Aramaic
fragments of T.Levi.It is almost certain that these
fragments and the corresponding Greek chapters go back
to a common source(see,among others,De Jonge,<u>The Testa-</u>
<u>ments...</u>,pp.38-52;129-131).In the case of T.Levi 13 the
question of which of the two texts is nearest to the
original cannot be solved with any certainty(see also De
Jonge,<u>The Testaments...</u>,p.43).It is,however,noteworthy
that in the Aramaic fragments Joseph is explicitly
mentioned in connection with wisdom : 'My sons,behold
Joseph my brother,Who gave instruction in the writings
and discipline of wisdom'(Charles,<u>Translation</u>,p.234;cf.
Charles,<u>Edition</u>,p.255).If it is true that in T.Levi 13
the fragments are nearer to the original than the corresponding Greek text -which is quite probable in other
passages(see also De Jonge,<u>The Testaments...</u>,p.42)-,it
is the more striking that in the Greek T.Levi 13 the
connection between Joseph and wisdom was not taken over
from the original source.

SYNTACTICAL EVIDENCE OF A SEMITIC VORLAGE OF
THE TESTAMENT OF JOSEPH

R. A. Martin

A. Method

In my book *Syntactical Evidence of Semitic Sources in Greek Documents* (SBL Septuagint and Cognate Studies, 3; Missoula: Scholars Press, 1974) a number of Greek syntactical features were isolated by means of which it may often be determined whether a Greek document, or part of it, is a translation of a Hebrew or Aramaic original. These syntactical features are as follows:[1]

(a) Syntactical features which are <u>less frequent</u> in Greek which is a translation of Hebrew or Aramaic than in original Greek prose writings:

(1) eight prepositional usages: <u>dia</u> with the genitive; <u>dia</u> with all its cases; <u>eis</u>; <u>kata</u> with the accusative; <u>kata</u> with all its cases; <u>peri</u> with all its cases; <u>pros</u> with the dative; <u>hypo</u> with the genitive;

(2) the use of <u>de</u>;

(3) the separation of the article from its substantive;

(4) the placement of a genitive before the word upon which it depends;

(5) the placement of attributive adjectives before the words they qualify;

(6) the use of the adverbial (circumstantial) participle;

(7) the use of the dative case; other than its use as the object of <u>en</u>.

(b) Syntactical features which are <u>more frequent</u> in Greek which is a translation of a Semitic original than in original Greek:

(1) the use of the preposition <u>en</u>;

(2) the use of <u>kai</u> to join main (independent) clauses;

(3) the use of genitive personal pronouns;

---

1. Cf. Martin, <u>Syntactical Evidence</u>, pp. 1-43.

(4) the use of genitive personal pronouns dependent on an anarthrous substantive.

These syntactical features were studied in a variety of
Greek documents. For original Greek writers typical of the
Koine period the following were selected:

Plutarch (<u>Lives</u>)	325 lines
Polybius	192 lines
Epictetus	138 lines
Josephus (<u>Contra</u> <u>Apionem</u>, <u>Antiquities</u>)	215 lines
Papyri (300 B.C. to A.D. 100)	630 lines
Total	1500 lines

For translation Greek the following books were selected
as being representative of various levels of Greek in the LXX:

Genesis	382 lines
1 Samuel	194 lines
1 Kings	58 lines
2 Kings	71 lines
Daniel (Hebrew) -- LXX	482 lines
Daniel (Hebrew) -- Theodotion	460 lines
Daniel (Aramaic) -- LXX	595 lines
Daniel (Aramaic) -- Theodotion	634 lines
Ezra -- Hebrew	328 lines
Ezra -- Aramaic	211 lines
Total	3415 lines

In this study it was found that whenever these syntactical features occur with the following frequencies, the Greek
is characteristic of translation Greek rather than original
Greek:

1. <u>dia</u> with genitive 6% - 1% as frequent as <u>en</u>;

2. <u>dia</u> with all cases 18% - 1% as frequent as <u>en</u>;

3. <u>eis</u> 49% - 1% as frequent as <u>en</u>;

4. <u>kata</u> with accusative 18% - 1% as frequent as <u>en</u>;

5. <u>kata</u> with all cases 19% - 1% as frequent as <u>en</u>;

6. <u>peri</u> with all cases 27% - 1% as frequent as <u>en</u>;

7. <u>pros</u> with dative 2.4% - 1% as frequent as <u>en</u>;

8. <u>hypo</u> with genitive 7% - 1% as frequent as <u>en</u>;

9. <u>kai</u> (coordinating main clauses) 2.1+ times more frequent than all occurrences of <u>de</u>;

10. 5% or fewer articles separated from their substantives;

11. 22 or more dependent genitives following the word they qualify for each such genitive preceding the word qualified;

12. 9 or fewer lines of Greek text for each dependent genitive personal pronoun;

13. 77 or fewer lines of Greek text for each genitive personal pronoun dependent on an anarthrous substantive;

14. .35 or fewer attributive adjectives preceding the word they qualify for each such adjective following the word qualified;

15. 10.1 or more lines of Greek text for each attributive adjective;

16. 6 or more lines of Greek text for each adverbial participle;

17. 2 or fewer datives not used as the object of <u>en</u> for each occurrence of <u>en</u>.

In the above-mentioned study of these syntactical features two aspects were found to be particularly significant. First of all, these frequencies are most valid for amounts of text more than 50 lines in length. (They are also valid to a modified degree for smaller units of text.)

Further, it was found that the <u>net</u> number of translation Greek or original Greek frequencies <u>was</u> most significant. These <u>net</u> figures are arrived at as follows: Whenever a section has more occurrences of original Greek frequencies than occurrences of translation Greek frequencies, the number of occurrences of translation Greek frequencies was subtracted from the number of occurrences of original Greek frequencies, and the resulting number is the <u>net occurrences of original Greek frequencies</u>.

Conversely, whenever a section has more occurrences of translation Greek frequencies, the number of occurrences of original Greek frequencies was subtracted from the number of occurrences of translation Greek frequencies, and the resulting number is the <u>net occurrences of translation Greek frequencies</u>.

For convenience of representation, <u>net</u> original Greek frequencies in the charts are expressed as positive numbers and <u>net</u> translation Greek frequencies are expressed as negative numbers.

Using these net original Greek and net translation Greek frequencies, a range of 35 spaces extending from +17 to -17 can be established.

In the above-mentioned study it was found that the Greek documents originally written in Greek and consisting of 138 to 630 lines fell within a limited area at one end of the range (in the area occupied by +17 to +15 net original Greek frequencies) whereas the Greek documents known to be translations of Semitic originals, consisting of 58 to 634 lines, fell in a limited area at the opposite end of the range (in the area occupied by -4 to -14 net translation Greek frequencies), separated from the area occupied by original Greek documents by 18 spaces (+14 to -3). These data can be seen in Chart 1[1] which follows below.

Similar ranges were established for smaller units of Greek text, as will be seen in the subsequent discussion of the Testament of Joseph data.

B. Testament of Joseph

The above 17 syntactical features were calculated for the Testament of Joseph (using the De Jonge text). The data are listed in the charts in Appendix 1 and 2 at the end of this paper, classified by chapter and by subdivisions within each chapter. The last two columns of those data in Appendix 1 give the net original Greek frequencies and the net translation Greek frequencies for each section.

From those data it will be seen that the Testament of Joseph taken as a whole consists of 329 lines[2] and has -6 net translation Greek frequencies, which places the Testament of Joseph as a whole in the range occupied by translated documents -- equal in this instance to the position of 1 Kings in Chart I above.

There seems little doubt that the present Greek text of the Testament of Joseph goes back to a Semitic Vorlage.

Subsections of Testament of Joseph

The relative frequencies of these 17 syntactical features were also calculated for each chapter and for subdivisions in the longer chapters. These data are also found in the charts in Appendix 1 and 2.

In Syntactical Evidence (pp. 49, 51 and 53) ranges were established for units of 31 to 50 lines, 16 to 30 lines and 4 to 15 lines in length in texts of both original and translated Greek.

---

1. Cf. also Martin, Syntactical Evidence, p. 42.
2. These are "adjusted" lines, since the line length of De Jonge's text are slightly greater than the standard line length used in my study (Cf. Appendix 1, p. 109f of that study for details).

Chart I

Net Original Greek or Translation Greek Frequencies Appearing in Each Document

Columns 0–17 record the **Net No. of Frequencies Characteristic of Original Greek**; columns −1 to −14 record the **Net No. of Frequencies Characteristic of Translation Greek**.

Name	No. of Lines	17	16	15	14	13	12	11	10	9	8	7	6	5	4	3	2	1	0	-1	-2	-3	-4	-5	-6	-7	-8	-9	-10	-11	-12	-13	-14
Genesis 1-4,6,39	382																						X										
1 Samuel 3,4,22	194																													X			
1 Kings 17	58													X																			
2 Kings 13	71																														X		
Dan. - Heb. -- LXX	482																													X			
Dan. - Heb. -- Theod.	460																											X					
Dan. - Aram. -- LXX	595																													X			
Dan. - Aram. -- Theod.	634																														X		
Ezra -- Hebrew	328																															X	
Ezra -- Aramaic	211																																X
Plutarch-Selections	325		X																														
Polybius--Bks I,II	192			X																													
Epictetus--Bks III,IV	138	X																															
Josephus--Selections	215		X																														
Papyri--Selections	630	X																															

The chapters and smaller divisions of chapters in the
Testament of Joseph fall only in the last two categories --
units 16 to 30 lines in length and units 4 to 15 lines in
length.

Testament of Joseph Units 16 to 30 Lines in Length

There were 12 units in the Testament of Joseph with between 16 and 30 lines of text. As Chart II[1] below indicates
all except 3 such units fell within the range occupied by
translation Greek (+1 to -3 net frequencies). Two (Chapter 6
and Chapter 13) fell within the area occupied by some units of
translation Greek and also by 2 units of original Greek. One
unit (Chapter 3) fell outside the area occupied by any of the
units of translation Greek and within the lower portion of the
area occupied by a few units of original Greek. It would
appear that in the case of Chapter 3 either the translator
translated quite freely or parts of that chapter may be original Greek composition (Cf. discussion at end of this paper).

Testament of Joseph Units 4 to 15 Lines in Length

There were 45 units in the Testament of Joseph with between 4 and 15 lines of text. As Chart III[2] below indicates,
6 of these fell within the range occupied only by translation
Greek and the rest (39 units) fell within the area occupied
by both translation Greek and original Greek units. None fell
within the range occupied only by original Greek units.

The distribution of the small units of the Testament of
Joseph is most similar to the pattern of distribution of such
small units of the LXX translation of the Aramaic portions of
Daniel found in Chart III above.

Comments on the Syntax of Chapter 3 of the Testament of Joseph

Without intending to be exhaustive, the following tentative comments on certain Greek constructions in Chapter 3 of
the Testament of Joseph suggest that Chapter 3 is free translation rather than original Greek composition.

a) Greek Constructions which are not usual in Greek but
are literal translations of underlying Semitic idiom:

3:2   despotēs hēmōn   The use of a genitive
                              personal pronoun with an
                              anarthrous substantive is un-
                              common in Greek. Of course the
                              Hebrew or Aramaic equivalent
                              could not have an article in
                              such cases. Cf. also patros mou
                              in 3:3.

---

1. Cf. also Martin, Syntactical Evidence, p. 51.
2. Cf. also ibid., p. 53.

Chart II

Net Original Greek or Translation Greek Frequencies in Each Unit of Text 16 to 30 Lines in Length

	No. of Units	Net No. of Frequencies Characteristic of Original Greek																	Net No. of Frequencies Characteristic of Translation Greek													
		17	16	15	14	13	12	11	10	9	8	7	6	5	4	3	2	1	0	-1	-2	-3	-4	-5	-6	-7	-8	-9	-10	-11	-12	-13	-14
Genesis 1-4,6,39	5																1		2	1													
1 Samuel 3,4,22	4																			1	1	2											
1 Kings 17	-																																
2 Kings 13	1																		1														
Dan. -- Heb. -- LXX	6															1			2	2													
Dan. -- Heb. -- Theod.	4																			2						2							
Dan. -- Aram. -- LXX	10														1				3	2							2						
Dan. -- Aram. -- Theod.	13															1				1		3	2		1	1	1						
Ezra -- Hebrew	10																			2	1		1	1	5								
Ezra -- Aramaic	7																		1	1		1	2					2					
Plutarch-Selections	7						1	1	1	1	1			2																			
Polybius--Bks I,II	5						1	2	1	1																							
Epictetus--Bks III,IV	5						1		1	1	1	1																					
Josephus-Selections	5						1			3	3																						
Papyri-Selections	12						2		2	3	3	1	1																				
Testament of Joseph	12						1								2				2	3	3												

Chart III

Net Original or Translation Greek Frequencies in Each Unit of Text 4 to 15 Lines in Length

	No. of Units	Net No. of Frequencies Characteristic of Original Greek																		Net No. of Frequencies Characteristic of Translation Greek													
		17	16	15	14	13	12	11	10	9	8	7	6	5	4	3	2	1	0	-1	-2	-3	-4	-5	-6	-7	-8	-9	-10	-11	-12	-13	-14
Genesis 1-4,6,39	13																2	3	2	3	3	3											
1 Samuel 3,4,22	12														1	1		1	1	5		1	1	2	2								
1 Kings 17	5																1	1	1	1	1	1	1		1								
2 Kings 13	5																1	1	1	1	1	1	1		1								
Dan. -- Heb. -- LXX	35											1				1	3	2	5	7	8	4	3	1	1	1							
Dan. -- Heb. -- Theod.	37																2	3	3	2	7	8	10	2									
Dan. -- Aram. -- LXX	38												1	1	3	4	3	4	6	3	6	4	2	3	1	1							
Dan. -- Aram. -- Theod.	36															2	5	1	4	6	3	6	5	2	2	1							
Ezra -- Hebrew	15															1	2	2	3	3	6	2	2	2	1								
Ezra -- Aramaic	6														2			1	1	2	1												
Plutarch-Selections	49								1	5	3	6	12	8	4	6	2	2	2														
Polybius--Bks I,II	12							1	3	2	1	2	3																				
Epictetus--Bks III,IV	2							1			1				1																		
Josephus-Selections	22								1	2	3	3	6	6	1	2		2															
Papyri-Selections	75						2	1	2	5	7	16	9	13	12	2	3		8	3	2												
Test. of Joseph	45											1	4	4	5	4	4	5	8	3	2		1										

3:3 <u>logous pateron</u>   The Greek idiom would more commonly have an article with <u>logous</u>. Hebrew would not be able to have an article in such a case. Aramaic often would use a construction without an article for the equivalent of <u>logous</u> also. Cf. also <u>rhēmata hupsistou</u> in 3:10.

3:10 <u>tēs epithumias autēs tēs ponēras</u>   While the occurrence of the article with <u>epithumias</u> would not be possible in a Hebrew or Aramaic equivalent, the order (substantive, possessive pronoun, attributive adjective) is uncommon in Greek and reproduces exactly the word order of the Semitic idiom.

b) Constructions which are normal in Greek and cannot literally reproduce a Semitic syntactical construction.[1]

3:2 <u>pantōn tōn emōn</u>   Semitic languages do not have possessive adjectives.

<u>heauton</u>   Semitic languages do not have reflexive pronouns. Cf. also <u>emauton</u> in 3:9.

3:3 <u>to tamieion</u>   The use of the article to express the possessive pronoun is usual in Greek and not possible in Hebrew or Aramaic.

3:4 <u>tois hepta etesin</u>   The separation of the article from its substantive is not possible in either Hebrew or Aramaic. Cf. also <u>hoi ... nēsteuontes</u> later in this verse and <u>ta ... prōta</u> in 3:7.

<u>tou prosōpou tēn charin</u>   The placement of the genitive before its governing substantive is common in Greek and impossible in Semitic languages. Cf. also <u>mou</u> in 3:5 and <u>Memphias</u> in 3:6.

---

1. Greek constructions like these do occur in translated documents of the LXX, but are non-literal, idiomatic renditions of the Semitic <u>Vorlage</u>. Thus these Greek constructions in the <u>Testament of Joseph</u> can indicate <u>either</u> free, idiomatic translation <u>or</u> original Greek composition.

While the Greek idioms in b) above would be possible either in original Greek or as a relatively idiomatic translation of a Semitic Vorlage, the Semitic features noted in a) above suggest that Chapter 3 of the Testament of Joseph is most probably a relatively free translation of Hebrew or Aramaic.

Thus it would appear that the Greek text of the Testament of Joseph as a whole and in all its smaller units is a translation of a Semitic Vorlage.[1]

R. A. Martin
Wartburg Theological Seminary
Dubuque, Iowa

---

1. In Appendix 3 the larger units of the Testament of Joseph according to one proposed outline are analyzed.

Appendix 1

Frequencies of the 17 Criteria in *Testament* of *Joseph*

Translation Frequencies	Net translat. Grk freq.	Net original Grk freq.	No. of lines where occ. of criter. are too few to be indic.	Grk freq. Tot. no. of orig.	Grk freq. Tot. no. of transl.	No. of dat. not used w. en for ea. occur. of en	adverb. participle No. of lines: each	attrib. adjec. No. of lines: ea.	adj. post position / No. of prec. attr.	Lines/ea. gen. pers. pron. dep. on anarth. subst.	pers. pronoun dep. gen. No. of lines/ea.	dep. gen. post ea. prec. / No. of dep. gen.	Percent of separ. article	No. of occ. of kai for each occ. of de	Hupo w. gen.	Pros w. dative	Peri w. all cases	kata W. all cases	W. accus.	eis	dia W. all cases	W. gen.	No. of occur. of en	Greek text No. of lines
Entire Test. of J.	17				17	2.	6.	10.1	35.	77.	9.	22.4	.05	2.11	.07/.01	.024/.01	.27/.01	.19/.01	.18/.01	.49/.01	.18/.01	.06/.01	75	329.
1:1,2	-6		1	5	11	1.0/.00	4.4	10.0	.83	10.0/5.0	2.8	22.0/6	.07	4.8	.03/1.0	-	.17	.03	.01	.44	.17	.07	1	5
3-7		+1	10	4	3	.33	5.0/14	5/7.0	-	-	1.3/4.7	6.0/12.0	-	-	-	-	-	-	-	.33	-	-	9	14
Chap 1			8	4	5	.30	19.0	9.5	1.0/1.0	19.0	2.7		.07/.05	14/14	.10	-	-	-	-	.30	-	-	10	19
2:1-3	-1/-3	0/+2	11		7	-	7/10	7.0	-	-	3.5/10	4/1.0	-	4/2.0	-	-	-	-	-	1/.20	-	-	-	7
4-7			9	3	3	.80	10.0	5.0	2.0	-	8.5	1.0	-	6.0	-	-	-	-	-	.40	-	-	5	10
Chap 2	-2		9	5	3	1.0	17.0/17	5.7	2.0	-		5.0	-		-	-	-	-	-		-	-	5	17
3:1,2		+5/+1/+4	8	3	5	1.3	2.5	5.0	1.0	5.0/11.0	5.0/11.0	1/2.0/3	.22/.20	2.0/8.0/8	-	-	.33	-	-	1/.33	.33	-	-	5
3-6			6	7	2	-	3.7	11/4.5	-	-	4.5				-	-	-	-	-	2	-	-	3	11
7-10			9	6	5	-	4.5		-	-					-	-	-	-	-		-	-	3	9
Chap 3		+6/+6	5	6	2	3.0	3.6	8.3	.50	12.5	6.3	4.0	.19	9.0	-	-	.67	-	-	1.3	.33	.25	3	25
4:1-3			7	9	3	.25	3.0	9.0/10	1.0	-	2.3/5.0	4	-	2/2.0	-	-	.50	-	-	-	.25	.14	4	9
4-8			9	8	2	.67	5.0	19.0	-	10.0/19.0	3.2	5	-	3.0	-	-	.29	-	-	-	.14	-	3	10
Chap 4	-1	0	6	4	4	.43	3.8	10.0	1.0	-		9	-		-	-	-	-	-	-	-	-	7	19
Chap 5		+3	10	5	6/2	4.0	3.3/4.0	-	-	-	3.3	6	-	5.0	-	-	-	-	-	1.0	-	-	1	10

Frequencies of the 17 Criteria in Testament of Joseph

Translation Frequencies	No. of lines of Greek text	No. of occur. of en	dia W. gen. (.06-/.01)	dia W. all cases (.18-/.01)	eis (.49-/.01)	W. accus. (.18-/.01)	kata W. all (.19-/.01)	Peri W. all cases (.27-/.01)	Pros W. dative (.024/.01)	Hupo W. genitive (.07-/.01)	No. of occ. of kai for each occ. of de (2.1-)	Percent. of separ. articles (.05-)	No. of dep. gen. post ea. prec. dep. gen. (22+)	No. of lines ea. gen. dep. pers. pronoun (9.)	Lines ea. gen. pers. pron. dep. on anarth. subst. (77.)	No. of prec. attr. adj. for each attr. adj. post position (35.)	No. of lines ea. attrib. adjc. (10.1+)	No. of lines each adverb. participle (6')	No. of dat. for ea. occur. of en used w. en, not (2.)	Tot. no. of transl. Grk. frequencies (17)	Tot. no. of orig. Grk. frequencies	No. of inst. where occ. of criter. are too few to be indic.	Net original Grk. frequencies	Net translat. Grk. frequencies (17)
6:1-3	7	1	–	1	1.0	–	–	–	–	–	4	–	4	3.5	–	–	7.0	2.3	1.0	3	4	10	+1	
4-6	6	1	–	1	1	–	–	–	–	–	4	–	4	2.0	6.0	–	6.0	3.0	3	3	7	7	+4	
7-9	7	1	–	–	1.0	–	–	–	–	–	4	.13	5	3.5	–	–	7	2.3	.00	2	6	9	+4	
Chap 6	20	2	.50	.50	1.5	–	–	–	–	–	1.5	.06	13	2.9	20.0	–	10.0	2.5	2.0	4	7	6	+3	
7:1,2	6	1	–	1	1	–	–	–	–	–	.67	–	5	2.0	–	–	6	3.0	–	1	5	11	+4	
3-6	12	1	2	2.0	2.0	–	–	–	–	–	4	–	11	1.5	–	–	12	3.0	3.0	3	4	10	+1	
7,8	4	1	–	2	1	–	–	–	–	–	1	–	2	4.0	–	–	2.0	4	–	1	6	10	+5	
Chap 7	22	1	2.0	2.0	4.0	–	–	–	–	–	2.3	.00	18	1.8	–	–	11.0	3.7	5.0	4	5	8	+1	
8:1-3	7	1	–	–	1	–	–	–	–	–	1	–	1.0	7.0	–	1.0	7	1.2	–	1	6	10	+1	
4,5	8	5	–	.20	.40	–	–	1	–	–	5	–	6	2.0	4.0	1.0	8.0	4.0	.20	5	6	6	+5	
Chap 8	15	5	.20	.20	.60	–	–	.20	–	–	6	–	7.0	3.0	7.5	1.0	15.0	1.9	.40	6	6	5	+1	
9:1-3	8	4	–	–	.50	–	–	–	–	–	4.0	.38	2	8.0	8.0	–	8	8.0	.50	5	3	9	0	
4,5	8	2	–	–	.17	–	–	–	–	–	3.0	–	6	1.3	8.0	–	8	2.0	.00	4	4	9	0	
Chap 9	16	6	–	–	–	.17	–	–	–	–	3.5	.19	8	2.3	16.0	–	16	3.2	.33	6	3	8	0	-2
10:1-3	9	3	.33								1.0	.13	2	9.0	9.0	–	9	9.0	1.3	4	5	8	+1	-3
10:4-11:1	12	6	.17							.17	6	.06	12.0	1.3	12.0	–	6.0	6.0	.00	6	4	7		-2
10:1-11:1	21	9	.22							.11	7.0	.08	14.0	2.1	10.5	–	10.5	10.5	.44	6	4	7		-2

Frequencies of the 17 Criteria in Testament of Joseph

Translation Frequencies	No. of lines of Greek text	No. of en	W. gen.	dia W. all cases	eis	W. accus.	kata W. all cases	Peri w. all cases	Pros W. dative	Hupo W. genitive	No. of occ. of kai for each occ. of de	Percent of separ. articles	No. of dap post ea. prec. gen.	No. of lines/ea. pers. pronoun gen. dap	Lines ea. gen. dep. pers. pron. dap on anarth. subst.	No. of prec. attr. adj. for each attr. position	No. of lines/ea. attrib. adjec.	No. of lines each adverb. participle	No. of dat. not used w. en for ea. occur. of en	Tot. no. of transl. Grk. frequencies	Tot. no. of orig. Grk. frequencies	No. of inst. where occ. of criter. are too few to be indic.	Net original Grk. frequencies	Net translat. Grk. frequencies
	.06-.01	.18-.01	.49-.01	.18-.01	.19-.01	.27-.01	.024-.01	.07-.01	2.1-	.05-	22+	9-	77-	.35-	10 1+	6+	2-	17					
11:2,3	6	1	1	1	1	1	1	1	1	.67	1	5	1.2 3.0	1	6	6.0	1	3	3	9		+2	17
4-8	8	3	1	.67 1.0	1	1	.33 .67	1	1	5.0 1.8	1	5	2.7 4.0	1	8	4.0	.67 1.0	4	5	8		+1	
11:2-8	14	3	1	1.0	1	1	1	1	1	1.8	1	10	1.8 3.5	1	14	4.7	1.0	4	5	8		+1	
Chap 12	9	1	1.0	1.0	1.0	2.0	2.0	1	1	4.0	.08	7	3.0 9.0	2.0	4.5	9	2.0	5	8	4		+3	
13:1-4	10	1	1	1	1	1	1	1	1	1.0 8.0	.09	3	5.0 10.0	1	10.0	2.0 2.3	.4 2.0	2	7	8 11		+5	
5-9	9	1	1.0	1.0	1	1	1	1	1	2.8	1	.00 3.0	9.5 19.0	1	9 19.0	2.1 6.0	2.0 6.0	3	6	8		+3	
Chap 13	19	1	1	1.0	1	1	1	1	1	2.8	.06	3.0	9.5 19.0	1	19.0	2.1	6.0	3	6	8		+3	
14:1,2	6	1	1	1	1	1	2.0	1	1	.50 3.0	.17	3 2	3.0 8.0	2.0	6 4.0	2.0 8	2.0 8.0	1 4	7 6	9 7		+6 +2	-1
3-6	8	1	1.0	1	1	1	2.0	1	1	1.3	.17	5	4.7	2.7 8.0	7.0 8	4.7	8.0 4.0	2	6	6		+7	
Chap 14	14	1	2.0	1	1	1	2.0	1	1	5.0 1	.17	5	4.7	2.7 8.0	7.0	4.7	4.0	2	6	6			
15:1-3	8	2	1	1	1	1	1.0	1	1	5.0	1	3	2.7 8.0	1	8.0 8	8.0 4.0	8.0 5.3	4	3	10		0	
4-7	8	3	1	1	1	1	.40	1	1	1	1	3	4.0	1	8	4.0	4.0	4	4	9		0	
Chap 15	16	5	1	1	1	1	1	1	1	6.0	1	6	4.0	1	16.0	5.3	5.3	5	3	9		0	-2
16:1-3	6	1	1	1	1	1	1	1	1	1.0 3.0	.33	1 1	6.0	1	6	3.0 1.5	3.0 1.5	1 1	7 3	9 13		+6 +2	
4-6	6	1	1	1	1	1	1	1	1	3.0	1	1	6.0	1	6	1.5	1.5	1	3	13		+2	
Chap 16	12	1	1	1	1	1	1	1	1	1.7	.22	2	12.0	1	12	2.0	2.0	1	7	9		+6	

Frequencies of the 17 Criteria in Testament of Joseph

Translation Frequencies	No. of lines of Greek text	No. of occur. of en	die W. gen (06-.01)	die W. all cases (18-.01)	eis (49-.01)	kata W. accus (18-.01)	kata W. all cases (19-.01)	Peri w. all cases (27-.01)	Pros w. dative (024-.01)	Hupo w. genitive (07-.01)	No. of occ. of kai for each occ. of de (2.1-)	Percent of separ. articles (.05-)	No. of dep. gen. post ea. prec. (22-)	No. of lines ea. dep. gen. pers. pronoun (9-)	Lines ea. gen. pers. pron. dep. on anarth. subst. (77-)	No. of prec. attr. adj. for each adj. post position (.35-)	No. of lines ea. attrib. adjec. (10.1-)	No. of lines each adverb. participle (6-)	No. of dat. not used w. en for ea. occur. of en (2-)	Tot. no. of transl. Grk frequencies (17)	Tot. no. of orig. Grk. frequencies	No. of inst. where occ. of criter. are too few to be indic.	Net original Grk. frequencies	Net translat. Grk. frequencies
17:1-3	5	1	-	-	1.0	-	-	-	-	-	2	-	3.0	5.0	1.3	2.0	5	5	2.0	2	-	10		17
4-8	13	4	-	.25	.25	-	-	-	-	-	6	.11	19	.76	1.8	2.0	6.5	13	.25	6	5	6		
Chap 17	18	5	-	.20	.40	-	-	-	-	-	8	.08	22.0	1.0	5.5	-	9.0	18	.60	7	5	6	+3	-1
Chap 18	11	5	.20	.40	.40	-	-	-	-	-	5	-	6	5.5	-	-	11	11	.60	7	4	7		-3
19:1,2,8,9	9	-	-	-	1	-	1	-	-	-	8	.20	2	4.5	4.5	2.0	4.5	9	-	4	3	9	0	
10-12	8	3	-	-	.33	-	.33	-	-	-	1.0	.11	5	2.7	4.0	.67	2.7	8.0	.67	5	4	7	0	
Chap 19	17	3	-	-	.33	-	.33	-	-	-	5.0	-	7	3.4	4.3	-	3.4	17.0	1.3	6	5	6		-4
20:1,2	7	2	-	-	.50	-	-	-	-	-	2	-	6	1.4	-	-	7	7.0	.00	3	5	10	+1	
3-6	8	-	-	-	-	-	-	-	-	-	5	-	2	4.0	-	.50	2.7	2.7	5	2	4	10	+3	
Chap 20	15	2	-	-	.50	-	-	-	-	-	7	-	8	2.1	-	.50	5.0	3.8	2.5	2	6	9	+4	-1

Appendix 2 - Numerical Count

Chapter Totals - Testament of Joseph

	LINES	DIA EN	DIA G	DIA T	KATA EIS	KATA A	KATA T	PLOT T	PROS D	HUPO G	KAI	DE	ART. UN-SEP.	ART. SEP.	DG PREC.	Art. c GS D N	Art. c GS D P	No Art. c GS D N	No Art. c GS D P	ATTR. PREC.	ATTR. POST	ADVERB. PART.	DATIVES
Chap 1	19	10	-	-	3	-	-	-	-	1	14	-	18	1	1	2	6	3	1	1	1	1	3
2	17	5	-	-	2	-	-	-	-	-	6	1	11	-	1	2	2	1	-	2	1	1	5
3	25	3	-	1	4	-	-	2	-	-	18	2	13	3	2	-	2	4	2	1	2	7	9
4	19	7	1	1	-	-	-	2	-	-	6	2	13	-	-	-	5	3	1	1	-	5	3
5	10	1	-	-	1	-	-	-	-	-	5	1	8	-	-	1	3	2	-	-	1	3	4
6	20	2	1	1	3	-	-	-	-	-	11	2	17	1	-	3	6	3	1	-	2	8	4
7	22	1	-	2	4	-	-	-	-	-	7	3	23	-	-	3	12	3	-	-	2	6	5
8	15	5	1	1	3	-	-	1	-	-	6	-	14	-	1	-	3	2	2	1	-	8	2
9	16	6	-	-	1	-	-	-	-	-	7	2	13	3	-	-	6	1	1	-	-	5	2
10:1-11:1	21	9	-	2	-	-	-	-	-	1	7	1	22	2	1	1	8	3	2	-	2	2	4
11:2-8	14	3	-	-	3	-	-	2	-	-	7	4	7	-	-	-	4	2	4	-	-	3	3
12	9	1	-	-	1	1	1	2	-	-	4	1	11	1	-	2	2	2	1	2	-	-	2
13	19	1	-	-	1	-	-	-	-	-	11	4	16	1	1	-	1	1	1	-	1	9	6
14	14	1	1	2	-	-	-	2	-	-	4	3	10	2	-	1	3	1	-	2	-	3	2
15	16	5	-	-	-	-	-	2	-	-	6	1	8	-	-	1	3	1	1	-	1	3	3
16	12	-	-	-	1	-	-	-	-	-	5	3	7	2	-	1	1	1	-	-	-	6	3
17	18	5	-	1	2	-	-	-	-	-	8	-	11	1	1	-	8	4	10	2	-	-	3
18	11	5	1	2	2	-	-	-	-	-	5	-	4	-	-	1	-	3	2	-	-	-	3
19	17	3	-	-	1	-	1	-	-	-	10	2	17	2	-	2	1	-	4	2	3	1	4
20	15	2	-	-	1	-	-	-	-	-	7	-	14	-	-	1	7	-	-	1	2	4	5
Total	329	75	5	13	33	1	2	13	-	2	154	32	257	19	8	20	83	40	33	15	18	75	75

Smaller Units - Testament of Joseph

LINES	EN	DIA G	DIA T	E:S	KATA A	KATA T	PERI T	PROS D	HUPO G	KAI	DE	ART UN-SEP	ART SEP	PREC	ART c GS D S	ART c GS D P	No ART c GS D S	No ART c GS D P	ADJ PREC	ADJ POST	ADVERB. PARTICIPLES	DATIVES
1:1,2	5	1	-	-	-	-	-	-	-	1	-	-	5	-	-	-	3	2	1	-	-	1	-
3-7	14	9	-	-	3	-	-	-	-	-	14	-	13	1	1	2	3	1	-	1	1	-	3
Chap 1	19	10	-	-	3	-	-	-	-	1	14	-	18	1	1	2	6	3	1	1	1	1	3
2:1-3	7	-	-	-	1	-	-	-	-	-	4	-	4	-	-	2	2	-	-	-	1	-	1
4-7	10	5	-	-	1	-	-	-	-	-	2	1	7	-	1	-	-	1	-	2	-	1	4
Chap 2	17	5	-	-	2	-	-	-	-	-	6	1	11	-	1	2	2	1	-	2	1	1	5
3:1,2	5	-	-	-	1	-	-	-	-	-	2	1	2	-	-	-	-	-	1	1	-	2	4
3-6	11	3	-	1	1	-	-	1	-	-	8	1	7	2	2	-	-	3	1	-	-	3	4
7-10	9	-	-	-	2	-	-	1	-	-	8	-	4	1	-	-	2	1	-	-	2	2	1
Chap 3	25	3	-	1	4	-	-	2	-	-	18	2	13	3	2	-	2	4	2	1	2	7	9
4:1-3	9	4	1	1	-	-	-	2	-	-	2	-	7	-	-	-	4	-	-	1	-	3	1
4-8	10	3	-	-	-	-	-	-	-	-	4	2	6	-	-	-	1	3	1	-	-	2	2
Chap 4	19	7	1	1	-	-	-	2	-	-	6	2	13	-	-	-	5	3	1	1	-	5	3
Chap 5 5:1-4	10	1	-	-	1	-	-	-	-	-	5	1	8	-	-	1	3	2	-	-	1	3	4
6:1-3	7	1	-	-	1	-	-	-	-	-	4	-	5	-	-	-	2	2	-	-	1	3	1
4-6	6	-	1	1	1	-	-	-	-	-	4	-	5	-	-	1	2	-	1	-	1	2	3
7-9	7	1	-	-	1	-	-	-	-	-	3	2	7	1	-	2	2	1	-	-	-	3	-
Chap 6	20	2	1	1	3	-	-	-	-	-	11	2	17	1	-	3	6	3	1	-	2	8	4
7:1,2	6	-	-	-	1	-	-	-	-	-	2	3	6	-	-	1	3	1	-	-	-	2	-
3-6	12	1	-	-	2	-	-	-	-	-	4	-	15	-	-	2	8	1	-	-	-	4	3
7,8	4	-	-	2	1	-	-	-	-	-	1	-	2	-	-	-	1	1	-	-	2	-	2
Chap 7	22	1	-	2	4	-	-	-	-	-	7	3	23	-	-	3	12	3	-	-	2	6	5
8:1-3	7	-	-	-	1	-	-	1	-	-	1	-	6	-	1	-	1	-	-	-	-	6	1
4,5	8	5	1	1	2	-	-	-	-	-	5	-	8	-	-	-	2	2	2	1	-	2	1
Chap 8	15	5	1	1	3	-	-	1	-	-	6	-	14	-	1	-	3	2	2	1	-	8	2

Testament of Joseph

| | LINES | DIA | | | LIS | KATA | | ΠΛΗΝ Τ | ΔΕ Δ | ΥΠΟ G | ΚΑΙ | ΔΕ | ARTICLE | | PREC | DEPENDENT GENITIVES | | | | ATTRIBUTIVE ADJECTIVES | | ADVERB PARTI-CIPLES | DATIVES |
| | | EN | G | T | | A | T | | | | | | UN-SEP | SEP | | Art. c GS | | No Art. c GS | | | | | |
																D S	D P	D S	D P	PREC	POST		
9:1-3	8	4	-	-	-	-	-	-	-	-	4	1	5	3	-	-	1	1	-	-	-	1	2
4,5	8	2	-	-	1	-	-	-	-	-	3	1	8	-	-	-	5	-	1	-	-	4	-
Chap 9	16	6	-	-	1	-	-	-	-	-	7	2	13	3	-	-	6	1	1	-	-	5	2
10:1-3	9	3	-	1	-	-	-	-	-	-	1	1	7	1	-	-	-	1	1	-	-	-	4
10:4-11:1	12	6	-	1	-	-	-	-	-	1	5	-	15	1	1	1	8	2	1	-	2	2	-
10:1-11:1	21	9	-	2	-	-	-	-	-	1	7	1	22	2	1	1	8	3	2	-	2	2	4
11:2,3	6	-	-	-	1	-	-	1	-	-	2	3	4	-	-	-	3	-	2	-	-	1	1
4-8	8	3	-	-	2	-	-	1	-	-	5	1	3	-	-	-	1	2	2	-	-	2	2
11:2-8 Chap 11	14	3	-	-	3	-	-	2	-	-	7	4	7	-	-	-	4	2	4	-	-	3	3
12:1-3	9	1	-	-	1	1	1	2	-	-	4	1	11	1	-	2	2	2	1	2	-	-	2
13:1-4	10	-	-	-	1	-	-	-	-	-	3	3	10	1	-	-	1	1	1	-	1	5	4
5-9	9	1	-	-	-	-	-	-	-	-	8	1	6	-	1	-	-	-	-	-	-	4	2
Chap 13	19	1	-	-	1	-	-	-	-	-	11	4	16	1	1	-	1	1	1	-	1	9	6
14:1,2	6	-	1	1	-	-	-	-	-	-	1	2	5	1	-	1	2	-	-	-	-	3	-
3-6	8	1	-	1	-	-	-	2	-	-	3	1	5	1	-	-	1	1	-	2	-	-	2
Chap 14	14	1	1	2	-	-	-	2	-	-	4	3	10	2	-	1	3	1	-	2	-	3	2
15:1-3	8	2	-	-	-	-	-	2	-	-	5	1	5	-	-	-	3	-	-	-	1	1	-
4-7	8	3	-	-	-	-	-	-	-	-	1	-	3	-	-	1	-	1	1	-	-	2	3
Chap 15	16	5	-	-	-	-	-	2	-	-	6	1	8	-	-	1	3	1	1	-	1	3	3

122

Testament of Joseph

	Lines	DIA EN	DIA G	DIA T	EIS	KATA A	KATA T	PERI T	PROS D	HUPO G	KAI	DE	Article UN-SEP	Article SEP	Dep.Gen. PREC	Art.c GS DS	Art.c GS DP	No Art.c GS DS	No Art.c GS DP	Attr.Adj PREC	Attr.Adj POST	Adverb. Participles	Dative
16:1-3	6	-	-	-	1	-	-	-	-	-	2	2	4	2	-	-	1	-	-	-	-	2	3
4-6	6	-	-	-	-	-	-	-	-	-	3	1	1	3	-	-	-	1	-	-	-	4	-
Chap 16	12	-	-	-	1	-	-	-	-	-	5	3	7	2	-	-	1	1	-	-	-	6	3
17:1-3	5	1	-	-	1	-	-	-	-	-	2	-	3	-	1	-	1	2	-	-	-	-	2
4-8	13	4	-	1	1	-	-	-	-	-	6	-	8	1	-	-	7	2	10	2	-	-	1
Chap 17	18	5	-	1	2	-	-	-	-	-	8	-	11	1	1	-	8	4	10	2	-	-	3
Chap 18 18:1-4	11	5	1	2	2	-	-	-	-	-	5	-	4	-	-	1	-	3	2	-	-	-	3
19:1,2, 8,9	9	-	-	-	1	-	1	-	-	-	8	-	9	-	-	-	-	-	2	-	2	-	2
10-12	8	3	-	-	-	-	-	-	-	-	2	2	8	2	-	2	1	-	2	2	1	1	2
Chap 19	17	3	-	-	1	-	1	-	-	-	10	2	17	2	-	2	1	-	4	2	3	1	4
20:1,2	7	2	-	-	1	-	-	-	-	-	2	-	9	-	-	1	5	-	-	-	-	1	-
3-6	8	-	-	-	-	-	-	-	-	-	5	-	5	-	-	-	2	-	-	1	2	3	5
Chap 20	15	2	-	-	1	-	-	-	-	-	7	-	14	-	-	1	7	-	-	1	2	4	5

Appendix 3

Frequencies of the 17 Criteria in the Larger Units of the Testament of Joseph

Translation / Frequencies	No. of lines of Greek text	No. of occur. of en	dia W. gen (06-/01)	dia W. all cases (18-/01)	eis (49-/01)	eis W. accus (18-/01)	kata W. all (19-/01)	Peri W. all (27-/01)	Pros W. dative (024/-.01)	Hupo W. genitive (07-/01)	No. of occ. of kai for each occ. of dé (2.1+/20.0)	Percent. of separ. articles (.05-)	No. of dep. gen. post. ea. prec. dep. gen. (22+)	No. of lines ea. dep. gen. pers. pronoun (9-)	Lines/ea. gen. on anarth. subst. pers. pron. dep. (77-)	No. of prec. attr. attr. adj. for each attr. adj. post position (35-)	No. of lines ea. attrib. adjec. (10.1+)	No. of lines each adverb. participle (6+)	No. of dat. not w. en for ea. occur. of en (2-)	Tot. no. of transl. Grk. frequencies (17)	Tot. no. of orig. Grk. frequencies	No. of inst. where occ. of criter. are too few to be indic.	Net original Grk. frequencies	Net transl. Grk. frequencies (17)
Intro₄ 1:1-2:7	36	15	—	—	.33	—	—	—	—	.07	20.0	.03	8.5	4.0	36.0	1.5	7.2	18.0	.53	8	3	6		-5
First Story 3:1-9:5	127	25	.12	.24	.64	—	—	.20	—	—	5.0	.06	23.0	2.9	18.1	.43	12.7	3.0	1.2	7	6	4		-1
Parenesis 10:1-3	9	3	—	.33	—	—	—	—	—	—	1.0	.13	2	9.0	9.0	—	9	9	1.3	4	5	8		
10:4-11:1	12	6	—	.17	—	—	—	—	—	.17	.6	.06	12.0	1.3	12.0	—	6.0	6.0	.00	6	4	7		-2
10:1-11:1	21	9	—	.22	—	—	—	—	—	.11	7.0	.08	14.0	2.1	10.5	—	10.5	10.5	.44	6	4	7		-2
Second Story 11:2-16:16	84	11	—	.18	.55	.09	.09	.73	—	—	2.3	.09	33.0	4.0	12.0	2.0	14.0	3.5	1.7	9	6	2	+1	-3
Parenesis 17,18	29	10	.10	.30	.40	—	—	—	—	—	—	.06	28.0	1.5	2.4	2.0	14.5	29	.60	8	4	5		
Vision & Forecast 19:1-20:2	24	5	—	—	—	—	—	.20	—	—	13	—	13	2.4	6.0	.67	4.8	12.0	.80	6	4	6		-4
Instruction & Burial 20:3-6	8	—	—	—	—	—	—	—	—	—	6.0	.07	2	4.0	—	.50	2.7	2.7	5	2	5	10	+3	-1

THE NEW EDITION OF THE TESTAMENT OF JOSEPH

M. de Jonge and Th. Korteweg

Further research into the history of the textual tradition of the Testaments of the XII Patriarchs, carried out during the preparation of the new *editio maior*, has shown that certain alterations in the stemma presented by H.J. de Jonge in his "Die Textuberlieferung der Testamente der zwolf Patriarchen", *Z.N.W.* 63 (1972), pp. 27-44 are necessary. This article has now been incorporated in a volume of essays entitled *Studies on the Testaments of the Twelve Patriarchs: Text and Interpretation* to be published as vol. III in the series *Studia in Veteris Testamenti Pseudepigrapha* (E.J. Brill, Leiden 1975). For a detailed analysis and presentation of the evidence, one should now also consult H.J. de Jonge, "The Earliest Traceable Stage of the Textual Tradition of the Testaments of the Twelve Patriarchs"; Th. Korteweg, "Further Observations on the Transmission of the Text"; and M. de Jonge, "The Greek Testaments of the Twelve Patriarchs and the Armenian Version", all to be found in the forthcoming volume.

The following list gives all instances where the *editio maior* will differ from the edition of MS. *b* in M. de Jonge, *Testamenta XII Patriarcharum*, edited according to Cambridge University Library MS Ff 1.24 fol. 203a-261b, (Ps. V.T.Gr.I), Leiden 1970. A number of these variants are simply orthographical and need no further comment. In all other cases the variant chosen represents the hyparchetype of the rest of the tradition over against *b(k)*. Often family I stands over against all other witnesses to the text (family II), and in each of these cases we have to choose between the reading of *b(k)* and that of (the reconstructed hyparchetype of) the rest of the tradition. The decision is not always easy and in many cases not even possible. In the end we have decided to follow the text of family I where its text is clearly superior, or stands at least an equal chance of being original as that of family II. Consequently the following list contains only those cases where family II gives a text which, in our opinion, is decidedly nearer to the original than that of family I (=*bk*). The most important witnesses for the text of family II are *g*, *l*, and *e*. In some cases A gives useful corroborative evidence.

I 7	σὺν δόλοις	]	συνδούλων
II 2	ἐπειγούσηι	]	ἐπείγουσαν
II 3	ἐτυπτίθην	]	ἐτυπτήθην
II 5	ἀποθεῖται	]	ἀπωθεῖται
III 2	ἑαυτόν	]	σεαυτόν
III 3	πατέρων	]	<
III 5	ἐπεδίδη μοι	]	ἀπεδήμει,
III 5	οἶνον,	]	οἶνον
III 6	εἰσίει	]	εἰσήιει
IV 3	ἐχαμοκοίτων	]	-τουν
IV 6	λέγει	]	θέλει
VI 2	ἐπιδιδοῦντα	]	ἐπιδιδόντα

125

VI 2	περιεργεία	]	περιεργία
VI 3	αὐτῆς[1]	]	αὐτοῦ
VIII 4	ἐσυκοφάντισε	]	-τησε
VIII 4	πρὸς τὸν ἄνδρα αὐτῆς	]	<
VIII 4	φυλακὴν[2]-Αἰγύπτιος	]	τὴν εἰρκτὴν τοῦ Φαραώ
IX 2	ταμείοις	]	+ βασιλείων
IX 4	ἐσιώπουν	]	-πων
X 3	συκοφαντίαι	]	+ ἢ σκοτίαι
X 6	ἐτίμουν	]	-μων
X 6	ἐσιώπουν	]	-πων [ὀφθαλμῶν
XI 1	πράξει ὑμῶν	]	πάσηι πράξει ὑμῶν πρὸ
XI 2	ἠρώτουν	]	-των
XII 1	παρίει	]	παρήιει
XII 1	Μεμφία	]	+ ἐν λαμπήνηι, ἡ
XII 1	Πετεφρί	]	-φρή,
XII 2	ἐπλούτισεν	]	-τησεν
XII 2	κλοπῆι	]	καὶ κλοπῆι
XIII 1	Πετεφρίς	]	-φρής
XIII 4	αὐτοῦ	]	+ τοῖς λόγοις
XIII 4	Πετεφρίς	]	-φρής
XIII 5	ἀρχευνούχωι	]	-χιευνούχωι
XIII 8	τῆς Χ.	]	γῆς Χ.
XIV 3	σου	]	σοι
XV 2	ἑαυτόν	]	σεαυτόν
XV 2	τῆι	]	γῆι
XV 2	λάκκωι	]	σάκκωι
XV 6	Πετεφρί	]	-φρή
XVI 2	Ἰσμαηλίταις	]	+αἰτοῦσά με εἰς διάπρασιν. Καλέσας οὖν ὁ ἀρχιμάγειρος [τοὺς Ἰσμαηλίτας
XVI 4	ἀγάγετε	]	ἄγαγε
XVI 5	δεδῶσθαι	]	δεδόσθαι
XVII 2	μακροθυμίαις	]	μακροθυμίαι
XVII 7	ἡ βουλή μου βουλὴ αὐτῶν	]	ἡ βουλὴ αὐτῶν βουλή μου
XVII 8	ἀλαζονήαι	]	ἀλαζονείαι
XVIII 3	ἐδούλευσε	]	ἐδούλωσε
XIX 6	σώζων	]	σώιζων
XIX 7	παρασαλεύσεται	]	-λεύεται
XIX 8	ὀποροφυλάκιον	]	ὀπωροφυλάκιον
XX 2	τὴν ἐπαγγελίαν	]	γῆν ἐπαγγελίας

JOSEPH IN THE TESTAMENT OF JOSEPH, PSEUDO-PHILO, AND PHILO

Daniel J. Harrington

This report takes the two major themes of the *Testament of Joseph* (hereafter T Jos)--Joseph as the model of *sōphrosynē* and as the example of forgiving love for his brethren--and compares them with the interpretations of Joseph found in Pseudo-Philo's *Biblical Antiquities* (hereafter Ps-Philo) and the writings of Philo of Alexandria. By choosing these two authors as the terms of comparison, we do not mean to imply that they come from the same milieu. On the contrary, we are suggesting that they may give us some clue to the understanding of the OT figure Joseph in the Palestinian and Alexandrian exegetical traditions respectively. Many factors point to Palestine as the place where Ps-Philo originated: It was apparently composed in Hebrew. The biblical text that the author had at his disposal was a Palestinian one rather than a Babylonian or an Egyptian one, according to the categories of F. M. Cross, Jr. There are many verbal parallels with *4 Ezra* and *2 Baruch*, both seemingly of Palestinian origin. Some of the author's theological interests (the proper place for the cult, the rules of sacrifice, the covenant and the Law, and eschatology and angelology) point toward a Palestinian provenance. The work is best seen as a repository of interpretations of the Bible current in the Palestinian synagogues at the turn of the common era. That Philo represents the Alexandrian Jewish mode of interpretation hardly needs saying, though one can argue about the influence of Palestinian traditions on Philo[1] and about Philo's originality as a biblical interpreter.[2] Our point in this paper is a simple one: T Jos has much more in common with one strain of Philo's thought on Joseph than it has with Ps-Philo. If we knew only Ps-Philo and Philo as representatives of the Palestinian and Alexandrian traditions respectively, we would locate T Jos's composition in Alexandria.

1. The first section of the *Testament of Joseph* (1:1--10:4) depicts Joseph's struggle to avoid being seduced by Potiphar's wife. While in Gen 39:8-9 what seems to motivate Joseph is his refusal to betray his master's trust, here his strength in resisting the temptation to adultery is emphasized. The Egyptian woman uses every ploy at her disposal: the threat of death (3:1), flattering Joseph as a chaste and holy man (4:1-2), planning to poison her own husband (5:1), sending food mixed with a poison (or aphrodisiac?) potion (6:1), the threat of suicide (7:3), and self-display (9:5). Against these wiles, Joseph relies on prayer (3:3; 4:3,8; 6:7; 7:4; 8:1,5) and fasting (3:4; 4:8; cf. 6:3 and 8:1). In this section Joseph emerges as the model of *sōphrosynē*. In 4:1-2 Potiphar's wife tries to ensnare him by praising his *sōphrosynē*. In 6:7 Joseph says

that the wickedness of the ungodly has no power over those who worship God with *sōphrosynē*. 9:2 speaks of the combination of fasting and *sōphrosynē*, while 9:3 describes God's generosity toward the person who lives in *sōphrosynē*. Finally, the climax of the whole section is the statement that God loves *sōphrosynē* and exalts the man who practices it (10:2-3). The use and the context of the term suggest that the translation "chastity" is appropriate.

The second section (10:5--18:4) describes the great sufferings that Joseph had to endure because he did not want to put his brothers to shame (17:1). Rather than reveal that his brothers had sold him into slavery, Joseph refrained from telling the Ishmaelites that he was Jacob's son (10:5-6). Even when he had achieved so much success in Egypt at the merchant's house, he still refused to admit that he was a free man rather than a slave. Torture does not make him reveal his true identity (13:9). Confronted by the Ishmaelites who only want to avoid trouble for themselves (15) and sold to Potiphar (16), he steadfastly continues on in his resolve. He does not even report the dishonesty of the eunuch who purchased him "lest the eunuch should be put to shame" (16:6). His message is "love one another, and with longsuffering hide one another's faults" (17:2). The truth and value of this advice is confirmed by the good fortune that he later encountered--a wife, wealth, beauty, and a long life (18). The testament ends with a vision of Israel's future (19) and some instructions concerning Joseph's burial (20). Thus, the picture of Joseph that emerges from T Jos is that of a model of heroic chastity and of heroic brotherly love.

2. In Ps-Philo, Joseph is described as the son of Rachel (8:6), the one who was sold by his brothers and later visited by them as clients in Egypt (8:9-14). His brothers' failure to recognize him is compared to the Israelites' failure to recognize Moses when he came down from the mountain (12:1). His refusal to marry a Gentile woman and his subsequent exaltation are contrasted with Samson's willingness to marry Delilah and his subsequent degradation (43:5). Joseph is not a major character in Ps-Philo, and most of what is said about him is merely a repetition of the biblical account. At two points, however, Ps-Philo does come close to T Jos. Ps-Philo 8:10 says that Joseph "did not deal vengefully with them" (i.e. his brothers). The Latin has *et non malignatus est cum eis*. This is, of course, the major theme of T Jos 10:5--18:4, but it really is not developed in Ps-Philo at all. Ps-Philo 43:5, which contrasts Samson and Joseph, explains his refusal to marry Gentile women as stemming from his desire "not to afflict (or damage) his own seed" *(contristare semen suum)*. The context makes it clear that this passage is one more example of Ps-Philo's very negative attitude toward marriages with Gentiles. Other instances are these: Tamar had relations with her father-in-law rather than marry a Gentile (9:5). Balaam plots to have the Midianite women lead Israel astray (18:13-14). Joshua sees a close connection between intermarriage and idolatry (21:1; cf. also 30:1). The list of evils in 44:7 culminates in lusting after foreign women. The levite's concubine was abused because she had intercourse with the Amalekites (45:3). What is most important for Ps-Philo in all these instances is preserving

Israel's racial purity in order to preserve also its religious and moral purity. But this is not at all the same as the heroic chastity practiced by Joseph in T Jos. In fact, one wonders how Ps-Philo reacted to the description of Joseph's wife in Gen 46:20 as "Asenath the daughter of Potiphera the priest of On." But he makes no comment on this text. T Jos 18:3 describes her as "the daughter of the priest of Hieropolis," with no visible embarrassment.

3. Philo of Alexandria begins his *De Josepho* with the observation that Joseph was well prepared to be a statesman by his training as a shepherd (3). Then he contrasts the brothers' envy with Joseph's innocence (5-6) and places moving speeches on the lips of Reuben (17-21) and Jacob (23-27). In 28-36 he shows how Joseph was suited to be a politician: His name "Joseph" means "addition of the Lord," and this mirrors the fact that the political structure of states is something added to the law of nature. His coat of varied colors befits the politician whose life is "varied and multiple, liable to innumerable changes." Just as Joseph was sold into slavery, so the politician is sold from master to master. As Joseph was claimed to have been attacked by wild beasts, so the politician is attacked by vainglory. In 37-124 Philo explains how Joseph resisted the attempt of Potiphar's wife to seduce him (on this section, see below). In 125-147 there is a discussion of the statesman as an interpreter of dreams: since all life is dream, the statesman must find the truth behind the dream. In 148-156 Joseph's position on the second chariot is taken to signify that the statesman has the place between the king and the general public; other details such as the ring, the chain, and the eunuchs are explained allegorically. The remainder of *De Josepho* is basically a paraphrase of Gen 41:46--47:12 and 50:1-426: the famine, Joseph's encounter with his brothers, their descent to Egypt with Benjamin and their reception by Joseph, Joseph's testing of his brothers, the revelation of his true identity, his appraisal of the events as God's will, his meeting with his father, and his own death.

Philo's negative estimate of Joseph, which is only glimpsed in *De Josepho* 28-36, is much more explicit in his other writings. For example, he is censured by Jacob in *Legum Allegoria* 3:179, and he is blamed for saying that he would interpret dreams through God rather than by God in *De Cherubim* 128. *Heres* 256 and *De Somniis* 1:78 call him "the body" as opposed to the mind. In *Quod Deus* 120 Joseph "follows in the train of the body and bodily things." In *De Mutatione* 89 he is the controller of bodily necessities. *De Confusione* 71 equates him with "the many-sided pride of worldly life." According to *De Somniis* 2:11 he had a keen desire for outward things and so was an unstable character.

Philo's generally unfavorable evaluation of Joseph makes the positive portrayal of him in *De Josepho* 37-124 all the more remarkable.[3] There, as in T Jos, his resistance to the advances of Potiphar's wife shows him to be the model of *sōphrosynē*. He refused her because "so strong was the sense of decency and *sōphrosynē* which nature and the exercise of control had implanted in him"(40). Philo contrasts the strict sexual morality of the Hebrews with that of other peoples: Prostitutes are not allowed to live. Sexual intercourse before marriage is not permitted. The end of marriage is not pleasure but the begetting of children (43). Joseph is unwilling to commit an act that would be at the same time fornication, idolatry, and breach of his master's trust. In 54-79 his self-control in resisting the woman's advances is extolled: "If the results of licentiousness are civil strife and war and ill upon ill without number, clearly the results of *sōphrosynē* are stability and peace and the acquisition and enjoyment of perfect blessings" (57). While in prison Joseph impressed all as the model of *sōphrosynē* and every virtue (87). His release from prison and his exaltation prove that the pious, "though they be bent they do not fall, but arise and stand upright, firm and strong, never to be brought low any more" (122).[4] In *De Josepho* 40, 57 the translation of *sōphrosynē* as "chastity" seems appropriate, though in 87 (a passage concerned with the impression that Joseph made while in prison) a more general term such as "temperance" may be in order.[5]

The idea that Joseph kept secret the shameful deed done to him by his brothers when they sold him into slavery, which is so prominent in T Jos 10:5--18:4, is also present in *De Josepho* 248-250. Even when Joseph had been appointed the overseer in Egypt, he still said nothing to prevent the belief "that he was of obscure and ignoble station, whereas he was really a noble, no slave by birth, but the unfortunate victim of a ruthless conspiracy of those who should have been the last to treat him so." He refrained from taking vengeance on his brothers. In fact, "the story of their conspiracy and selling of him into slavery was completely unknown and remained secret...."

Conclusion: Our report shows that Ps-Philo depicts Joseph as an example of one who resists marrying a Gentile woman and as one who did not deal vengefully with his brothers. It does little to illumine T Jos. On the other hand, both T Jos 1:1--10:4 and Philo's *De Josepho* take him as the model of *sōphrosynē* ("chastity"). Furthermore, both T Jos 10:5--18:4 and *De Josepho* present the motif that Joseph preferred passing himself off as a slave rather than drawing attention to the shameful behavior of his brothers. The fact that Philo's portrayal of Joseph here conflicts with his usually negative attitude toward him leads us to suspect that he is transmitting some Alexandrian exegetical traditions and that these same traditions were also used in the composition of T Jos. A relationship of literary dependence is difficult to prove.

Daniel J. Harrington
Weston College
Cambridge, Massachusetts 02138

Notes

1. H. A. Wolfson, *Philo*, vol. 1 (3rd printing, rev.; Cambridge, Mass.: Harvard, 1962), pp. 90-91.

2. See E. R. Goodenough, *By Light, Light. The Mystic Gospel of Hellenistic Judaism* (New Haven: Yale, 1935), as well as his many other writings on Hellenistic Judaism.

3. Goodenough in *The Politics of Philo Judaeus. Practice and Theory* (New Haven: Yale, 1938), pp. 42-63, saw *De Josepho* as Philo's advice to Gentile readers on the proper conduct of political affairs. He explained the two pictures of Joseph in Philo's works as due to the different audiences for which they were intended. For the Gentiles Joseph was portrayed as the ideal politician; for the Jews he was the enemy of what they hold sacred. In "Philo's Exposition of the Law and his De Vita Mosis," *HTR* 24 (1933) 116, he criticized the explanation that the two pictures of Joseph come from a chronic vaccillation in Philo's own character and his tendency to look at issues from all sides.

4. For the descent and exaltation of Joseph, see Wisdom 10:13-14.

5. U. Luck in *TDNT* 7, p. 1101, states that Philo's notion of *sōphrosynē* as "the basis of the possibility of the vision of God stands contrasted with *aphrosynē*." But this is not the sense of the term in *De Josepho*. Is this an indication that Philo here is drawing on an already traditional portrayal of Joseph as the model of *sōphrosynē*? Joseph's *sōphrosynē* is also prominent in Josephus' *Antiquities* 2:48, 50, 59, though his basic motive is seen as avoiding what would be an iniquity and outrage to his master (2:42).

Edgar W. Smith, Jr.

The purpose of this report is the identification of
aspects of the Joseph tradition in *Joseph and Asenath* (JA) and
Josephus that relate to the material about Joseph in T Jos.[1]
For the most part, only developments of (or departures from)
the biblical material relating to Joseph have been considered
worthy of mention.

Of the two sources thus compared with T Jos, JA yielded
more that is worthy of mention. The results are presented in
the following categories: similarities to the account of the
seductive woman; Asenath as an expression of motifs traditionally associated with Joseph; other common characteristics of
Joseph; and miscellaneous similarities.

Because so much of T Jos has to do with Joseph's response
to the seductive woman, the major points of similarity in JA
have to do with the figure of Asenath, even though the pure
virgin Asenath is a model of chastity.

Joseph's beauty (cf. T Jos 3:4) is mentioned when Asenath,
who had scornfully rejected her father's proposal that she
marry this "captive" and "son of a shepherd," sees Joseph enter
her father's courtyard in regal (or divine) splendor, at which
point she falls immediately in love with him (JA 5:2-6:8).

When Joseph sees Asenath looking at him out of her tower
window he is reminded of other women who annoyed (ἐνόχλουν)
him, so he orders that she be sent away. Although no special
emphasis is put upon Asenath's posture in JA (5:2; 7:2), it is
reminiscent of T Jos 14:1 (ἐώρα διὰ θυρίδος τυπτομένου μου),
and may well have been a characteristic position of the goddess
of love.[2]

Different developments of motifs found in T Jos are seen
in the explanation of Joseph's reaction to Asenath (JA 7:2b-6/
7:3-7 Ph):
> For Joseph was afraid and said, "Lest she also annoy me."
> For all the wives and daughters of the great men and
> satraps of all the land of Egypt annoyed him in order to
> sleep with him. And many wives and daughters of the
> Egyptians who saw him suffered (κακῶς ἔπασχον) at his
> beauty. And Joseph sent back the old women, whom the
> wives sent to him with gold and silver and precious gifts,
> with threats and outrage (ἀπειλή καὶ ὕβρις) saying,
> "I shall not sin before the Lord God and the face of my
> father Israel." For Joseph ever had God before his eyes,
> and always remembered the commands of his father. For
> Jacob often spoke and admonished his son Joseph and all
> his sons: "Children, guard yourselves from the strange
> woman in order not to commune (κοινωνῆσαι) with her, for
> her communion (κοινωνία) is destruction and ruin."
> Because of this Joseph said, "Let that woman depart from
> this house."[3]

The elaboration of the biblical account of Joseph's
problems with the one woman takes the form of detailed description in T Jos, while in JA it is done by turning the event
into a general situation.

In this section of JA the lovesickness is merely summar-

ized by the words κακῶς ἔπασχον. But elsewhere in JA there are
more specific descriptions of Asenath's reaction to Joseph that
have counterparts in T Jos. Thus the sighing and falling upon
the bed (T Jos 7:1; 9:4) are present, although mentioned in
different places, in JA 6:1 and 9:1. Like the woman in T Jos
7:2, Asenath feigns sickness (headache), so that her maidser-
vants inquire about her and wish to comfort her; but Asenath's
pretense is in order to do penance (JA 10:4-6/10:6-8 Ph) rather
than to seduce.

Although the sending of the eunuch to buy Joseph (T Jos 16)
has a similar purpose, T Jos has nothing directly corresponding
to the sending of old women with bribes of gold and silver and
precious gifts, as in JA 7:4. Nevertheless, the woman in T Jos
does use gifts (5:4), promises of power over her husband's
household (3:2; 5:1) and the promise to convert from the worship of idols (4:5), as well as threats and punishments. (In
JA it is Joseph who uses threats.)

Joseph's response to the annoying women, with a quotation
of the words of his father (JA 7:5/ 7:6 Ph) seems to be what is
referred to in T Jos 3:3, Joseph's remembering the words of his
father. (Cf. also προ ὀφθαλμῶν ὑμῶν in T Jos 11:1 v.1.)

Even after it is clear that Asenath is a virgin, Joseph
must reject her kiss of greeting because she is still an idol-
worshipper (JA 8:5-6).[4] Joseph's rejection causes Asenath
great sorrow, and brings on sighing, longing looks and tears
(JA 8:8; cf. T Jos 6:8; 9:4). Joseph's merciful response is a
blessing of Asenath that results in her conversion (μετάνοια)
from the worship of idols. Although Joseph's ῥήματα ὑψίστου εἰ
ἄρα ἀποστρέψει (T Jos 3:10) are directed against ἐπιθυμία
πονηρός rather than idol-worship, they do lead to that woman's
offer to turn from her idols (T Jos 4:4-5).

After Joseph's blessing the account of Asenath's conversion has even less in common with the description of the
seductive woman in T Jos.[5] In fact, the figure of Asenath in
JA acquires some of the motifs associated with Joseph in T Jos.
For example, the term ταπείνωσις (T Jos 10:2) is important in
JA as a general term for Asenath's penance. It includes the
προσευχὴ μετὰ νηστείας (T Jos 10:1), although the terms are not
used together in JA.

It is interesting that in T Jos 8:1 Joseph is portrayed as
praying from the sixth hour until dawn. Although Asenath is
blessed by Joseph shortly after noon (when he arrives), she
does not begin her praying until evening; but then she does
pray through the night (JA 10:15-16/10:17-18 Ph). Asenath's
crying during this night of prayer is portrayed much more
vividly than is done by the use of the simple δακρύων of T Jos
8:1.

In a more general sense, Asenath in JA may function, as
does Joseph in T Jos, as a representative of a particular
virtue, for JA, although not sharing the literary genre of
T 12 Patr, can be seen as emphasizing a virtue in each of its
two parts. In JA I this is μετάνοια,[6] of which Asenath becomes
almost the personification. Asenath also shares (with some of
Joseph's brothers, but not Joseph himself) in the proclamation
of the virtue that predominates in JA II, the merciful treatment of enemies (JA 28:10, 14).

Asenath does this to protect the sons of the handmaidens,
who had sought to kill Joseph, from revenge by the loyal
brothers. In this respect she takes on another characteristic

of Joseph, the refusal to take revenge on his brothers.

The plot of JA II is centered about the fact that Asenath is desired by the Pharaoh's firstborn son, who sees her from a wall (cf. T Jos 14:1) and decides to abduct her. Furthermore, as is the case with Joseph, the reason for this desire is the surpassing beauty of Asenath (JA 23:1/23:2 Ph). In the description of this beauty in JA 16:16 the use of flowers for comparison and the expression "your youth will not see old age" are reminiscent of the description of Joseph's beauty in T Jos 18:4.[7]

Joseph himself in JA is not only physically attractive (cf. JA 6:7; 13:14/13:11 Ph; and T Jos 3:4), but the bearer of χάρις from heaven (JA 4:7/4:9 Ph; cf. T Jos 12:3).[8] Although the term σωφροσύνη is not used for him in JA, he is once (4:7/4:9 Ph) described as σώφρων.[9] He shows a merciful concern for the woman he has rejected (JA 8:8/8:9 Ph; cf. T Jos 3:6, 9). The chastity of Joseph is illustrated in JA both in reaction to the women who annoy him (JA 7:2-6/7:2-7 Ph) and in his rejection of the possibility of sleeping with Asenath before marriage (JA 21:1/20:8 Ph).

One other similarity between T Jos and JA, which does not concern the figure of Joseph, deserves some mention: T Jos 19:12, whatever its origin, has a conceptual and formal counterpart in Asenath's prayer of confession: 'Ιδού γὰρ πάντα τὰ δώματα τοῦ πατρός μου Πεντεφρῆ ἃ δέδωκέ μοι εἰσ κληρονομίαν προσκαιρά εἰσι καὶ ἀφανῆ· τὰ δὲ δώματα τῆς σῆς κληρονομίας, κύριε, ἄφθαρτά εἰσι καὶ αἰώνια.[10]

In spite of some superficial resemblances the Joseph material in JA is quite distinct from that in T Jos. This is not surprising in view of the entirely different origins of the two documents with regard to time, place and theological milieu. What they share are basic elements of the biblical story, which are usually developed in ways that are quite distinct.

The same is true of Josephus' typical elaborations of the biblical account in his retelling of the Joseph story, for few of these elaborations have direct counterparts in the added details found in T Jos.

As in the comparison of T Jos with JA, the most interesting correspondence has to do with the account of the attempted seduction. Both Josephus (Ant. 2.4.3 [45, 47]) and T Jos (7:1-3) portray the woman as feigning sickness, although only in Josephus is it made clear that this is a device for being alone with Joseph (cf. Gen 39:11, 16). Both also portray the husband as questioning the woman about her appearance, but in T Jos (7:2) this is related to the feigned illness, while in Josephus (2.4.5 [55]) it occurs as part of the accusation of Joseph.

Elaborations of the plot by examples of persuasion are found in both T Jos and Josephus, and in one case the same reasoning is used. Both T Jos 3:2 and Ant. 2.4.3 (48) mention the woman's offer of more benefits in the household. Both accounts also portray Joseph as attempting to persuade the woman to desist (T Jos 7:5; Ant. 2.4.4 [51-52]), although in these instances different reasonings (both having to do with the marriage relationship) are offered. It is also interesting that both Ant. 2.4.3-4 (49-50) and T Jos 3:1 add threats (ἀπειλαί or ἀπειλεῖν) to the biblical account.

Naturally, both accounts have some mention of Joseph's beauty, although different terms are used. In Josephus there is a reference to Joseph's εὐμορφία (2.4.2 [41]) and ἀξίωμα τῆς μορφῆς (2.5.1 [60]). T Jos refers to ὡραιότητα and κάλλος (18:4). These terms in T Jos are related to Joseph's being like his father, which is reminiscent of the expression σώματος εὐγένεια in Ant. 2.2.1 (9) (cf. also εὐγενῆ in T Jos 14:3).

Both accounts mention Joseph's virtue, but in T Jos the term used most frequently is σωφροσύνη (4:1, 2; 6:7; 9:2, 3; 10:2, 3), while in Josephus this term does not occur. Rather, there is more varied terminology, with more use of φρόνησις (2.2.1 [9]; 2.5.7 [87]), φρόνημα (2.4.1 [40]) and σύνεσις (2.5.5 [80]; 2.6.1 [91]; cf. also σοφία in 2.5.7 [87]).

An attribute of Joseph that is common to both accounts is ὑπομονή (Ant. 2.4.2 [43]; 2.4.4 [50]; T Jos 2:7; 10:2; 17:1; cf. also the related μακροθυμία in 2:7; 17:2; 18:3). This is illustrated in T Jos 16:6 and 17:1 by Joseph's being unwilling to put the eunuch or his brothers to shame. With this may be compared Joseph's lack of self defense and silent submission to imprisonment in Ant. 2.5.1 (60) (to which T Jos 5:2, Joseph's threat to reveal the woman's plan, may be contrasted), and Joseph's desire, expressed in Ant. 2.6.9 (163) that his brothers not be burdened with shame for their sins.

Finally, both accounts illustrate the virtue of Joseph by some paraphrase and elaboration of Gen 50:15-21, Joseph's treatment of his brothers after Jacob's death (T Jos 17:5-8; Ant. 2.8.1 [197; cf. also 195]).

NOTES

[1]Texts used are: for T Jos, R. H. Charles, *The Greek Versions of the Testaments of the Twelve Patriarchs* (repr. Hildesheim: Olms, 1964), and M. deJonge, *Testamenta XII Patriarchum* (Leiden: Brill, 1964); for JA, P. Batiffol, "Le livre de la Prière d'Asenath" in *Studia Patristica* (Paris: Leroux, 1889-90), and M. Philonenko, *Joseph et Aséneth* (Leiden: Brill, 1968); for Josephus, H. St. J. Thackeray's edition (LCL). JA is cited according to the method proposed by C. Burchard, "Zum Text von 'Joseph und Aseneth,'" *JSJ* 1 (1970) 4 n. 1: the chapter numbers of Batiffol's edition and the verse numbers supplied by Riessler are given first, followed by the numbers of Philonenko's edition when it differs.

[2]Cf. Wolfgang Fauth, *aphrodite Parakyptusa* (Wiesbaden: Steiner, 1967), and the review by W. Schottroff in *ZDPV* 83 (1967) 206-8; cf. also the princess who sees and desires Moses in Josephus, *Ant.* 2.10.2 (252-3).

[3]Philonenko's shorter text does not differ in any way that affects comparison with T Jos.

[4]Asenath's blessing of the idols, and eating food offered to them, means that ἐμιάνθη τὸ στόμα (11:9; cf. 12:5). This adds interest to the *v.l.* στόμασιν ἀμιάντοις (T Jos 4:6) in the context of idol-worship.

[5]It is inconsequential, for example, that Asenath is both ὡραία (JA 1:4/1:6 Ph) and κοσμουμένη (JA 4:1/4:2 Ph), as is the seductive woman (T Jos 9:5).

[6]Cf. Philonenko, 53.

[7]Also with regard to T Jos 18:4, cf. the description of Jacob's beauty in JA 22:7.

⁸The similarity of the expressions has been noted by C. Burchard, *Untersuchungen zu Joseph und Aseneth* (Tübingen: Mohr, 1965) 115.

⁹Cf. Philonenko, 143, for a note on σωφροσύνη as a traditional virtue of Joseph.

¹⁰There is also some similarity between T Jos 18:2 and the prohibition against rendering evil for evil expressed in JA 23:9; 28:5, 10, 14; 29:3, on which cf. C. Burchard, *Untersuchungen zu Joseph und Aseneth*, 100-102, esp. 102 n. 1.

Edgar W. Smith, Jr.
Wm. B. Eerdmans Co.
255 Jefferson, S.E.
Grand Rapids, Michigan   49502

JOSEPH IN THE TANNAITIC MIDRASHIM

Barbara Geller

This essay compares the portrayal of Joseph in the Testament of Joseph with that of the tannaitic Midrashim, herein understood to include the Mekiltas of Rabbi Ishmael (MI) and Simon ben Johai (MS) to the book of Exodus, Sifra to Leviticus (SL), Sifre (SN) and Sifre Zutta (SZ) to Numbers, and Sifre (SD) and the Midrash Tannaim (MT) to the book of Deuteronomy.[1] The latter portrayal consists primarily of haggadic material found in MI and SD which, despite their designation as halachic midrashim, embody mainly haggadic interpretations of Scripture. The importance of the haggadic passages, to at least some of the Tannaim, is reflected in a portion of SD 11:22, attributed to the "interpreters of haggadah: "if it is your desire to discern Him who spoke and the world came into being, study haggadah, for in its midst you will discern Him who spoke and the world came into being, and you will cling to his ways." The significance of the non-legal material is revealed further in noting that the tannaitic Midrashim are running commentaries of only selected portions of their respective biblical books.

Many passages juxtapose Joseph with Moses and the Exodus, a response to the scriptural context from which these haggadic passages arose, the importance of the exodus in the rabbinic understanding of history, and the apparent fascination of the authors and compilers of these elaborations and clarifications of the legal traditions with Moses, the law-giver. Similarly, many lines are devoted to Joseph's bones and coffin; again, a reflection of the biblical verses under discussion, and the scripturally based relationship between Joseph's bones, and Moses and the Exodus (Gen. 50:25; Ex. 13:19; Josh. 24:32). Some of the passages suggest also

---

[1] The conventional manner of citation for these works has been replaced with the form, book and scriptural passage, in order to indicate the biblical stimulus for the given midrash. My translations derive from the following editions of the Hebrew: *Mekilta of R. Ishmael*, ed. and trans. Lauterbach (Philadelphia, 1933); *Mekilta of R. Simon b. Johai*, ed. Epstein, Melamed (Jerusalem, 1955); *Midrasch Tannaim zum Deuteronomium*, ed. Hoffman (Berlin, 1908-09); *Siphre ad Deuteronomium*, ed. Horovitz (Berlin, 1939); *Siphre ad Numeros adjecto Siphre zutta*, ed. Horovitz (Jerusalem, 1966). This paper cites also *The Mishnah*, trans. Danby (London, 1933); *The Testaments of the XII Patriarchs*, trans. Charles (London, 1913); *The Tosephta*, ed. Zuckermandel (Jerusalem, 1937).

the concern of the rabbis with a situation in which an oath
imposed by Joseph upon Israel (Gen. 50:25; Ex. 13:19) required
that they transport the remains of a dead man, an object of
uncleanliness and unholiness (Num. 19:15).

In a passage illustrative of the above, the nations
inquired of Israel, "What is its nature that a coffin should
accompany the ark of the Eternal?" She answered, "The one
lying in this coffin has fulfilled that which is written on
what lies in that ark (MI 13:19)." The parallel passage in
MS is more emphatic: travellers used to ask, "Is it really
possible that a corpse accompanies the Shekinah?" Israel's
response is the same (MS 13:19). In like manner, R. Ishmael,
in a dispute with R. Akiba, maintained that the men alluded
to in Num. 9:6, who were unable to keep the passover because
of their contact with the dead body of a man, were the
bearers of Joseph's coffin (SN 9:6).

Conversely, the Joseph material illustrates also the
tannaitic belief in the importance of, and honor in trans-
porting bones for reburial in Palestine.[2] This is exemplified
in the following comparison between Joseph and Moses: the
latter complained to the Master of the Universe that Joseph's
bones were permitted to enter the land of Israel, while his
were not. It was explained to Moses that whereas Joseph had
acknowledged his country when he said, "For I was indeed
stolen out of the land of the Hebrews (Gen. 40:15)," Moses
did not acknowledge his country in failing to correct the
daughters of Jethro whom he heard tell their father, "An
Egyptian delivered us out of the hand of the shepherds
(Ex. 2:19) (MT 31:14)."[3]

The Midrashim inform us that Joseph, than whom none of
his brothers was greater, behaved meritoriously in burying
his father. No one was greater than Joseph, for none other
than Moses, than whom no one in Israel was greater, attended

---

[2]For archaeological and literary evidence concerning
the prevalence and theological significance of secondary
burial in Palestine in tannaitic times, see Eric Meyers,
Jewish Ossuaries: Reburial and Rebirth (Rome, 1971). Professor
Charlesworth draws my attention to possible references to
secondary burial in The Testaments of the Twelve Patriarchs:
T. Zebulun 10:7; T. Dan 7:2; T. Gad 8:5; T. Joseph 20:6. For
a description of the advantages of burial in Palestine, in
the tannaitic Midrashim, see *Midrasch Tannaim*, p. 58, a frag-
ment of a Mekilta to Deuteronomy of the school of R. Ishmael.

[3]This differs from the biblical account of Moses'
failure to enter the promised land. P attributes this to his
lack of faith, manifested in striking the rock that it might
yield water (Num. 20:10-13); D attributes it to God's anger
with Moses on account of the transgressions of the Israelites
(Deut. 1:37; 3:26; 4:21).

to his bones (MI 13:19; MS 13:19; SN 12:15). The bones went
up from Egypt with the ark, the Shekinah, the priests, the
Levites, all Israel, and the seven clouds of glory (MI 13:19;
MS 13:19).

Although the above forms part of passages, the intent of
which is to illustrate "with what measure a man metes, it is
measured to him," it reveals also the importance attributed
to burial in the family tomb and in the homeland of Palestine.
This is probably inherent in R. Judah's statement that not
only the bones of Joseph went up from Egypt, but also the
bones of all of the tribes of Israel (SD 33:7; see similarly,
MI 13:19; MS 13:19). It may well be reflected in the
likening of the love of Zelophehad's daughters for Israel
with the love of their ancestor Joseph for the land (SN 27:1).
Finally, one finds possible evidence of the same in Simon
of Kitron's statement that the parting of the sea was for
the sake of Joseph's bones: "for it is said, 'And he left
his garment in her hand and fled (Gen. 39:12),' and it also
says, 'The sea looked and fled (Ps. 114:3)' (MI 14:15;
MS 14:15)."[4]

All of the passages cited heretofore assume Joseph to be
an embodiment of righteousness. It is stated further that
Joseph was appointed king over the land of Egypt because of
his righteousness (SD 32:44; MT 32:44), having been sent
there in order that it might be made known (SD 32:44). "He
paid regard to royalty saying, 'It is not in me; God will
give Pharaoh an answer of peace (Gen. 4:16)' (MI 12:31)."
Joseph's making ready his chariot to meet his father is
contrasted with Pharaoh's activity of the same to pursue the
Israelites (MI 14:6; MS 14:6). Both Mekiltas adduce scriptural passages which disclose that Joseph adhered to the
Decalogue and Levitical laws before they were revealed at
Sinai (MI 13:19; MS 13:19).[5] He is envisioned similarly in
the pronouncement that "he carried out the will of Him who
was revealed to Moses in the thorn-bush (SD 33:17; MT 33:17)."
Joseph is to be rewarded for his righteousness; just as he
was first in Egypt, he will be first to enter the world to
come (SD 33:17; MT 33:17).

Joseph's righteousness will reap benefits for his
descendants. Moses blesses the tribe of Joseph declaring
that its land will be the most blessed among all of the
lands, rich in dew, fruit, and wells. It will lack nothing

---

[4]Joseph's bones retain some of his vitality. One observes with Professor Meyers, "According to the Israelite
view, man is a solitary unit in death, even when the bones of
a man possess a shade of their strength in life. The body in
the Israelite conception is merely the soul in its outward
form, while the bones of the dead represent a manifestation
of that soul in a weakened state." Meyers, p. 12.

[5]Lauterbach notes that it was assumed that the ark
contained the tablets of the Decalogue and the Book of the
Law; see Jer. Sot. 8.3. Lauterbach, I, p. 181.

such that a man might dwell in its midst, and never have need
to leave (SD 33:13-17; MT 33:13-17).

Two legends concerning the manner in which Moses obtained
Joseph's coffin are found in MI and MS 13:19. In addition to
answering the questions of where, when, whom, and how raised
by the verse, the passages emphasize further both the honor
due Joseph and his relationship with Moses and the Exodus;
Serah b. Asher, who had survived from the generation of
Joseph, showed Moses the site of Joseph's grave. The Egyptians had placed him in a metal coffin which they had sunk
in the Nile. Moses stood by the river into which he threw
a gold tablet upon which he had engraved the Tetragrammaton,
and cried, "Joseph, son of Jacob, the oath which God swore
to our father Abraham has reached its fulfillment. If you
come up, it is good, but if not, we are not sworn to your
oath." Immediately, Joseph's coffin rose to the surface,
and Moses took it.

Vestiges of the myth of Isis and Osiris may be seen
behind this story. If this is so, it is another example
of the manner in which Israel adapted the cultural motifs
of the surrounding nations to suit her unique temperament.[6]

The second legend places Joseph's grave in the capitol
of Egypt in the mausoleum of the kings. Moses stood among
the coffins and cried out, informing Joseph that the oath
which God swore to Abraham had reached its fulfillment.
Immediately, Joseph's coffin began to sway, and Moses took it.[7]

It is interesting to note that the Mishnah and the
Tosephta, which are bound by the literary constraints of
explicating and arranging the legal traditions by subject
area, rather than biblical verse, as in these works, make
mention of Joseph's burial. Indeed, the sole mention of
Joseph in the Mishnah (M. Sot. 1.9) is the previously cited
midrash of SN 12:15 which is found also in MI and MS 13:19.
Again, it serves to illustrate the principle of retribution
of deed, but discloses incidentally the importance attributed
to reburial in Palestine. It forms part of the only passage
in the Tosephta in which Joseph is mentioned other than in
passing. The Tosephta section embraces also the two legends
concerning Joseph's coffin, and an additional midrash of

---

[6]For details concerning the relationship between this
legend and the myth of Isis and Osiris, see B. Heller, "Die
Sage von Sarge Josephs und der Bericht BEnjamins von Tudela
über Daniels schwebenden Sarg" *MGWJ* 70 (1926), pp. 271-276.

[7]T. Simon 8.3 states that the Egyptians guarded Joseph's
bones in the tombs of the kings. This indicates that the
motif was not unique to the rabbinic academies. The Genesis
account mentions only that Joseph died, and was embalmed,
and placed in a coffin in Egypt (Gen. 50:26). It is
interesting to note that the Egyptian sorcerers of T. Simon
attribute vital qualities to Joseph's bones; their departure
would give rise to a plague of darkness (T. Simon 8.4).

Joshua 24:32, found also in MS 13:19; "but if Moses had not occupied himself with Joseph, would not the Israelites have occupied themselves with him...Furthermore, if the Israelites had not occupied themselves with him, would not his own sons have done so...They said, 'Leave him; his honor will be greater (when the burial is performed) by the great rather than the small' (Tos. Sot. 4.7)."

Although the references to Joseph in the tannaitic Midrashim are few in number, they engender some interesting observations. The passages are found primarily in works emanating from the school of R. Ishmael.[8] However, the material gives no evidence of the hermeneutical differences between the schools of Akiba and Ishmael. To be sure, one would be more likely to discover such testimonies in expositions of legal passages. Many of the midrashim, especially those which are unattributed, derive probably from shared traditions some of which may antedate the schools. One notes that some of the passages, for which an authority is named, and which belong to works of the school of Ishmael. are identified with students of Akiba (see SD 33:7, 17). Most of the passages are not attributed to individual teachers. There is seemingly no pattern to be derived from those who are mentioned by name. The Joseph material in MI is nearly identical with that of MS. This reflects probably both the influence of common traditions and the possible literary dependence of MS on MI.

---

[8]The theory that the tannaitic Midrashim reflect the works of the schools of Ishmael and Akiba is explicated in David Hoffmann's, *Zur Einleitung in die halachischen Midraschim* (Berlin, 1887). He observed that MI and SN cite the students of R. Ishmael frequently, in contrast to SL and SD which cite mainly the students of Akiba. The former group makes greater use of the hermeneutical rules of the school of Ishmael, the latter of the school of Akiba. They employ different technical terms. Chanoch Albeck offers noteworthy criticisms of Hoffmann's theory in his book, *Untersuchungen über die halakischen Midraschim* (Berlin, 1927). He concurs with Hoffmann's recognition that MI and SN form one group, SL and SD another, to which belong also MS and SZ. However, he notes that with the exception of the differences in terminology, Hoffmann's criteria were based on relative frequencies of teachers and hermeneutical devices. Albeck concludes that there was not sufficient reason for assigning these groups to the schools of Ishmael and Akiva, respectively. He represents a minority opinion. One notes that the largely haggadic passages at the beginning and end of SD, sections 1-54 and 304-357 (Deut. 1-11, 31-34) emanate probably from the school of Ishmael unlike the midrashim of chapters 12-26, which are the work of the school of Akiba. MT, which consists of passages gathered from the Midrash ha-Gadol, coincides generally with the parallel passages in SD, especially in chapters 1-12 and 33-34. It also contains legal material not found in SD which probably formed part of a Mekilta to Deut. of the school of Ishmael. See Hoffmann, "Vorwort" *Midrasch Tannaim*, pp. iii-viii.

The degree of thematic uniformity in the Joseph material of the tannaitic Midrashim and legal codes is striking. To what might this be attributed? Some explanations have been advanced already. It is important also to remember that these earliest midrashic works comment only on the legal books of the Torah. The destruction of the Jerusalem Temple and the cultural disorientation which must have followed may well have given rise or, at least, given urgency to a need to elaborate, clarify, and codify the extant legal traditions. In filling the vacuum created by the destruction of the cultural nucleus of Judaism, the rabbis had to not only make provisions for the new situation but, equally important, make evident the continuity between old times and the present. An arrangement and clarification of the Law contributed to that end. The haggadic midrashim gave strength to the preceding by serving as a literary vehicle for exemplifying the manner in which the events of history fall into place to reveal the unifying principle of God's plan for His people behind them. They served to uncover the patterns and inter-relationships among the events and peoples of the Torah. The information was there, if one could tap it. Midrash was a method for recovering this information; the haggadah allowed the insightful to "discern Him who spoke, and the world came into being (SD 11:22)."

The Joseph material served the above purposes. The passages which associate Joseph and, to a lesser extent, Jacob, with Moses and the Exodus tacitly point to the promise made by God to the patriarchs. Jacob asked Joseph to bury him in Canaan, and, at his death, informed him of God's promise made to him (Gen. 47:29-31; 48:3-4). Joseph buries his father, and, in turn, at his death, tells his brothers of God's promise to Jacob. He alludes to the preceding, and makes the children of Israel swear that they will transport his bones (Gen. 50: 7-14, 24-25; Ex. 13:19).[9]

Joseph is able to fulfill his oath with his father; Moses is the instrument by which the children of Israel can fulfill their oath with Joseph. He is also the instrument by which God will fulfill His promise which, in Gen. 50:25, is linked with the taking up of Joseph's bones. The Midrashim begin with these scripturally established relationships, and offer entertaining and instructive details and explanations missing in the written word (see MI 13:19; MS 13:19; SN 12:15; M. Sot. 1.9; Tos. Sot. 4.7). Contemporary beliefs concerning the expiatory character of the land of Israel, as well as those which held that the resurrection would begin there, augmented the importance of burial in Palestine.

---

[9] The Midrashim explain why Joseph's oath was made with the children of Israel, and not with his sons: Joseph was afraid that Pharaoh would not permit the latter to bury him, and would declare that Joseph had been allowed to bury his father only because he was a king. Furthermore, it was the children of Israel who had caused him to be stolen from his home, and therefore should return him (MI 13:19; MS 13:19).

Joseph and Moses are intertwined in God's plan for His people. The misfortunes of the former, and the migration of his family to Egypt following his change in fortune, are not to be construed as deviations in the Divine plan. Moses acts to resolve the seeming complications and loose ends engendered by the Joseph story. God's promise is always operant. Thus, "God will visit you (Ex. 13:19)" is interpreted to mean that just as God was with the children of Israel at the sea and at the wilderness, He will be with them in this world and in the world to come (MI 13:19; MS 13:19).

All of the passages pertaining to Joseph in these works describe or suggest his righteousness, a theme common to most Joseph literature.[10] If Moses is the quintessential law-giver, Joseph is the quintessential law-keeper (MI 13:19; MS 13:19; SD 33:17; MT 33:17). He is praised also for having buried his father, as previously discussed, and for his love for the land of Israel (MT 31:14; SN 27:1). His righteousness is to be rewarded in this world and in the world to come (SD 32:44; 33:7; 33:17; MT 32:44; 33:17). God is with the righteous; He was with Joseph even when the latter was in prison, which suggests that the Shekinah is with Israel when she is enslaved (SN 10:35).

One can well appreciate the comforting and useful character of the sentiments expressed in the Joseph material for the men of the academies, especially in light of the events of the first and second centuries C.E. These passages add a human dimension to the larger works, cushioning and strengthening the drier discussions of the Law by providing them with a framework in which teachers and students could conceive of themselves as part of a purposeful historical continuum. Joseph is a model of behavior in adverse conditions.[11]

The portrayal of Joseph in the tannaitic Midrashim shares little with that of the Testament of Joseph (TJ). Both depict him as a man rewarded by God for his righteousness. However, while both envision Joseph as a paradigm of righteousness, the latter manifests this righteousness through Joseph's chastity and asceticism, and in his loving-kindness towards his brothers for whose sake he endured great hardship, lest he put them to shame. These themes are not considered in the Midrashim. Joseph's resistance to

---

[10] Joseph enjoys frequently the appellation *ha-tzadik* in rabbinic and pseudepigraphic literature. For references, see Louis Ginzberg, *The Legends of the Jews*, V (Philadelphia, 1925), pp. 324-325.

[11] One notes that the precise date of composition for most of the midrashim cannot be determined. However, their significance in the above discussion rests not on their date of composition, but in their inclusion in these early legal works. It is assumed that the midrashim do not post-date the tannaitic period. Their significance would not change, if it were to be proved that some of the passages antedate 70.

the wiles of Potiphar's wife is a testimony to his adherence to the Law and avoidance of sin, and not to a pursuit of chastity (MI 13:19; MS 13:19; MI 14:11; MS 14:11).

TJ makes two references to Joseph's bones. They share with the analogous passages of the Midrashim a basis in Scripture. In a passage lacking in the Armenian version, Joseph tells his sons, whom he has commanded to carry up his bones when God fulfills his promise to their fathers, "for when my bones are being taken up thither, the Lord will be with you in light, and Beliar shall be in darkness with the Egyptians (TJ 20.2)." The vocabulary and the world view behind them characterize the apocalyptic and probable Essene circles from which this document emerged. They would be foreign to the academies which produced the tannaitic Midrashim.

TJ 20.6, found only in the important Greek manuscript, Vatican Library, Cod. Graec. 731, places Joseph's burial in Hebron, the burial place of his fathers. This conforms to the remaining Testaments whose subjects are buried there also. Both Mekiltas and the Tosephta place Joseph's burial spot at Shechem, therein following Josh. 24:32 (MI 13:19; MS 13:19; Tos. Sot. 4.7). SN 12:15 reflects another tradition in recording his burial place as the land of Nebo, Moses' burial spot (Deut. 34: 1-6).

The absence of greater similarity between the portrayals of Joseph in the tannaitic Midrashim and TJ is not surprising, given the very different spheres of Judaism from which they emerged, and the different literary vehicles the authors selected. The difference in genre limits the possibility of greater similarity since each genre has its own literary constraints; it also bears witness to the differences in the intent of the authors in producing their respective works.

Barbara Geller
Duke University
Durham, North Carolina

JOSEPH IN THE SAMARITAN TRADITIONS

James D. Purvis

One would expect to find Samaritan traditions laudatory of Joseph, inasmuch as the Samaritans (i.e., the lay members of that community) claim to be the descendants of the Joseph tribes. This is indeed the case: Joseph is frequently cited in lists of revered heroes of the ancient faith; he is regarded as the good patriarch whose noble character reflects favorably upon those descended from him; and he is often represented as one whose righteousness provides an exemplary model for the Samaritan people. Joseph also figures in the theological argument for one of the major tenets of Samaritanism, the primacy of Mt. Gerizim: Joseph's burial at Shechem (acknowledged also in Jewish tradition, see Joshua 24:32) is cited as one of several indications of the sanctity of Gerizim as the chosen place of true Israelite worship. It is by virtue of his possession of Gerizim (in burial) that Joseph has been accorded the title malkâh, an Aramaic term which appears to have been used with the double meaning, possessor/king.[1] It should be noted, however, that the honor given Joseph in no way approaches the magnitude of the honor accorded Moses -- Samaritanism's only Prophet, Savior, and Celestial King. In fact, the highest honor which could be given Joseph by the Samaritans was the linking of his name with Moses: "There is none like Yôsēf malkâh and there is none like Mōšē nebi'âh. Each of them possessed high status; Moses possessed prophethood, Joseph possessed the Goodly Mount. There is none greater than either of them" (Memar Marqah IV. 12).[2]

It should be noted that there is a complex of Samaritan texts which makes little reference to Joseph. Included in this category are (1) texts magnifying Joshua (such as the early part of the Samaritan Arabic Book of Joshua,[3] and the Joshua portion of the chronicle tradition published by John Macdonald as Chronicle No. II[4]); (2) other Samaritan chronicles following the outline provided by the chain of high priests;[5] and (3) the Môlād Mōšēh texts.[6] These texts are clearly literary products of the priests of Nablus: Joshua had established the miškan-cultus on Gerizim; historic leadership had been in the hands of the priests; and the Light of the World manifest in Moses had been transmitted through the tribe of Levi.[7] It is difficult to avoid the conclusion that there was a conscious downplaying of Joseph within the Levitical priestly circles of the Samaritan community, with a corresponding emphasis upon Joseph among the laity. In fact, early tensions between priests and laymen (represented by traditions concerning Joseph and Levi) are reflected in several portions of the Memar Marqah. Marqah notes a dispute over the question of who is to offer the blessing on Mt. Gerizim: Levi (the priests) or Joseph (the laymen)? Answers from both sides are given, with the judgement finally being pronounced that it is the prerogative of the priests to bless (following Deut. 21:5), even though Joseph (the laity) possesses "the house" (Gerizim) (MM III. 4). With Marqah, this seems to have been a concession. His sympathies were mostly with the laity: Joseph is given dominion over his brothers (MM VI. 10); he is honored for his

wisdom and purity (see below); and he is contrasted in his
holiness with Judah, Simeon, Reuban, and Levi, who were sinners
(MM VI. 4). Marqah was not, however, anti-priestly. He was
frequently laudatory of Levi, and noted that Moses was from
that tribe (MM IV. 11). It was this latter consideration which
precluded the possibility of the laity ever gaining the upper
hand over the priests within the Samaritan community.

Samaritan texts which magnify Joshua mention Joseph in
connection with his burial by Joshua. In this tradition we do
not read of Yôsêf malkâh, but rather of Yehôšuaᶜ hammelek.[8]
The linkage is not Joseph/Moses but Moses/Joshua -- although
it may be argued that the assumed linkage is Joseph/Moses/
Joshua. At any rate, the connecting link with Joseph is not
stressed, and Joshua has usurped Joseph's title. Although
Joshua was from the tribe of Ephraim (Numbers 13:8), it does
not appear that his promotion was an activity of the Samaritan
laity. Rather, Joshua was remembered for having set up the
Tabernacle on Mt. Gerizim, and, thus, as having established
the historic Samaritan cultus. The magnification of Joshua at
the expense of Joseph appears, again, to have been an activity
of the Samaritan priesthood to maintain preeminence over the
laity.[9]

The following observations concerning Joseph in the Samaritan traditions should thus be regarded as traditions concerning Joseph as he was understood and represented among the
Samaritan laity.

1. Joseph as Preeminent over his Brothers

> When Joseph was mine, I gave him dominion over
> his brothers (MM VI. 10).

Thus spake Righteousness, in a laudatory poem (by Marqah)
praising Noah, Abraham, Isaac, Jacob, Joseph, and Moses. So
too, Marqah has YHWH declare, in a list of those whom God had
delivered, "I rescued Joseph and dealt with him lovingly; I
made all the people submit to him" (MM I. 2). The praise of
Joseph is here, as almost everywhere in Marqah, tied to his
righteous behavior in fleeing from the compromising situation
with Potiphar's wife (Genesis 39:6-23). This became the prime
example of Joseph's righteousness as an exemplary model (see
below). Joseph's righteousness is contrasted with the wickedness of his brothers, especially Reuben, Simeon, Levi, and
Judah (who "did not know that the heart of Joseph was pure, no
evil ever touching it," MM VI. 4). If it had not been for
Joseph, God would not have accepted the repentance of Judah
and Reuben (MM IV. 6, 8). The negative comparison of Judah
and Joseph is a typical Samaritan ploy, reflecting Jewish/
Samaritan antipathies. The negative comparison of Levi and
Joseph probably reflects dissensions within the Samaritan
community

Joseph is also cited for his wisdom (so MM I. 9; VI. 8-10).
The wisdom motif is probably present also in the statement
that Joseph understood the meaning of YHWH's creation: "Joseph
knew it and fled to it; it saved him from any evil deed" (MM
VI. 2). It was Joseph's wisdom which enabled him to flee
from evil.

2. Joseph as the Good Samaritan

> Come with us. Let us wholeheartedly make petition;
> let us worship sincerely before Him . . . like
> Joseph when he fled (MM III. 2).

> How will the Lord have compassion for you? How can
> he deal favorably with you? You seek the covenant
> with Abraham and do not do his actions. You seek
> the glory of Isaac and do not act sincerely like
> him. You seek too the devotion of Jacob and do
> not make his words efficacious. You seek the king-
> ship of Joseph and do not flee as he did (MM III. 2).

> See Joseph and Ephraim addressing all Israel, an
> address wholly of admonishment to them. It was as
> though Joseph was saying, "You will come to my
> house. Do what I did." (MM III. 5).

Joseph is represented by Marqah as the exemplary model of
the good Samaritan. Those who would worship in his house
(i.e., Gerizim, the place Joseph possesses) must do as he did.
The specific example of Joseph's rectitude, when cited, is the
flight from adultery. Other Samaritan traditions refer also
to Joseph's kindness towards his father and brothers (which
may be tacitly assumed by Marqah). An example of this is
found in a writing by the Samaritan high priest Jacob (1841-
1917): "The reason why our lord Jacob (upon whom peace) gave
particularly Nablus to our lord Joseph (upon whom be peace) in
preference to his brothers can be found in Jacob's desire to
recompense his son's beneficent deeds and favors which the
latter accorded to his father and brothers in supplying with
abundance their deficiencies and needs in those years of famine, as the report is given in Genesis 47:12, where we find
the following: 'And Joseph nourished his father, brothers, and
all his father's family, with bread, according to their fami-
lies.'"[10]

3. Joseph Malkâh

The kingship of Joseph in Marqah is understood in several
ways: first, in reference to Joseph's position of authority
and political leadership in Egypt while vizier under Pharaoh
(the "crown of Joseph" which was cast down until Moses rescued
the Israelites, MM I. 2); second, as representative of the
high status of the Samaritan people, the sons of Joseph (the
malkûth the Samaritans are to seek, MM III. 2); and, third, as
representing the sanctity of Gerizim and the territorial rights
of the Samaritans to that place by virtue of Joseph's burial
(see especially MM II. 10; IV. 10, 12). The third of these
aspects is that which is most frequently alluded to by Marqah.
In this connection, the title malkâh clearly means possessor,[11]
but probably with the double meaning, king. But to Marqah,
God is king and his kingdom is eternal (MM II. 10; III. 4; IV.
4, 8, et passim). Nonetheless, his kingdom belongs to Israel.
Of his kingdom it could be said that Moses was its chief deni-
zen, that the angels dwelt within it, and that "Adam arranged
it, Abraham built it, Isaac renewed it, Jacob dedicated it,
and Joseph the king established it" (MM IV. 10). There is a
fluidity in the use of the term kingdom in Marqah, both in
respect to time (and eternity) and space (heavenly or earthly),
and there is also a fluidity in the use of the title king.

There is at least one text in Marqah in which it is affirmed
that Moses inhabits a heavenly place and Joseph an earthly
place, with the suggestion that Moses is possessor/king in
heaven as Joseph is possessor/king on earth (MM IV. 9).[12] The
discrepancy between Yôsēf malkâh in Marqah and Yᵉhôsuaʿ hammelek in Chronicle II probably reflects a difference of opinion
within the Samaritan community as to whether leadership on
earth rested with the laity or the priesthood.

It is sometimes affirmed that Joseph served as an eschatological model among the Samaritans,[13] and that there were perhaps several models employed in the development of their concept of the Taheb (including Moses, Joseph, and Joshua). I
have elsewhere treated this problem,[14] with the conclusion that
if Joseph served as a model for future leadership it was as a
wise and righteous leader who would rule under a benign,
Pharaoh-like soverign. This is the only type of local govern-
ance the Samaritans have known from the Persian period to mod-
ern times, although too often the overlord has not been benign. The model here is one of a secular, this-worldly order.
The "kingship of Joseph" did not provide the Samaritan community with an archetypal historical kingdom for eschatological
development, in the sense that the kingship of David did in
Jewish eschatology. H.G.Kippenberg has also considered the
question of whether the Taheb was viewed as a returning Joseph,
and has concluded that although this eschatological figure may
have absorbed some of Joseph's functions (specifically, the
possession of Gerizim) he was not understood as Joseph-
redivivus.[15]

Postscript: The Samaritan Joseph and the Testament of Joseph

There are some points of agreement between the portrayal
of Joseph in the Samaritan materials and in the Testament of
Joseph: e.g., (1) the emphasis upon Joseph's righteous behavior in fleeing from the Egyptian woman (T.Jos. 8:1-5), and
(2) the kindness shown to his brothers (T.Jos. 17:6-8). We
note, however, the absence in the Samaritan texts of embellish-
ments (be they literary or homiletical) depicting the crafty
wiles of the temptress (T.Jos. 2-9). Also, Joseph's patience
does not appear to be stressed (as in T.Jos. 10:1), and Joseph's concern for his brothers is not manifest in a desire to
conceal their treachery (so T.Jos. 10:5-18:4). Also, and
extremely important to note, the Samaritan traditions do not
emphasize the chastity of Joseph as virtuous (compare T.Jos.
10:2, "He [God] loveth chastity"), but rather his fleeing from
an illicit relationship.

Some points of comparison may also be noted between the
Samaritan Joseph and the portrayal of Joseph in other portions
of Test. XII: The wisdom of Joseph, which is emphasized in the
Samaritan materials, is mentioned in T. Levi 13. This emphasis, however, does not appear elsewhere in Test. XII (so Harm
Hollander). The statement in T. Simeon that Joseph was comely
in appearance "because no wickedness dwelt in him," is quite
similar to the statement in Marqah that "the heart of Joseph
was pure, no evil ever touching it" (MM VI. 4). Other similar
points of agreement could probably also be noted; indeed they
should be expected. What seems more important to note is that
the paraenetical character of affirmations concerning Joseph

(both In Test. Jos. and other parts of Test. XII), which so
many scholars have observed, may be noted also in Marqah's
speeches.

It may be argued that there are some anti-Samaritan elements in the Testament of Joseph. We note the statement (in
one ms. tradition) that Joseph was buried at Hebron (T.Jos. 20:
6). This is not only contrary to Samaritan tradition, but also
to the explicit statement of the Jewish scriptures (Joshua 24:
32 locates Joseph's burial at Shechem). This in itself may
not be an anti-Shechemite (i.e., anti-Samaritan) polemic, inasmuch as Test. XII locates the burial of all twelve patriarchs
at Hebron. What seems more significant is Joseph's statement
in T.Jos. 19:11-12 that the salvation of the Lord shall arise
from Levi and Judah, and that his (Joseph's) kingdom shall
come to an end. This would appear to be an overt reference to
the Samaritan community, although it is more of a subtle jibe
than a polemic.

This latter text should probably be seen as relating to
anti-Samaritan texts found elsewhere in Test. XII, specifically T.Levi 5-7 and T.Judah 3-7. I have argued elsewhere that
these passages (and also Jubilees 30:1-26; 39:1-11; Judith 5:
16; 9:1-4) most likely reflect a positive Jewish reaction to
the pillaging of Shechem and Gerizim by John Hyrcanus in 128
B.C.E., and the destruction of the city ca. 107.[16] The anti-
Samaritan statement in T. Levi 7:1-4 roughly parallels Ben
Sira' 50:25-26, which I have interpreted as reflecting Samari-
tan/Jewish hostilities in the time of Simon the Just.[17] George
Nickelsburg has called my attention to a number of literary
parallels between T.Simeon and Ben Sira' 49-50 (e.g. 49:15/
TS 8:3; 49:16/TS 6:5; Simon the Just/Simeon the patriarch;
50:8/TS 6:2 in extenso; 50:25f./6:3-4). The statement in
T.Simeon 6:3 ("Then shall perish the seed of Canaan, and a
remnant shall not remain unto Amalek.") may be an oblique
reference to the Shechemites -- i.e., with the parallel between the destruction of the Shechemites by Simeon and the
later devastions brought upon Shechem by Simon the Just and/or
John Hyrcanus.

Notes

[1] On which see H.G.Kippenberg, Garizim und Synagoge:Traditions-
geschtliche Untersuchungen zur samaritanischen Religion der
aramäischen Periode (Berlin, 1971), pp. 257-265.

[2] References to the Memar Marqah (henceforth, MM) are cited
from the edition of John Macdonald, Memar Marqah: The Teaching
of Marqah, vol. I: The Text, vol. II: The Translation (Berlin,
1963). On the linking of Moses and Joseph see also MM IV. 9.
(see note 12).

[3] T.G.Juynboll, Chonicon Samaritanum, arabice conscriptim, cui
titulus est Liber Josuae (Leiden, 1848), pp. 130-175; O.T.
Crane, The Samaritan Chronicle or the Book of Joshua (New York,
1890), pp. 13-98.

[4] The Samaritan Chronicle No. II (Berlin, 1969), pp. 77-99.
See also Moses Gaster, "Das Buch Josua in hebräische-samaritan-
ischer Rezension," ZDMG, 62(1908), 209-279, 494-549.

[5] For example, the Tolidah (John Bowman, Transcript of the Original Text of the Samaritan Chronicle Tolidah [University of Leeds, 1955]); the Shalshalat (Moses Gaster, "The Chain of Samaritan High Priests," in Studies and Texts [London, 1925-28], vol. I, pp. 483-502; vol. III, pp. 131-138); Abu'l Fath (E.Vilmar, Abulfathi annales samaritani [Gotha, 1856]); and Chronicle Adler (E.N.Adler and M.Seligsohn, "Une nouvelle chronique samaritaine," REJ, 44[1902], 188-222; 45[1902],70-98, 223-254; 46[1903], 123-146).

[6] See S.J. Miller, The Samaritan Molad Mosheh (New York, 1949); cf. also T.H.Gaster, "A Samaritan Poem about Moses," in A. Berger, et al., The Joshua Bloch Memorial Volume: Studies in Booklore and History (New York, 1960), pp. 115-139.

[7] Miller, Molad Mosheh, p. 250: "And of them [i.e., the twelve sons of Jacob], Levi became the portion and lot of God, for he was the bearer of the ray of light for the sake of prophecy. In him He placed His glory. From his seed the house of the priesthood grew. For God selected him to minister and to bless his congregation, and his seed for all time. The Levite tribe with all the blessings which he had, carried the mystery of Moses, and in goodness the essence was carried when he transmitted his seed. For from the seed of this holy tribe arose the exalted of all men."

[8] For example, Macdonald, Samaritan Chronicle No. II, p. 80.

[9] Against John Bowman, who has maintained that the promotion of Joshua (specifically of an eschatological Joshua) was an activity of the lay-led Dosithean sect (see "Identity and Date of the Unnamed Feast of John 5:1," in H. Goedicke (ed.), Near Eastern Studies in Honor of William Foxwell Albright [Baltimore, 1971], pp. 45-47; "Pilgrimage to Mount Gerizim," in M. Avi-Yonah, et al., Eretz Israel, vol. VIII [Jerusalem, 1964], pp. 17-28). Also against A.D. Crown who has contended that the orthodox priestly circles of Samaritanism modeled their eschatological figure after Joseph (see "Some Traces of Heterodox Theology in the Samaritan Book of Joshua," BJRL, 50 [1967], 185-186). For a critique of both views, see J.D. Purvis, "The Fourth Gospel and the Samaritans," Novum Testamentum (forthcoming).

[10] From the essay, "Mount Gerizim, the One True Sanctuary," edited by W.E.Barton, reprinted from Bibliotheca Sacra 64, (1907), 385-426, and published in booklet form, p. 17.

[11] As pointed out by Kippenberg, see note 1.

[12] The text is found in Macdonald, Memar Marqah, vol. I, p.102, vol. II, p. 169. "Behold two were coupled together; the one inhabited a place and the other inhabited a place. Joseph inhabited the place of his father and received what was his and acquired it for himself, so that it became his portion. The great prophet Moses inhabited the place of his Lord which he had chosen. God chose both places and rewarded both men."

[13] For example, Crown, loc. cit.; G.W.Buchanan, "The Samaritan Origin of the Gospel of John," in J.Neusner (ed.), _Religions in Antiquity: Essays in Memory of E.R.Goodenough_ (Leiden, 1968), pp. 159-160.

[14] "The Fourth Gospel and the Samaritans," forthcoming in _Novum Testamentum_.

[15] Kippenberg, _Garizim und Synagoge_, p. 293.

[16] See my chapter on "The Samaritans," forthcoming in W.D. Davies and L. Finklestein, _Cambridge History of Judaism_, vol. I (Cambridge University Press).

[17] On which, see Purvis, "Ben Sira' and the Foolish People of Shechem," appendix in _Samaritan Pentateuch and the Origin of the Samaritan Sect_ (Cambridge, Mass., 1958), pp. 119-129.

James D. Purvis
Department of Religion
Boston University
232 Bay State Road
Boston, Massachusetts 02215